Eighteenth-Century Writing from Wales

Writing Wales in English

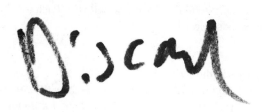

CREW

CREW series of Critical and Scholarly Studies
General Editor: Professor M. Wynn Thomas
(CREW, Swansea University)

This *CREW* series is dedicated to Emyr Humphreys, a major figure in the literary culture of modern Wales, a founding patron of the *Centre for Research into the English Literature and Language of Wales*, and, along with Gillian Clarke and Seamus Heaney, one of *CREW's* Honorary Associates. Grateful thanks are extended to Richard Dynevor for making this series possible.

Other titles in the series
Stephen Knight, *A Hundred Years of Fiction* (978-0-7083-1846-1)
Barbara Prys-Williams, *Twentieth-Century Autobiography* (978-0-7083-1891-1)
Kirsti Bohata, *Postcolonialism Revisited* (978-0-7083-1892-8)
Christopher Wigginton, *Modernism from the Margins* (978-0-7083-1927-7)
Linden Peach, *Contemporary Irish and Welsh Women's Fiction* (978-0-7083-1998-7)

Eighteenth-Century Writing from Wales

Bards and Britons

Writing Wales in English

SARAH PRESCOTT

UNIVERSITY OF WALES PRESS
CARDIFF
2008

© Sarah Prescott, 2008

www.uwp.co.uk

British Library Cataloguing-in-Publication Data
A catalogue record for this book is available from the British Library.

ISBN   978-0-7083-2053-2

THE *A*SSOCIATION FOR
*W*ELSH *W*RITING IN *E*NGLISH
*C*YMDEITHAS *L*LÊN *S*AESNEG *C*YMRU
Recommended text

Published with the financial assistance of the Welsh Books Council

Typeset by Keith James Design
Printed by CPI Antony Rowe, Wiltshire

I IDLOES, BETSAN A MARI ROBERTS

gyda llawer o gariad

CONTENTS

General Editor's Preface

The aim of this series is to produce a body of scholarly and critical work that reflects the richness and variety of the English-language literature of modern Wales. Drawing upon the expertise both of established specialists and of younger scholars, it will seek to take advantage of the concepts, models and discourses current in the best contemporary studies to promote a better understanding of the literature's significance, viewed not only as an expression of Welsh culture but also as an instance of modern literatures in English world-wide. In addition, it will seek to make available the scholarly materials (such as bibliographies) necessary for this kind of advanced, informed study.

M. Wynn Thomas,
Director, CREW (*Centre for Research into the English Language and Literature of Wales*)
Swansea University

ACKNOWLEDGEMENTS

Material from chapter 1 has appeared as '"What Foes more dang'rous than too strong Allies?: Anglo-Welsh relations in eighteenth-century London', *Huntington Library Quarterly*, 69, 4 (2006), 535–54; from chapter 2 as 'The Cambrian Muse: Welsh identity and Hanoverian loyalty in the poems of Jane Brereton (1685–1740)', *Eighteenth-Century Studies*, 38, 4 (2005), 587–603; and from chapter 3 as '"Gray's pale spectre": Evan Evans, Thomas Gray, and the rise of Welsh bardic nationalism', *Modern Philology*, 104, 1 (2006), 72–95. I am grateful to the editors and readers of these journals for their extremely useful comments on these essays. The Department of English, Aberystwyth University, granted me study leave to work on the project, and the AHRC granted me a Research Leave Scheme award which enabled me to bring the book to completion. A Sir David Hughes Parry Award, Aberystwyth University, provided me with further financial support for researching material in chapters 1 and 3.

I would like to thank various colleagues and friends at Aberystwyth and elsewhere for their advice and support in the course of writing this book, especially the following: Jane Aaron, Peter Barry, Mary-Ann Constantine, Damian Walford Davies, Louise Marshall, Francesca Rhydderch, David E. Shuttleton, Jane Spencer, Diane Watt, Cathryn Charnell-White and David Womersley. I also thank Geraint H. Jenkins and Mary Burdett-Jones for sharing their knowledge and expertise. Sarah Lewis and M. Wynn Thomas have been very helpful in the final stages of the book's completion. Special thanks as ever to Claire Jowitt.

I owe a special debt of gratitude to Betty and Cliff Moon, Gwenda and Gareth Morgan, and to my family, to whom this book is dedicated.

INTRODUCTION

In a letter to Evan Evans in July 1761 concerning Evans's 'authentication' of the tradition of Edward I's supposed massacre of the Welsh bards, Thomas Percy declares to the Welshman: 'Your nation and ours are now happily consolidated in one firm indissoluble mass, and it is of very little importance, whether Llewelyn or Edward had the advantage in such a particular encounter.'[1] Through emphasising the positive outcome of united Britishness, Percy effectively empties Edward's conquest of Wales and the act of bardicide of any political import, as Wales is seamlessly absorbed into England. Recent scholarship on the literary construction of British national identity in the eighteenth century has also underplayed the role of Wales.[2] This critical neglect is partly due to the general sense expressed by Percy that, in contrast to Scotland and Ireland, Wales was not only dutifully acquiescent in the Anglicisation processes of the eighteenth century, but actively rejoiced in their happy union. In keeping with Welsh enthusiasm for the Tudor Union, it is assumed that Wales was eager to be part of a post-1707 political consensus which emphasised Protestant solidarity and foregrounded loyal patriotism to the British nation and its monarchy. This book aims to complicate the view that the Welsh were passively assimilated into an Anglo-British consensus in the eighteenth century. Although many eighteenth-century Welsh writers did express pro-British loyalty to the Protestant and Hanoverian succession, for most Welsh writers and readers of the period the idea that Edward's triumph and the conquest of Wales were devoid of contemporary relevance or empty of political and cultural significance was unthinkable.

In a rather belated response to J. G. A. Pocock's call in 1975 for an 'archipelagic' approach to British history, the last ten years have produced a wealth of scholarship – initially historical but increasingly literary – on the question of British national identity.[3] Archipelagic approaches to literary history can, broadly, work in two ways. On the one hand, scholars emphasise that British history is not, in fact, the history of England, but of four nations. The focus from this perspective centres on British inclusiveness and the potential for reciprocity between Britain's constituent parts. On the other hand, archipelagic criticism can uncover a more conflicted sense of Britishness, with the additional sense that the 'Celtic' components of Great Britain are engaged in active resistance to Anglo-British incorporation, preferring instead to highlight cultural, literary and national difference. However, although a substantial body of literary scholarship exists on early modern British identities and archipelagic approaches to literary history, the role of Wales in these debates is rarely touched on despite the urgency of some of the calls for 'inclusiveness'. This neglect is mostly due to the lack of knowledge of a body of texts and scholarship in the Welsh language. However, literary scholars in particular also seem to be unaware of a pre-1900 anglophone tradition in Wales. A notable exception to this is the work of Philip Schwyzer, whose *Literature, Nationalism and Memory in Early Modern England and Wales* (2004) makes Wales and Welsh writing central to his thesis that 'national consciousness in Tudor England was largely "British" rather than narrowly "English" in its content and character'.[4] This study aims, then, to add to our understanding of the writing of archipelagic literary history through attention to the piece of the jigsaw usually missing in this context: eighteenth-century Wales. Although work in this area has been mainly based in early modern studies, the eighteenth century is especially pertinent in this respect since, as Linda Colley has influentially observed in *Britons: Forging the Nation, 1707–1837*, the Act of Union between England and Scotland in 1707 marked the invention of Great Britain as 'a would-be nation'.[5] The years following Colley's 1992 study have witnessed a surge of critical interest in eighteenth-century conceptions of national identity. However, as might be expected given the nature of the 1707 Union, attention paid to eighteenth-century negotiations of Britishness has mainly concerned the often turbulent relationship between England and Scotland.[6] In contrast, the role played by Wales and English-language Welsh writers, especially from the earlier years of the century, has been neglected by literary scholars. Wales and England had been formally united by the Tudor legislation of 1536–43, and thus can be said to have a long history of political and religious assimilation prior to 1707. Nevertheless, this book argues that eighteenth-century literary negotiations of Wales represent a distinct national tradition which enriches, yet also unsettles, the broader creative re-imagining of Britain following the 1707 Act of Union.

Linda Colley's by now familiar argument in *Britons* emphasises the invention of a coherent British national identity in the eighteenth century in terms of a common Protestantism consolidated by ongoing wars with France and Spain. Through the construction of Catholic Europe as the 'Other', she argues, the disparate parts of the Isles could unite in a shared sense of Britishness. As such, Colley openly rejects another extremely influential model of British nationhood, Michael Hechter's theory of 'internal colonialism'.[7] Hechter views the processes of union (in Wales, Scotland and Ireland) as primarily serving English interests and suggests that the experience of England's domestic colonies was analogous to that overseas. From his perspective, Britain did not adopt a coherent national identity by consensual allegiance to a common cause; rather, this was an identity imposed by a dominant core on a politically and economically marginalised periphery. In Hechter's terms, potential Celtic sovereignty was progressively lost in the various unions of the British Isles from 1536 to 1801. By contrast, Colley states quite plainly that the genesis of Great Britain is not 'to be explained primarily in terms of an English "core" imposing its cultural and political hegemony on a helpless and defrauded Celtic periphery'.[8] She reiterates in her conclusion that it is a mistake 'to interpret the growth of British national consciousness in this period in terms of a new cultural and political uniformity being resolutely imposed on the peripheries of the island by its centre'.[9]

However, if we attend more closely to Colley's argument it appears that the gap between her and Hechter is not insurmountable. In fact, Colley never suggests that there was 'political and cultural consensus' throughout Britain at the expense of internal differences. Rather, she argues that

> The sense of a common identity here did not come into being, then, because of an integration and homogenisation of disparate cultures. Instead, Britishness was superimposed over an array of internal difference in response to contact with the Other, and above all in responses to conflict with the Other.[10]

Colley does, then, allow for a measure of both regional and national difference, which shows her idea of Britishness as capable of nuance and flexibility. Nevertheless, as I show in chapter 4, it was often the case that, from the perspective of English writers, Wales itself represented 'otherness' as much as countries overseas did. The Welsh language was at the heart of this perception of difference. As Geraint H. Jenkins states,

'The native language was not only the most distinctive badge of national identity, but also a more powerful dividing factor than religion and politics'.[11] However, rather than view a Welsh-British identity, for example, as a problematic and/or conflicted experience, Colley argues that dual identity (at least for the ruling class) could result in overall profit:

> Those Welsh, Scottish and Anglo-Irish individuals who became part of the British Establishment in this period did not in the main sell out in the sense of becoming Anglicised look-alikes. Instead, they became British in a new and intensely profitable fashion, while remaining in their own minds and behaviour Welsh, or Scottish, or Irish as well.[12]

Although Linda Colley's work has been widely acclaimed and extremely influential, she has also been criticised for over-emphasising the homogeneity of Britishness as 'a seamless fabric of Protestant and then imperial interests after the Union'.[13] In relation to the Scottish context, Leith Davis, for example, argues that *Britons* ultimately upholds 'the Whig interpretation of British history as a series of events that eventually led to a united identity for Scots and English as Britons'.[14] Murray Pittock, in his 'four nations' literary history of Britain, *Inventing and Resisting Britain*, is also critical of Colley's 'fashionable' views.[15] Pittock comments particularly on the resistance to jurant Anglicanism as only one of the 'questions of cultural complexity which lie behind the building of Britain, and which cannot be answered by seductive appeals to single motivating historical forces, be they religious or economic'.[16] By focusing on internal differences and spatial dynamics, rather than overarching teleological forces, Pittock's project contributes to 'the decolonization of British space in the eighteenth century', to allow for 'a clearer vision of difference than that permitted by teleological narratives or religious or economic integration through time'.[17] Colley can also be said to underplay what Colin Kidd calls 'the hollowness at the heart of Britishness': the fact that the Britain of 1707 was 'a freshly minted state which failed to inspire any emotional enthusiasm in its peoples and lacked an enduring *raison d'être*'. In one sense, then, the Union could be seen merely as 'an instrument of politics rather than an end in itself'.[18] More pertinent for my purposes in this study is Kidd's further point that 'the vital missing ingredient from Colley's work is the phenomenon of anglicization, whether in the fields of culture, economics or politics'.[19] Indeed, provincial aspiration to metropolitan tastes in the interests of fashion could be at least as powerful as enforced political union in terms of shaping common attitudes and lifestyles. As Kidd notes, 'Britain did not only unite against an external Other, but the emulation of Englishness acted – up to a point – as a glue of integration'.[20] In the anglophone literature of the period under discussion here, however, attitudes to Anglicization are not uniform and it is clear that the desire to conform to English expectations was indeed satisfied only 'up to a point'. My research suggests that the forces of Anglicisation are most clearly apparent in Welsh fiction of the period. While poets could draw on a bardic persona to articulate a specifically Welsh poetic identity which was markedly different from that of their English counterparts, novelists were more bound by English standards of taste and generic limits. Such limitations can be clearly seen, for example, in *Elisa Powell, or Trials of Sensibility* (1795), the only novel by Edward 'Celtic' Davies. As I demonstrate in chapter 5, Davies struggles to square his investigation of Welsh culture with the generic limits of the novel of sensibility. These limitations are even more pressing in novelistic representations of Welsh heroines, whose background and behaviour are often seen to be lacking in relation to expectations of femininity based on Anglicised standards of behaviour and metropolitan accomplishment.

Katie Trumpener's *Bardic Nationalism: The Romantic Novel and the British Empire* (1997) is an example of a literary study which is implicitly critical of Colley's integrationist thesis. Trumpener's work grows out of the broader interest in 'archipelagic' literary history and internal colonialism which I have sketched out above. Throughout her study she emphasises the parallels that can be drawn between domestic and imperial colonial processes as well as highlighting English appropriation of Celtic literary traditions. Her work shows that renewed attention needs to be paid to the cultural specificity of Ireland, Scotland and Wales and to how the literature of these Celtic nations challenges notions of hegemonic Britishness in the eighteenth century. In her recent study *Antiquaries* (2004), Rosemary Sweet has argued that the version of eighteenth-century Britishness emphasised by Linda Colley only 'operated at what was often a largely political and rhetorical level' and does not account for the fact that 'the stronger sense of national identity which historians have identified in the eighteenth century was arguably more evident in the formulation of Scottish, Welsh and English, not to mention Irish, identities during this period'.[21] Like Sweet, Trumpener foregrounds antiquarianism as crucial to the formation of these national identities. Her concept of a 'bardic nationalism', which draws authority from the exploration and reinterpretation of each nation's literary and historical past, is especially helpful for literary studies of nationhood in that it can accommodate the seemingly apolitical while realising the oppositional politico-cultural potential of poetry, fiction and the figure of the bard as national mouthpiece. Indeed, as literary scholars are beginning to recognise, post-1707 Irish, Scots and Welsh antiquarian writers consciously reinvented and championed distinctive national literary traditions and historiographies in response to the promotion of an increasingly Anglocentric 'British' identity. The work of these eighteenth-century antiquarians had profound implications, not only for the development of popular genres, such as historical fiction and the national tale, but also for the rise of specifically Irish, Scots and Welsh cultural nationalism. However, despite the usefulness of the bardic model for politicising antiquarian endeavours, Welsh fiction is actually the least likely place to find the kind of bardic nationalism Trumpener identifies in Scottish and Irish novels, as I show in chapter 5.[22]

One of the broader aims of this study is to explore how the work of eighteenth-century Welsh writers in English endorses, complicates and/or revises the theoretical/historical models sketched out above. On what terms and in what ways was Wales imagined in literary texts? Was Protestant loyalty the most crucial factor in shaping Welsh allegiance to Britain, as Linda Colley argues, or were there other, more unexpected, ways in which Welsh writers configured their national 'belonging'? In what ways does the work of anglophone Welsh writers challenge or uphold the belief in an acquiescent and Anglicised Wales? Can Welsh writing in English speak for a Welsh-speaking nation, or are these texts simply the product of an Anglicised upper echelon of society? More specifically, the study explores how history and historical narratives are used in a literary context. Are historical narratives of especial pertinence to Wales – Galfridian (Geoffrey of Monmouth's *The History of the Kings of Britain*), Tudor, Ancient British, the Edwardian conquest – used to further incorporation into Britain or to resist assimilation? In what ways are Welsh mythologies and literary traditions – St David, Arthur, Merlin, bardic traditions, the poetry of prophecy, the massacre of the bards – employed by literary authors, and to what ends? In what ways does mid-century antiquarianism bolster Welsh literary culture, and does it constitute a form of 'bardic' resistance to English cultural dominance? Or, is Welsh antiquarian writing in English a form of 'contributionism', whereby the literary past of Wales is simply further fuel for a broader sense of Britishness in the period? Issues of gender also expand our understanding of the central questions raised by this study. Does the work of eighteenth-century Welsh women writers in English reveal different attitudes from those expressed by their male counterparts? Were women able to speak of and for the nation with the same freedom as men? As I demonstrate in chapter 2, the poet Jane Brereton was influenced by gendered expectations of what a women poet should be, as well as by the dominant views of her male peers. Although she is partially successful in speaking on behalf of the Welsh nation as a woman poet, her views were very probably circumscribed by her wish for male approval.

The answers to the questions raised thus far are varied and complex. Although certain attitudes do recur, the allegiance of a particular writer is often directly influenced by a number of factors, including geographical location, gender, political views, class position and, of course, language 'choice'. The proximity of the London Welsh to the centres of power in London, for example, immediately destabilises any fixed binaries of centre/periphery or core/margin, and complicates the notion that the Welsh were, by dint of their birth, automatically excluded from the Establishment. Viewing Wales exclusively as the disadvantaged side of a centre–periphery dichotomy, or coloniser–colonised model, misrepresents those groups who are no doubt excluded in some ways, but who in other respects have access to elite institutions and power-bases (the Welsh connections of Jesus College, Oxford, would be another case in point). Indeed, what characterises much of the writing I discuss in my first two chapters is the often simultaneous claims which are made for both integration and distinctiveness, and which further break down any simple binary opposition between Welsh and British cultures. Writers from the early to mid century often express pride in a distinctly Welsh culture at the same time as firmly declaring strong loyalty to the Hanoverian monarchy. For example, in the sermons and poetry produced by the London Welsh Society of Ancient Britons, discussed in chapter 1, there is a clear pro-Hanoverian stance and images of peaceful union are frequently employed. Yet, through the various dramatisations of bardic prophecy, the insistence on the Welsh identity of the Ancient Britons and the antiquity of the Welsh language, plus the use of Galfridian mythology and anti-Saxon rhetoric, the texts discussed can be said not only to resist Anglo-British assimilation, but also to pave the way for the more openly nationalist re-appropriation of Welsh historical and literary traditions that was to follow. This is just one example of what Philip Schwyzer, working in the early modern period, has called the 'Welsh paradox', which he explains thus: 'within those Welsh texts that provided the key materials for the development of British nationalism there is also encoded a resistance to such acts of appropriation, a refusal to relinquish a separate Welsh identity'.[23] An eighteenth-century example of this phenomenon is the way in which the Tudors are often employed as symbolic precursors of the Hanoverians, yet with the understanding that Henry Tudor also serves as one incarnation of the 'Mab Darogan/Son of Prophecy', or deliverer of the Welsh people from colonial oppression.

What is often confusing in discussions of Britishness in any period of history is the slippage between, or sharing of, common Welsh and English national traditions. Despite the focus on 1707 in studies of eighteenth-century national identity, it is clear that many of the narratives of Britishness employed by writers in this period are versions of those used by writers in earlier times. Writing of Tudor national consciousness, Philip Schwyzer argues that 'British nationalism, the nationalism of the English, had much in common with Welsh national consciousness . . . British nationalism took most of its facts, many of its tropes, and even more of its tone from Welsh sources'.[24] This sense of Britishness – for both Welsh and English – was based on the hugely influential account of ancient British history, Geoffrey of Monmouth's *The History of the Kings of Britain* (*c*.1136). In the Tudor period, the Galfridian myth of origins was shared by English and Welsh, but with the following, crucially important, caveat: 'the Welsh rarely if ever extended the category of Britishness to include the English, or saw themselves as participating with them in a national identity'.[25] As several of the following chapters will show, the Galfridian myth of the founding of Ancient Britain by Brutus the Trojan continued to be influential with Welsh writers in both English and Welsh well into the eighteenth century.[26] However, by the eighteenth century the English no longer relied exclusively on the old narratives of Britishness. English writers began to dissociate themselves from this way of shaping national identity and turned increasingly to re-evaluations of Saxon liberty and constitutionalism. Even when the English did identify with the Ancient Britons, they managed to achieve this identification without any association with the contemporary Welsh.[27] Furthermore, as Christine Gerrard has argued, while the English were happy to mix up Saxons, Goths and Celts in one eclectic national muddle, with no apparent sense of contradiction, Welsh writers continued to emphasise the historical clashes between Saxons and Britons.[28] For the Welsh, the Saxons were always the enemy.

The varying ways in which the terms 'Briton' and 'British' were used by eighteenth-century writers is often confusing, given the fact that they

could (often simultaneously) refer to post-1707 Britons under
Hanoverian rule and/or to the Ancient British, the Welsh. Throughout
this study I have tried to make it clear from the various contexts in what
sense these terms are being employed. In contrast to their English
counterparts, many eighteenth-century Welsh writers continued to
emphasise the Brutus myth and frequently refer to themselves as the
Ancient Britons. These writers therefore make a firm distinction between
themselves and the post-1707 'Britons' of Colley's study. For these
eighteenth-century Welsh writers, 'British' signifies Welsh (and/or the
Welsh language), and 'Briton' refers to those of the ancient variety.
Edward Lhuyd, for example, expressed his patriotism by referring to
himself as 'an old Briton'.[29] Indeed, from one perspective, to say Welsh
instead of British is, as Philip Jenkins notes, to admit that 'the island had
been lost to the English'.[30] Some writers, such as Jane Brereton, avoid
making a discrete choice between British and Welsh. Brereton describes
her poetry as the work of a 'Cambrian' muse and often refers to herself
as a 'Cambro-Briton'. Cambria is the name used for Wales in Geoffrey of
Monmouth's *History*, and thus to use this name could, on one level,
invoke a respect for Galfridian tradition. Cambria is also, of course, the
Latinate derivative of *Cymry* or *Cymru*, so to use 'Cambria', as Jane
Brereton does, is to create a learned persona working within a venerable
tradition. As a woman poet, she adopted such authorising strategies to
lend a gravitas to her poetry and her poetic persona. As I discuss in
chapter 2, the choice of 'Cambro-Briton' as a self-descriptor also implies
a broad identification with English-language culture and post-union
Britishness, although Brereton herself is playful with these different
terms and seems aware of their various inflections.[31]

   Another major aim of this book, and of the series 'Writing Wales in
English' as a whole, is to reassess critical treatment of the English-
language literature of Wales. Just as scholars have begun to extend the
paradigms (such as post-colonialism) which we can use to describe
Welsh writing in English, the dates of its inception are also being
questioned and revised. The main way in which this study challenges
conventional accounts of Welsh writing in English is through its focus on
the eighteenth century. Pre-twentieth-century texts have been
marginalised from a canon of Welsh writing in English due to the
dominance of one model of 'Anglo-Welsh' writing, which sees it as
beginning with the publication of Caradoc Evans's *My People* in 1915.
For example, the volume *Welsh Writing in English* (2003) has only one
chapter on pre-1900 texts, 'Prelude to the Twentieth Century', which

focuses mainly on Henry Vaughan and John Dyer.[32] However, as
M. Wynn Thomas has noted, there is a different model for Welsh writing
in English 'based on the undeniable fact that writers born, or living, in
Wales have been using English ever since the 15th century'.[33] This
alternative (but not necessarily mutually exclusive) model for the
English-language literature of Wales has recently been gaining ground,
especially in the fields of Romanticism and nineteenth-century studies.
Jane Aaron's important work on women's writing from the Romantic
period and the nineteenth century has been crucial in opening up the
field. Further recent scholarship which redresses this imbalance has
been, for example, the work of Moira Dearnley and Andrew Davies in
the field of eighteenth-century and Romantic fiction, and that of
Catherine Brennan on nineteenth-century women's poetry.[34]

Extending the chronology of Welsh writing in English backwards
does not only expand the canon in bibliographical terms; it also raises
fresh questions about the field itself. Unlike in the twentieth century,
eighteenth-century Wales did not have a substantial population of urban
English speakers who could act as an indigenous audience for
anglophone literature. As Geraint H. Jenkins notes of eighteenth-
century Wales, 'Nine out of every ten of the population spoke only
Welsh'.[35] At least since William Morgan's translation of the Bible in
1588, Welsh had also been the language of religion in Wales. The
eighteenth century built on this tradition through the printing of cheaper
editions of the Bible and the Welsh Prayer Book, which reached a wide
audience and helped to increase literacy.[36] Furthermore, Welsh scholars,
such as Lewis Morris and his circle (which included Evan Evans, the
subject of chapter 3), were labouring to preserve the literary and
historical treasures of Wales as well as to produce a body of Welsh
writing which could rival English 'Augustanism'.[37] Since the Acts of
Union in 1536 and 1543, however, Welsh had no longer been the official
language of the law, professions, business and administration in Wales, a
situation not rectified in a legal context until the Welsh Court Act of
1942. Wales had to wait even longer for the Welsh Language Act of 1993
to put Welsh and English on an equal footing in public life.[38] The
'downgrading' of Welsh as an official language affected its status in the
eyes of the English and Anglo-identified circles in Wales. As Geraint H.
Jenkins also points out, in the eighteenth century the Welsh language
was viewed by Anglicised groups as not reaching the status of 'a learned
tongue', despite its dominance as the language of religion in Wales.[39]

It might be expected, then, that English texts written by Welsh writers in this period were the product of an Anglicised minority who either did not speak or write Welsh, or who deliberately rejected their native tongue as unsuitable for literary expression. Furthermore, to invoke a post-colonial paradigm, it could be suggested that those eighteenth-century authors who wrote in English were attempting to mimic the voice of the coloniser, in the hope of being accepted into the English literary establishment. The reality is inevitably more complicated. Far from openly rejecting the Welsh language, eighteenth-century writers often use English to argue for the Welsh language as a source of national pride and, more broadly, to articulate resistance to incorporation into an Anglicised hegemony. Translation practices are also significant in this context, at a time when literary cross-fertilisation between Wales and England has been seen as particularly fruitful. Although translation of Welsh texts into English has been interpreted as yet another symptom of assimilation or 'cultural cringe', it could also be argued that, in the antiquarian work of Evan Evans for example, translation is a much more politically charged and radical proposition. Any simple generalisations are further complicated by the fact that writers wrote in English for different reasons at different times. It would appear, for example, that Jane Brereton did not have any knowledge of Welsh, which explains her language choice. On the other hand, Evan Evans wrote the majority of his poetry in Welsh, which makes his choice of English as a medium much more considered and driven by a variety of motives, of which defence of his native land was only one. Overall, while it is clear that some Welsh writers do use English to express integrationist sentiments, it is equally apparent that the use of English did not automatically preclude patriotic expression or a sense of national 'belonging'. Indeed, however we wish to categorise 'Welsh Writing in English' in this period, it is fair to say that, in all their variety of opinion and expression, the Welsh writers discussed in this study created a discernible and vital body of writing which starts well before the twentieth century. Nevertheless, while this body of writing does not simply reject or oppose its Welsh-language equivalent, neither is the relationship between the two one of peaceful coexistence, but is lived out, in M. Wynn Thomas's phrase, on 'terms of tense and uneasy intimacy'.[40]

This book does not claim, however, to be an authoritative or comprehensive survey of eighteenth-century Welsh writing in English. Its main purpose is to investigate the place of Wales and Welsh writing in the context of emergent Britishness in the eighteenth century. The book is, nevertheless, structured in a broadly chronological fashion. Chapter 1 considers the (ostensibly) pro-Hanoverian sermons and poetry produced under the auspices of the London Welsh Society of Ancient Britons, which was established in 1714. Staying in the early eighteenth century, chapter 2 explores the poetry of Jane Brereton in terms of her construction of her poetic persona as 'the Cambrian muse'. Chapter 3 investigates the politics of Evan Evans's translations of *Some Specimens of the Antient Welsh Bards* (1764), but also takes a more comparative approach through its investigation of the literary representation of the Edwardian conquest in the poetry of Evans and Thomas Gray. Patriotic poems of Wales are the focus of chapter 4, where I compare English and Welsh treatments of this topic in order to gauge in what ways they differ in their attitudes to Welshness and Britishness. Chapter 5 considers the way in which three novelists – Tobias Smollett, Anna Maria Bennett and Edward Davies – attempt to represent the Welsh nation in relation to dominant ideas of Anglo-Britishness. In a study such as this there are some inevitable omissions. For example, I have not discussed the poetry of John Dyer in any depth here. Dyer's *Grongar Hill* (1726) is one of the better-known poems by a Welsh writer from the eighteenth century and, as such, I have chosen to concentrate on lesser-known writers whose work provides new insights into my field of research.[41] Similarly, although my study includes texts from the 1790s, I deliberately avoid treading on the toes of those working in Welsh Romanticism, currently an extremely vibrant area.[42] However, it is to be hoped that one of the effects of this book will be not only to provide a fresh context for reading the poetry of John Dyer, for example, but also to stimulate further discussion about what constitutes the range and scope of 'Welsh Writing in English'.

1

'What Foes more dang'rous than too strong Allies?': The Society of Ancient Britons and Anglo-Welsh Relations in Eighteenth-Century London

Now shall the Rose, *the* Thistle, *and the* LEEK
Each a due Mixture in one Garland seek;
Henceforth with decent Pomp for ever spred,
Incircling Yearly CAROLINA's *Head.*[1]

It might seem self-explanatory that the most straightforward expressions of Welsh support for British unity might be found in London, the centre of British political and cultural life and also the capital city of England. As the first London Welsh society to be established, the Society of Ancient Britons (founded in 1714, the same year as the Hanoverian succession) might equally be expected to voice such sentiments, especially as its members were geographically closer to the centre of power. However, as I will demonstrate, the texts (mostly sermons, but also poetry) published by, or inscribed to, the Society often reveal more unexpected configurations of Welsh identity, which unsettle an integrationist emphasis on British unity. In many ways, the Society of Ancient Britons is the ideal place to assess Welsh–English relations in the eighteenth century, in that, although its members were mostly Welsh, it also included prominent Englishmen and was acutely aware of how its activities might appear to an English audience. Furthermore, as befits any society of this type, the views of its members encompassed a spectrum of opinions on Welsh and British national identity from a variety of different religious backgrounds. On one level, therefore, the opinions expressed by some of the Society's members are valuable precisely for showing the forms which Welsh loyalty to the Hanoverian state could take in the eighteenth century and for demonstrating how Welshmen could articulate their support for the post-1707 British Establishment. From another perspective, if we can locate resistance here – in the views expressed by London Welshmen, who might be expected to be more Anglicised than their countrymen living in Wales itself – it is my contention that such opposition raises serious questions about the extent of Welsh-British solidarity in the period.

Unlike the later scholarly societies such as the Cymmrodorion and the Gwyneddigion, which were set up primarily to further the literary culture and language of Wales, the Society of Ancient Britons was founded as a patriotic and charitable institution to help impoverished Welsh families living in London.[2] Sir Thomas Jones's account of the founding of the Society, *The Rise and Progress of the Most Honourable and Loyal Society of Antient Britons* (1717), outlines the initial impetus.[3] The creation of the Society in 1714 was in direct response to the Protestant succession: it was established in order to demonstrate the 'uncommon Zeal' of the Welsh in favour of the Hanoverians (and in the face of Catholic and Jacobite threat), as well as to celebrate St David's Day, 'the Tutelar Saint of their *Antient Country*' (p. 11), which 'providentially' fell on the birthday of Princess Caroline (1 March). The public face of the Society was presented by the annual St David's Day charity sermon, usually preached in Welsh, 'the *Antient British Language*' (p. 15), in a prominent London location: the first sermon was in St Paul's, Covent Garden. These high-profile sermons were attended by members of the Court and House of Commons, as well as the Bishop of Bangor and various representatives of the '*Welsh* nobility, Gentry and Clergy' (p. 15). The company would then proceed to Haberdashers' Hall to have dinner, make toasts and choose the stewards for the following year. At the first meeting in 1714, the Society also chose its president: George, Prince of Wales. In addition, the Society collected subscriptions and donations, which were controlled by the current Bishop of Bangor and used 'for the Benefit of the *Welch* Nation in general, as they shall think proper' (p. 21). In 1716, for example, the money was used to put out two Welsh boys as apprentices, one in north and one in south Wales, together with ten pounds each. Charity was also dispensed to 'other poor Persons, Natives of the Principality' (p. 53). In 1718, the Society was successful in its plan to establish a charity school, which aimed to educate Welsh children who were born in London, but not entitled to a parochial settlement. By the end of the century, a schoolhouse had been built in Gray's Inn Road which was able to accommodate 60 children. By 1793, 773 boys and 72 girls had passed through the school.[4]

In addition to its charitable function, the Society of Ancient Britons worked as a London showcase for Welsh Hanoverian and Whiggish loyalty. The after-dinner toasts display the avowed loyalties of the members: King George and the Church of England; the Prince and Princess of Wales; the Lord Mayor of London; King and Parliament; Prosperity to Trade; Prosperity to the Principality of Wales.[5] As Alexander Murdoch explains,

> When the London Welsh ostentatiously displayed the three ostrich plumes of the Prince of Wales's standard at the ceremonies of the Order of Ancient Britons, this was done to show the loyalty of the Welsh to the Hanoverian kings, in contrast to the Irish or Scots.[6]

Furthermore, the St David's Day sermons were very public events which attracted an influential and wealthy audience and gave Welsh clerics the opportunity to speak on issues pertinent to their native land. Accordingly, many of the sermons printed by the Society express a positive view of British integration, although, as Prys Morgan has noted, opinions varied in line with the particular viewpoint of the preacher.[7] These ranged from the nationalistic outrage of the scholar Moses Williams to the rather condescending tone used towards the Welsh by the Hanoverian bishops.[8] In the English dedication to *A Sermon Preached in Welsh before the British Society* (1723), William Wotton writes about Welsh–English relations from the perspective of a Welsh-speaking Englishman.[9] In the context of praising the design of the Society, Wotton remarks: 'It was a mutual Happiness to both Nations, that after long and bloody Struggles we at last coalesced into one People' (2 [no pag.]). Wotton goes on to promote the Tudor Union as simultaneously enabling successful Anglo-Welsh integration and continuing a sense of distinctness through an emphasis on the Welsh lineage of the Tudor monarchs:

> You have now, for near two hundred and fifty Years been governed by Princes of your own Blood, and We have all had the same common Sovereigns. We rejoice to see a People under the same Allegiance with Ourselves praising God in their own Language in Our Capital City. We desire your Happiness equally with our own. And there can be no Happiness where Brethren do not *dwell together in Unity*. (2–3 [no pag.])

Such a positive view of British unity between England and Wales can also be found in the preface to *The Goodness and Severity of GOD*, a sermon preached to the Society in 1716 by the Welsh Presbyterian Jeremy Owen.[10] Owen seemingly went even further, in his attempt to link Welsh identity to patriotic British pride and Hanoverian loyalty, by claiming a direct bloodline from the Tudors to George I:

> We find flowing in his Veins the Blood of the *Tudors*, derived from our own *Ancient Stock*, that we may justly triumph in him as one from among ourselves, by far the most worthy of any that could be found *to bear rule over us.* (2 [no pag.])

Owen links Union and Reformation together as a joint blessing for the Welsh. It was the Welsh and the English together who produced the 'First king that threw off the Pope's supremacy', and the 'Blessing of the *Reformation* reach'd us not until we were thus united' (p. 23). Due to these blessings, Owen asks: 'May not the Oppressed now sing for Joy, that their Oppressors are so no more, but their reconciled Friends and dear Brethren in Christ?' (p. 16). However, although both Wotton's and Owen's views of the Tudor Union seem positive overall, the repeated references to past bloodshed and to the English as oppressors, even though they may now be friends and Christian brothers, nevertheless alerts listeners and readers to a less than amicable history between the two nations. Furthermore, the use of the phrase 'compleatly incorporated' in the next quotation suggests that Wales was subsumed under English law, rather than assuming an equal position:

> And in the time of *Henry* VIII of the *British* Blood, we were compleatly incorporated into the *English* Nation, and enjoy'd thenceforth the same laws and Privileges with themselves. And tho' there had been such Contention and shedding of Blood, yet from thenceforward no Subjects more peaceable, or made more easy. Neither have we any separate Interest from theirs; nor are we to reckon ourselves as Two distinct Bodies, but as one and the same Body Politick with the *English*. (p. 15)

Present amity and political unity are again unsettled by the constant references to a bloody and contentious past which clearly still rankles in the Welsh national consciousness. Furthermore, the passage also shifts uneasily between claiming total incorporation into the English nation in the first instance, and then retracting to imply merely that unity is only really operative through a shared 'body Politick', not a merged nationhood.

Nevertheless, such positive and pro-Unionist interpretations of Tudor history as a providential deliverance for the Welsh persisted into the mid eighteenth century. In *The Christian Soldier* (1750), a sermon preached by John Evans at St Andrews, Holborn, Evans declares that Providence rewarded the 'brave' and 'honest' Welsh with 'Kings and Princes of *their own Blood* to govern Them, in so much that, now for many Successions, It had been a *Distinguishing* Part of the *Title* to the British Throne, *to be descended from a Tudor*'.[11] The connection between Welshness and post-Reformation Protestantism is made through the figure of Henry VIII of '*Ancient-British Blood*' (p. 24). Evans reminds his audience that 'Ye owe the *Beginning* and the *Establishment* of the *Reformation*, to a *Tudor*' (p. 24). As a result, English worship is practised in the '*Same Purity* in which Ye *at first* received *it* from *us*' (p. 24). Evans also emphasises the unity between the English and Welsh, albeit in a slightly different manner from either Wotton or Owen. In his emphasis on shared bloodlines and linguistic hybridity with the English he extends the context of the Welsh bloodline of the Tudors to include the English nation as a whole. To further his attempt to get the English audience to be charitable to the Welsh children in London – the main purpose of the sermon – Evans claims that it is extremely likely that most English people (not just the monarch) will have a fair proportion of Welsh blood in their veins:

> Lastly, as it is hardly credible that there are many, if any, Englishmen of the *Saxon* or *Norman* Race, at this Day in Great Britain, whose Blood is not mingled with the Ancient British: And as We have been taught for Ages past, to look upon ourselves as one People; permit me to apply myself to you ALL, as *such*; and to observe that These children, for whom I have taken upon me to plead with You, are All intended for Your future Service. (pp. 25–6)

Evans qualifies his statement by rehearsing British history to argue that the Saxons descend in part from some of the Ancient Britons left in England:

> The *Welsh* know no other Name for *Englishmen*, at this Day, than *Saison*, or *Saxons*: to whom, I do believe, they were the more readily reconciled, as looking upon them, at the time of their Reconciliation, as *Descendants*, in part, from *those Britons* whom they left in England; when *They*, the *Nobility* and *Gentry*, who refused to submit to the *Saxons*, retreated, with their Adherents, into Those Parts now call'd *Wales*. . . . It is not Rational

to suppose, that *so small* a Spot as *Wales* could have contained and maintained *All* the Inhabitants of this whole Kingdom. (pp. 25–6)

Although his overall aim is to argue for reconciliation, the use of the word 'Saison' for the English points to the potentially problematic connection between the ancient Saxon conquerors and the present-day English. In addition, the claim that the English descend in part only from those Britons who were left behind after the nobility and gentry fled contains the rather unflattering suggestion that it was only the lower order of Britons who mixed with their Saxon rulers. Nevertheless, Evans backs up his assertions of Welsh–English concord by claiming linguistic hybridity as well as a mixture of bloodlines. In the first English dictionary, he argues, the words contained were 'near half British. And it will be Difficult for him to persuade Himself, that there could be such a mixture of *languages*, where there was *none* of *Bloods*' (p. 26). He ends with a domestic vision of intermarriage based on linguistic and cultural synthesis: 'it is natural and easy to imagin [*sic*] that the Children of a *Saxon* and a *Briton* would make a Language out of *those* of *Both Parents*' (p. 26). The intermarriage of Welsh and Saxon produces children who speak an English language which uses words of both Welsh and Saxon origin. As such, Evans argues that the English language is not only one of Anglo-Saxon provenance, but is also Welsh-British in make-up. By the same token, the monarchical lineage is configured as a mixing of Tudor and Hanoverian blood, which together form the present united British monarchy. In terms of genealogical make-up as well as political consensus, Evans suggests, the Welsh and English really are 'one body'.[12] Overall, then, the imagery of mixed blood is used on the level of the domestic, the linguistic and the political.[13]

Such configurations of a mixed Welsh-Saxon British identity through shared blood and language are clearly problematic when taken out of the context of symbolic monarchical myth-making. In fact, there are remarkably few borrowings from Welsh into English, and the mingling of blood on a domestic level was, at this point, also rare. Indeed, Evans's claim about the Welshness of the English language is not repeated in any of the writers I discuss in this study, nor does it seem to have been used by anglophone Welsh writers as a way of inflecting their use of the medium of English for literary expression. However, as Kathleen Wilson, among others, has noted, in the early to mid eighteenth century older biblical ideas of the nation as a 'breed, stock or race' were still competing with newer ideas of the nation as 'a political-territorial entity'.[14] Although the more recognisable racialised assumptions about the origin of nations are apparent in the idea that the English were the 'one superior Island race', such assumptions became more commonplace only towards the end of the eighteenth century.[15] Indeed, despite the ground-breaking philological work of Edward Lhuyd (1660–1709), who began to define the Celtic languages as a distinct grouping, it was only towards the end of the eighteenth century (in the wake of Thomas Percy's edition of Paul-Henri Mallet's *Northern Antiquities* in 1770) that the Celts began to be distinguished from the Gothic or Teutonic nations.[16] As Colin Kidd's work has demonstrated, 'Mosaic' notions about 'the ethnic consanguinity of Britain's Celtic and Germanic stocks' who are all seen originally to derive (albeit in different branches) from Noah's grandson Gomer persisted into the eighteenth century.[17] It was only when the Celts and Saxons came to be understood as identifiable and distinct 'races' that it was possible to categorise the Celts as 'primitive' and 'savage' in comparison with the 'virtuous' and 'liberty-loving' Saxons.[18] Such racial distinctions also 'undermined the notion of shared political customs of Briton and Saxon', as 'Liberty' became appropriated by the English as the staple of a specifically Saxon identity.[19] As I show in chapter 4, English commentators from the end of the eighteenth century tend to emphasise the separate racial and linguistic identity of the Welsh as Celtic 'others', in order to assert their own sense of superiority. By the end of the century it would be unusual to argue, as Evans appears to, for a unified Britishness based on common bloodlines and shared linguistic heritage.

Like that of their English contemporaries, however, the rhetoric of union and Reformation used by the Society of the Ancient Britons often assumes a virulently anti-Catholic (and, by association, anti-French) tone, which adds to the providential message of Protestant British triumph. However, for the Welsh, the central focus is again on the Tudor Union as a providential blessing. Jeremy Owen writes of 'our Henry VIII' as being the monarch who 'as he completed our Union with one another, so he laid the Foundation for our Separation from the *Mother of Harlots*' (p. 23). Owen then links the Tudors to the Hanoverians, who are jointly responsible for forming Great Britain as a great Protestant nation. George I's ancestors (Duke Ernest and Duke Francis), Owen claims, 'were some of the earliest Patrons of the Reformation; and the same hereditary Zeal for this noble Cause, has continu'd without Interruption, in the direct Line of that August Family, down to him whom Providence has made the great Defender of our Faith' (p. 28). The King is described as a 'Hereditary Nursing Father to our Religion', and the British have been 'reserv'd in the Womb of Providence, unto the cleanest and brightest day of *Great-Britain*' (p. 30). The biblical language of messianic rebirth, also associated with the poetry of prophecy, is now used to celebrate the Protestant succession of eighteenth-century Britain.[20] Similarly, in *The Rise and Progress* (1717), Thomas Jones displays strong anti-Catholic and anti-Jacobite sentiments. He presents the 1715 invasion as an 'unnatural Rebellion' by 'the Popish Pretender', which was promoted by 'Papists, Non-Jurors, and others their Adherents' who are all unequivocal 'Enemies' of the King (p. 32). The language employed criminalises Jacobite resistance: the Pretender is an 'outlaw' and the 'Rebellion' part of the 'Projects of guilty Men' (p. 36). In contrast, the members of the Society of Ancient Britons – 'We of your Majesty's Dominion of Wales' (p. 37) – are loyal and patriotic Protestants who are 'men full of Love and true Loyalty to their King and Country' (pp. 38–9). Jones offers an account of George I's genealogical descent in terms of whether previous monarchs were either Catholic or Protestant to prove that the Hanoverian George is the proper heir to the throne, in opposition to 'a Papist, who is excluded by our Laws and Acts of Settlement, as utterly incapable of being our King' (p. 64).[21] Jones adds conclusively: 'So that it's plain there can be, in point of Birth-right, no one Competitor with our King' (p. 64). The truth of this assertion, Jones argues, is absolutely clear to the 'true *Briton* and serious Protestant', even though, as Linda Colley explains, in order to secure a Protestant successor, Parliament 'passed over more than fifty individuals who were closer as blood relations to Queen Anne but ineligible because of their Catholic faith'.[22]

The sermons had a textual life beyond their initial performance and many were published at the behest of the Society. Thomas Jones states that four thousand copies of the first sermon were printed in Welsh, some of which were 'dispersed among the Common People for whose Good it was intended, that they might be instructed in the Duties of Brotherly Love, and of Loyalty to their King in their own Language' (p. 17).[23] Later sermons were also printed in English and Welsh: 'for the Benefit of the Natives of Wales, and others of this Nation' (p. 52). A significant point about the Society's sermons is that many were preached originally in Welsh and then translated into English for publication, sometimes with the use of parallel texts in Welsh and English.[24] Therefore, even if the original delivery was in the Welsh language, through the publication process the Society reached, and also perhaps anticipated, an English audience.[25] On one level, then, these sermons are preaching to the converted, in that the original Welsh would obviously be understood only by Welsh speakers in the audience. From this perspective, any comments about the cultural status of Wales and the Welsh language are made from within that language and are therefore self-justifying: the proof of the vitality of the language is in the preaching. However, the fact that these sermons must also have reached a wider English audience raises some very interesting questions as to whom exactly these sermons were being directed at, what their effect might be, and what they reveal further about eighteenth-century Anglo-Welsh relations.

It is my contention that many of the sermons used the fact of a projected English-speaking audience to argue the case for the cultural superiority of the Welsh language, and thereby to assert a sense of national pride. Ironically, given the Tudor enthusiasm of the Society of Ancient Britons, the sixteenth-century Act of Union was itself responsible for the abandonment of Welsh for legal and political matters.[26] Various Welsh commentators in the late seventeenth and early eighteenth centuries expressed anxiety about the demise of the Welsh language under the forces of Anglicisation.[27] At the same time, a variety of early eighteenth-century English writers published satirical pieces which undermined and belittled Welsh and those who spoke it.[28] It is against the combined forces of pessimism and satirical attack, as well as the more obvious religious context, that the treatment of the Welsh language by the Society of Ancient Britons should be considered. The printing of Welsh alongside English in a parallel translation proved that the two languages were on an equal footing. Furthermore, as I shall demonstrate, when the sermons discuss the Welsh language, this is in terms of its significance not only as a language of great antiquity, but also as a source of resistance to English power.

William Wotton again presents an interesting case, in that he is a Celtophile Englishman preaching in Welsh as a second language, whose text is then published in parallel translation. As befits a translator of the laws of Hywel Dda, Wotton links the preservation of the language and 'love for country' to the preservation of the Welsh laws. Wotton also stresses the ongoing distinctiveness of the Welsh in terms of language, religion and ancient constitution:

It is an Honour to You that You have the Book of God so accurately translated into Your own Language. You have also the Usages and Constitutions of Your Ancestors still extstant [*sic*] in Your Mother-Tongue. It argued a true Love for Your Country to preserve such a record so long entire. (1 [no pag.])

In contrast to France and Spain, he argues, whose people have nothing 'of their original Tongue to boast of', the Welsh continued 'a distinct People' despite being subject to Roman rule.

In *The Christian Soldier*, John Evans goes further to link language and freedom, comparing the fate of other great empires – Assyrian, Macedonian, Roman – to that of the Ancient British. He declares the Welsh 'a conquered People' and adds:

Which of All the Empires of the World made so brave and so long a struggle for Liberty as the Britons did, for eight hundred Years; and preserved themselves *so Free* to the last. We speak our *own Language* at this day, *That* which was the *Language of our Fathers* before the *Roman Conquest*: we still have our Possessions in *That* Country of which we were the *First Inhabitants*. And if our well meaning Simplicity was once imposed upon, to accept of a *Prince* from *England*; it was only to give *England* a *King* often since: for the *Prince of Wales* is always *Spes Altera Anglorum*. (pp. 21–2)

This is an openly patriotic interpretation of the status of the Ancient British and their relation to the English monarchy, as befits a founder member of the Cymmrodorion Society. The sermon is used as a way of defending the Welsh language, the longevity of which is a sign of the way in which the Ancient Britons fought for their liberty against colonial oppression.[29] By focusing on the 'liberty' for which the Ancient Britons fought so strenuously, Evans could be said to mount a challenge to England's claims to be the land of (Saxon) liberty. He also suggests that the Welsh have been imposed upon by the English in the creation of the title of Prince of Wales, but cleverly turns this on its head to imply that, by the same token, the English king is by definition Welsh (with the added suggestion that England's future hope, in fact, lies in Wales: '*Spes Altera Anglorum*'). Such pronouncements centring on the Welsh language suggest a much more resistant stance and a more oppositional identity than Linda Colley's view of widespread Protestant solidarity with the English.[30]

In *The Goodness and Severity of GOD*, Jeremy Owen had also stressed the antiquity of the Welsh language as a way of asserting national pride. Welsh is one of the original languages derived from Babel, Owen claims, and adds that "'tis not likely to have it's [*sic*] Ending till the Dissolution of the World' (p. 8). Owen's interpretation of the Welsh as the original inhabitants of Britain is circumspect. His tone is rueful as he describes the break-up of Britain as an irreparable division, indeed diaspora. The imagery here is that of loss and confinement and also suggestive of imprisonment and defeat:

> Britons were once the only Lords and Possessors of the Island, now mostly shut up within the Confines of *Wales*, besides a colony of them settled in a Part of *America*, and what remains of them in *Cornwall*, and a Province in *France*, where they have almost lost the ancient Language. (p. 9)

Although Owen turns this diasporic vision into a gain for Wales – the Welsh have, of course, *not* lost their language – the imagery employed demonstrates a clear consciousness of the political and cultural dimension to the preservation of the Welsh language:

> 'Tis hardly known but that the Language of a People is lost with their Liberty; the Conquest of a Land has generally issu'd (in process of Time) in the Conquest of the Language: The Conquerors have given Law to Words as well as Actions, and to the Tongue as well as to the Customs and Manners of the Nation conquer'd. (p. 9)

Owen is fully aware here of the link between linguistic and cultural domination and frames such awareness in a clearly colonial context.[31]

Statements such as these suggest a more critical view of the Tudor Union, which, of course, introduced English as the language of the law in Wales. Although Owen asserts that the Britons were successful in resisting Roman and Saxon incursions on their native tongue – 'In this one only thing they have maintain'd their Dominion' (p. 9) – there is a knowledge here of the insidious processes of Anglicisation on Welsh language and culture. Overall, the treatment of the Welsh language in the sermons of the Society of Ancient Britons reveals a much more oppositional stance than the integrationist approach taken elsewhere to interpret British history. This view of language as a site of struggle for articulating and preserving national identity can be said to coincide with the more openly radical linkage of language, literature, antiquarianism and specifically Welsh patriotism which was beginning to emerge in the early to mid eighteenth century in the work of scholars such as Edward Lhuyd, the Morris brothers and Evan Evans.

Indeed, some of the clerics who spoke to the Society, such as John Evans and Moses Williams, were key players in these areas.

Although many of the sermons were printed in English, there are exceptions. The sermons preached by Moses Williams for the Society in 1717 and 1721 were printed in Welsh only (in 1718 and 1722 respectively). It is no coincidence that these sermons are considerably more outspoken than those which were translated. As Brynley F. Roberts notes, his 1717 sermon for the Society of Ancient Britons is remarkable, in that the 'Welsh national note struck in the sermon is more unambiguously political than the cultural one which was more usual at the time'.[32] Williams was an antiquarian scholar and translator who had worked with Edward Lhuyd on the *Archaeologia Britannica* (1707) at the Ashmolean Museum in Oxford. He was also responsible for editing translations of the Bible into Welsh and assisted William Wotton on his translation of the Welsh laws, which he completed after Wotton's death in 1726. In keeping with this Welsh scholarship, and Lhuyd's work in particular, Williams emphasises the Celtic antiquity of the Welsh language and people. However, like many other Welsh commentators, such as Theophilus Evans in his *Drych y Prif Oesoedd* (1716),[33] he is also enthusiastic about the views of the Breton Abbé Pezron, especially his claims for a direct lineage from Gomer's descendants to the Welsh nation:

> A Breton author has recently written a Book on this subject, which very eruditely and accurately proves through a great deal of credible and judicious Reasoning that these People came directly from the lineage of Gomer the eldest son of Japheth and Noah, which is sufficient to show that the Welsh Nation is equal in terms of its Antiquity to any other in this part of the World.[34]

In keeping again with his own work in biblical translation, Williams stresses what was commonly seen as the close connection between Welsh and Hebrew: 'it is related so closely and is so appropriately matched to the old language of the Eastern world, there is no translation of the Holy Scriptures whose understanding of the Spirit is so perfect and so complete as the Welsh translation' (p. 14).

Williams does not only use the antiquity of the Welsh language as a way of affirming past glory, he also argues for immediate and practical action to prevent its threatened extinction in the present.[35] In the first instance he argues, in a side glance at the widespread practice of appointing English-speaking clergy to livings in Wales, that Welsh 'is the language which is generally understood best throughout Wales and therefore the best language in which to disseminate Knowledge and Godliness among the monoglot Peasantry to the everlasting good of their Souls' (p. 12). However, Williams goes even further than this to suggest that, due to the processes of Anglicisation, the Welsh themselves are partly responsible for the decline of the language. He declares that many of his own countrymen (particularly those in London, the immediate audience for the sermon) are guilty of 'Thinking it shameful to admit to being *Welsh* and that it is far more responsible and acceptable (especially away from home) to be *English*' (p. 12). Stating that it is 'difficult for me to believe that such an Absurdity exists, unless I knew it to be true', Williams goes on to argue that Anglicisation causes the Welsh 'to forget their Nationality, to scorn their Language, and to neglect their Country in which they were born and brought up' (p. 12). The sermon therefore acts as a clarion call – 'a public show of my good Will to my Nation' – to rouse the Welsh to defend the nation in the face of 'the Calumny of the Enemy whether they be Welsh or Foreign (*anghyfiaith*)' (p. 12). If organised properly, Williams suggests, the charitable work of the Society can work towards such a goal of galvanising the Welsh nation to practical action.

Throughout his 1717 sermon Williams politicises and critiques the processes of Anglicisation in ways which fundamentally undermine attempts to present a positive image of British unity with England. The Tudor union of Wales and England is seen by Williams as having been effected 'through English cunning rather than force of arms' (p. 13). By a similar token, the undermining of the Welsh language is politicised by pointing out not only the Anglicisation of the language into 'a corrupt, obscure, slipshod Patois' by the introduction of 'new Anglicised words' (p. 15), but also by making explicit the professional rewards for being Anglicised and the penalties for being Welsh:

> However, if the Welsh language is not only something of which we should not be ashamed but also so advantageous, useful and indispensable to us as well as to our Souls, why is there so much Hostility towards it on the part of its own People? Was the misfortune of losing England so insignificant that we are now giving Wales to the English as well, and becoming their complete Slaves throughout the Island? It is already an infrequent occurrence that any Welshman is appointed to an Office or Position, however worthy he may be, and where an Englishman may dare to employ him, either here or in Wales itself. (p. 14)

Commentators such as Linda Colley have emphasised the positive gains in buying into Britain for members of the 'Celtic' nations, but what Williams shows is a very clear awareness of the negative side of becoming British: the loss of language and nation. Indeed, Williams goes as far as to suggest that as a result of English mockery, Wales is in danger of extinction:

> It is my Hope that there will not be a single Welshman who is mad enough to convince them of this Misapprehension, in case the Progeny of this oppressive Nation which has already taken England from us, steal Wales too in the same Manner, and thereby, in time, eradicate our Name under the Heavens. (p. 15)

The role of the Society, as perceived by Williams, to defend the language and thereby to save Wales is therefore to preserve the nation as a distinct entity and to resist vigorously the processes of Anglicisation associated with becoming British.

Moses Williams's sermon makes explicit the undercurrent of discontent bubbling beneath the surface of the more openly unionist sentiments expressed by Evans and Owen. His text also draws attention to one area of Welsh history which is a recurring theme in the sermons of the Society and in much Welsh literature in English: the Saxon conquest. Williams makes constant allusions to the loss of England to the Saxons, and refers to the Britons as 'the best of the People' who were 'driven out of their Homeland and retreated to the mountains of Wales to avoid the cruelty of the Enemies (who were previously Servants to them)' (p. 13). It is clear that there is a direct connection between the Saxons and the English. Although his sermon was preached originally in Welsh, Jeremy Owen's term in the English translation is 'the English *Saxons*' (p. 14). Similarly, John Evans states that 'The *Welsh* know no other Name for *Englishmen*, at this Day, than *Saison*, or *Saxons*' (p. 26). Jeremy Owen's sermon is also quick to point out that the Britons (the Welsh) were the victims of oppression and invasion. In the first instance, Roman vice and excess brought the formerly valiant British to a state of indolence and ease. After the Romans departed, the now slothful nature of the British people meant that they were at the mercy of roving Picts and Scots. The overriding disaster, however, is the arrival of the Saxons:

> And now is the time of their Overthrow and Desolation at hand. Stupid and Insensate People! they open the Sheepfold, and let in the ravenous

Wolves to guard the Flock; they invite the bloody treacherous *Saxons* into the Kingdom as stipendiary Soldiers, to fight in their Defence against the Barbarians that incessantly harras'd them. (p. 13)[36]

The Saxons were soon to reveal their treachery and, as Owen comments, 'the Remedy prov'd much worse than the Disease' (p. 13). As a result of their stupidity, the Britons were forced into the hills or pushed into 'vowing perpetual Servitude' at the feet of their 'hired Servants' (p. 13). Others were, as Owen hinted earlier, forced to disperse to 'foreign Countries' and 'might very well (though their tunefull Harps were thrown upon the Willow-trees) if not sing, yet sigh and howl out this mournful *Song* of *Zion*, in *Psalm 43*' (pp. 13–14).[37]

Owen's depiction of Saxon treachery and enforced Welsh diaspora is angry and bitter, despite the fact that in the event it is smoothed over, as a result of the Reformation, when the Saxon oppressors become 'reconciled Friends and dear Brethren in Christ' (p. 16). As Geraint H. Jenkins has noted, for Owen, 'recent Welsh–English relations offered a splendid paradigm of Samson's riddle: out of the eater came forth meat, and out of [the] strong sweetness'.[38] Despite the stress on a positive outcome, however, the tensions involved in Owen's attempt to smooth over past conflict are palpable. The historical conflict between Ancient Briton and Saxon works to unsettle the veneer of British solidarity which these sermons might elsewhere preach. Moreover, it could be argued that, given the fact that many English writers were increasingly celebrating the Teutonic heritage of the Hanoverians, the negative treatment of British–Saxon relations by Welsh writers represents further resistance to Anglo-British incorporation and a more clear-cut division of Welsh and English national pasts.[39] In the dedication to his epic poem *Alfred* (1723), for example, Sir Richard Blackmore tells Prince Frederick that Alfred is 'a Prince sprung from the ancient S*axon* Race of your own native Land' (p. 6).[40] Furthermore, in 1722 Edmund Gibson (bishop of London) fulsomely dedicated the revised edition of William Camden's *Britannia* to George I in terms of the common Saxon ancestry of King and people.[41] As Rosemary Sweet notes, the lauding of the Saxons was a specifically English antiquarian concern, with its focus in a cult of King Alfred as well as 'the traditions of Parliament, limited monarchy, common law, the jury system, and Christianity in its truest expression – the Church of England'.[42]

The attitudes to St David displayed by the Society continue the paradoxical pattern of Welsh specificity and unionist integration at work elsewhere in the sermons. Nevertheless, as patron saint, David represents distinct Welsh pride in a unique culture and religious tradition. In *The Rise and Progress*, for example, David is characterised as of 'Blood Royal' (p. 12). He is uncle to King Arthur and 'son of a Prince of Wales' as well as the 'first Archbishop of the See of St. Davids', and emphasis is placed on the great benefits he brought to the religion and country of the Ancient Britons. As a mark of respect to the patron saint, the Welsh are said, 'with a sensible Pleasure and a becoming Pride' to 'distinguish themselves and their dear Country, by wearing a *Leek*, wherever they reside in any Part of the World' (p. 13). On the other hand, however, St David could be used to enforce further the idea that the Welsh were particularly loyal subjects of the British monarchs and the Protestant succession. As I have noted, much was made of the 'providential' coincidence of Princess Caroline's birthday falling on St David's Day, and often the Society members seem to dwell more on this fact than on David himself. As a national figure St David is, of course, of considerable significance, but in the early eighteenth century he was often used to provide further evidence for the special place of Wales within a broader British consensus. The key to this particular use of St David is his status as a symbol of the independence of the Ancient British Church from papal Rome, and as one of the early adherents to pre-Roman Christianity. Indeed, one of the major themes of Welsh history was that the Welsh were the original founders of (Celtic) Christianity in Britain, which they defended vigorously against the pagan Irish and Saxons.[43] However, given David's own position as one of the saints, the argument that he was a type of early Protestant reformer could be seen as forced, to say the least. Nevertheless, as E. G. Bowen points out, such an interpretation had a long history by the early eighteenth century:

> By an ingenious, though well based, interpretation of church history the Protestant Reformers rehabilitated the Celtic Church (the church of St. David in his lifetime) by looking upon it as a kind of Early Christian Church in the West – a church that was to be found in Wales long before the Church of Rome came to these parts via Canterbury.[44]

This vision of Saint David as 'a simple Celtic monk who served Christ alone as his Master' was 'acceptable to churchmen and nonconformists alike'.[45]

Such an interpretation of David's significance had obvious attractions for the Society of Ancient Britons in their bid to exhibit Welsh pride in the context of political and religious harmony with

England. In his account of the *Rise and Progress*, Thomas Jones aligns the virtues of St David with those of the Welsh nation, who 'have ever been famous in story for their Generosity, Valour and Bravery' (p. 58). He continues to link such virtues to 'true primitive Christianity':

And the Princes and Noblemen of *Wales*, have not been more conspicuous in the generous and steady Defence of their antient Civil Rights and Liberties, than have their Archbishops and Bishops in supporting and maintaining the true Primitive Christianity and the antient Rights of their Sees: For there was in *Wales*, an Archbishop of *Caerleon* upon *Usk* in *Monmouthshire*, and afterwards at St. *Davids*, long before Pope *Gregory* sent St. *Austin* the Monk hither, to convert the *Saxon* King *Ethelbert* to the Christian Faith. (pp. 58–9)

The primitive faith is evidence not only of the virtues of the Welsh people, but also of the 'purity' of the British religion in contrast to the taint of Popery. Moreover, it is evidence of the way in which the Britons defied any outside authority from either the Pope or 'any foreign Prince or Prelate' (p. 59). Jones claims that the 'good old *British* Bishops . . . kept their Churches clean and untainted from the Infection of Idolatry, and from all usurpations of the See of *Rome*' (pp. 59–60). St David is presented as particularly courageous for the way in which 'he and his Successors continued their Metropolitan Jurisdiction in the See of St. *David*' (p. 60), until King Henry I wrested it from them.

It could be argued that the emphasis Jones places on the defence of civil rights and liberties, and his celebration of the way in which the Ancient Britons defied foreign authority, strikes a rather discordant note, in that such language is often employed in relation to Welsh defence (by 'Princes and Noblemen') against Saxon (English) invasion. As I shall demonstrate, St David could also fulfil a more militaristic role as defender of the nation as well as defender of the faith. However, in the sermons discussed here St David is clearly being appropriated as a symbol of Welsh loyalty to the Protestant succession. Although *The Christian Soldier* repeats the idea that the Welsh have a particularly 'Pure Religion', Evans uses this to recommend them to the English in terms of economic advantage: 'a Religion as *This* cannot fail of recommending *Us* and *our Country* to an *Industrious* and a *trading* People (as it renders us in every way worthy of their *Confidence and Trust*, the very *Hinges* upon which all *Human Commerce* depends:)' (p. 19). Moreover, in many of the sermons discussed here the patron saint is used very specifically as a way of articulating anti-Catholic animosity.

In the context of his representation of the Reformation and the Tudor Union as blessings to the Welsh, Jeremy Owen, for example, manages a dig at Catholicism through his invocation of the purity of the Ancient British Church. He writes of the Ancient British 'Adherence to Primitive Christianity, and Abhorrence of the Papal Innovation', quoting Taliesin, 'the chief of the Bards', to back up his assertion:

> Wo be to him that will not keep
> From Roman wolves his Sheep
> With Staff and Weapons strong.
>
> (p. 23)[46]

The Christian Soldier, too, uses primitive British Christianity not only as a marker of Welsh pride, but also as a stick to beat Catholicism:

> For whatever the Pope may boast of the *Conversion* wrought *here* by the *Roman Missionaries*, it is plain, that they had little more to do among Your Ancestors, the Saxons, than to draw them away from That *Truth, as it is in Jesus Christ*, which they had been taught, long before, by the *Ancient Inhabitants*. And the *Pope* had *no other Quarrel* with their *Christianity*, than that they had received *It* from *Those Britons*, who would not acknowledge Him for the *Head of their Communion* . . . And well had it been for the English Nation if *They* also had refused Him *their* Submission. How happily they had prevented All that Expence of Blood and Treasure, which it afterwards cost them to reduce their Christianity to the *True, Primitive, British Standard*. (p. 24)

It took a Tudor, Evans argues, to make the English realise their errors. From this perspective, the Union with Wales actually benefits England, as it turns the nation back to the original British Christianity. By this rather precarious and convoluted route, the Welsh are figured throughout these sermons as historically the most loyal adherents to the Protestant religion. This was not a new configuration, but from the perspective of these early eighteenth-century Welsh clergymen, the battle between the Celtic Church and Rome is reconfigured as a conflict between post-1688 Catholics and Protestants; a conflict in which the Welsh play a major role as loyal subjects to the British Crown in its Hanoverian incarnation.

    In addition to the St David's Day sermons and the periodic accounts of the Society's activities, members and accounts, the Society of Ancient Britons also inspired various poets to write verses on patriotic themes. In *The Rise and Progress*, Thomas Jones included some examples of poetry and songs written for the Society, including an 'Ode for Two Voices, for the Birth-Day of Her Royal Highness the Princess of Wales' by John Hughes the librettist, whose dissenting and Whiggish views made him an obvious choice as the Society's Hanoverian panegyrist. The ode was performed to music at the first anniversary meeting of the Society (with two female vocalists taking the parts of 'Cambria' and 'Fame') and published in 1716.[47] At a meeting in May 1716, Jones notes that several further poems were received by the Society in honour of St David's Day. One of these was printed by Jones, a poem by a Monmouthshire schoolboy, John Morgan of Tredegar, which, like Hughes's ode, 'doubly celebrates' St David's Day and Princess Caroline's birthday (pp. 54–7). At a special meeting called in response to the Jacobite rebellion in 1715, another song was performed by one Mr Durfey, of his own composition, which was made deliberately 'easy and natural' so 'that every honest *Briton*'s Voice may readily resound the Loyal Sentiments of his Heart' (p. 23). The Song (also printed in *The Rise and Progress*), begins by establishing the leek as marker of Welsh patriotism:

> The *Fleur de Lis* and *English Rose*
>   May boast of their Antique Tales,
> But the *Leek* with the greatest Honour grows
>   For the lasting Renown of *Wales*.
>   (I, 5–8, p. 23)

Although Durfey is unclear when exactly the leek became a national symbol ('For Time, without Date, has the famous *Leek* / In tuneful Verse been sung', II, 3–4, p. 23), its martial significance is unquestioned: the leek signifies success in battle and works to 'exalt the Renown of Wales' (I, 8, p. 23). Durfey underlines his point by mentioning a sequence of 'brave *British* heroes' (III, 1, p. 24), including 'Cadwaladr, Concan, and Griffith' (III, 3, p. 24). However, at the end of the song this patriotism and fervour for Welsh renown is translated into a further, and by now familiar, affirmation of Hanoverian loyalty, couched, rather ironically given the earlier associations of James I with Cadwaladr, in terms of a rejection of the Stuart line and formed in specific response to the Jacobite rebellion.[48] George and his lineage banish all Pretenders to the throne and through their support for Prince Frederick – 'the Rose that in *Hanover* grows' (VI, 3, p. 25) – loyal Britons 'reject the Pretender's Claim' (VI, 8, p. 25). Yet again, it would seem, any specifically Welsh patriotism is consumed by the need to express support for the Anglo-British centre.

Given that many of these poems and songs appeared in the context of the Society's proceedings, it is clear that they are intended to bolster the public image of its members as post-1707 loyal Britons. However, the Society was also the recipient of poems which are 'inscribed', or dedicated, to the Society on the title-page. The poems inscribed to the Society had a more independent existence and therefore have the potential to be more resistant to the Society's proto-British sympathies.[49] In contrast to the sermons and odes, the poems did not have a pre-publication existence as a spoken or sung public performance. In this sense, it may be the case that the comparatively more private medium of poetry allowed for a greater level of resistance to the public agenda of the Society. Nehemiah Griffith's *The Leek. A Poem on St. David's Day* is a more extensive example of a poem inscribed to the Society of Ancient Britons and one which, as its title makes clear, expands upon the significance of the leek as national symbol. The poem was published in 1717 and reached a second edition in the following year. From a comment in one of three dedicatory poems to Griffith attached to the second edition, it appears that he wrote the poem in a bid to become a member of the Society. Thomas Brereton concludes his verses to the author by stating: 'may a Place Your bold Attempt requite, / In that SOCIETY to which You write'.[50] In the course of writing the poem, then, Griffith must have been attempting to gauge what kind of themes might interest the Society and reflect their image favourably. In keeping with one of the major preoccupation of the sermons, his long narrative poem is a historical account of successive British resistance to Saxon rule. The poem is topographical and leads the reader through ancient Wales via an account of the original tribes (the Silures, the Dimetae, the Ordovices) and the regions they were associated with (the south and border counties, the south-west, and the north, respectively). Appropriately again for the Society, the figure of St David is at the centre of the poem and responsible for gathering all the British troops from throughout Wales and throughout history in a unified attack on their Saxon enemies. Taking the purpose behind this poem into account, does Griffith endorse the public Hanoverian loyalty of the Society and its purported British sympathies? Or does the less immediately public medium of poetry allow for a greater expression of the ambivalence towards British incorporation which many of the Society's members articulate in more covert ways in their sermons?

Griffith's version of the patron Saint reveals a distinctly more martial David than the usual image of saintly abstinence and simplicity. Indeed, at one point in the poem David kills Arskwin with a javelin which 'nail'd his venom'd Tongue up to his Head', resulting in him vomiting 'out his Soul in Clots of Blood' (p. 21). The poem opens with this image of David as soldier-hero, and additionally uses the ancient bards and prophetic poetry as a way of stirring up patriotic feeling:

HAIL to the Day, that crown'd with DAVID's Name,
Stands consecrated to eternal Fame;
Thy glad Solemnities his Worth shall speak,
That foil'd the *Saxons*, and obtain'd the LEEK:
While in our glowing Breasts the Patriot's Praise
Shall warm Incentives to new Honours raise.
  So, sacred *Bards* of old, in Layes inspir'd,
The Youth to noble Emulation fir'd;
High Deeds of Ancestors to view they plac'd,
And urg'd to future Glory from the past.
                    (p. 1)

The animosity is specifically directed at the Saxons, who by treachery and deceit destroyed the unity and liberty of Ancient Britain: David asks at one point, in a potentially critical, and also extremely perceptive, view of contemporary Anglo-Welsh relations, 'What Foes more dang'rous than too strong Allies?' (p. 19). The saint's role is to urge his compatriots to rise up again, with the bravery of their forefathers, and scorn loss of liberty and a life of slavery:

Is it for Love of Life, we're Cowards grown?
Oh, what is Life when *Liberty* is gone!
Can we live Slaves beneath the Victor's Hand?
Or Fugitives in our own Native Land?
                    (p. 2)

As a result of David's battle-cry, all the tribes of Wales come together in an attempt to defeat the Saxon foe. Albeit shielded by the historical distance of the subject-matter, Griffith's dramatic rendering of Welsh loss of liberty chimes very strongly with the language of slavery and oppression used by Moses Williams in particular. As such, it could be argued that, like Williams, Griffith is suggesting that the Welsh are still in danger of enslavement and extinction at the beginning of the eighteenth century, and is therefore presenting a highly critical perspective on contemporary Anglo-Welsh relations. Griffith's poem is another example of Ancient Britain being figured as the land of liberty, which is lost as a result of the Saxon (not Norman) yoke.

Throughout the poem, Griffith blends key episodes and characters from Geoffrey of Monmouth's *The History of the Kings of Britain* with Rhigyfarch's eleventh-century narrative concerning David's miracle at the Synod of Brefi. Famously, the ground upon which the Saint is standing swells to form a hill so that the crowd can hear him preach against the Pelagian heresy.[51] In *The Leek*, as the battle between Saxons and Britons begins, the ground starts convulsing and David is raised up on a 'Throne of grassy Turf' (p. 17) to give a rousing battle-speech:

> Once more, O *Britons!* This in Arms we stand,
> T'attempt the Rescue of our Native Land.
> Our glorious Fathers oft in Battel try'd,
> What this Great Day for ever must decide:
> This the important Crisis of our Fate,
> Compleats our Slav'ry, or restores our State!
> (p. 17)

With Liberty as the cause, the Britons charge into battle and the Saxons flee. Here Griffith provides an interpretation of the significance of his titular leek:

> Along a dismal Havock mark'd the Road,
> With Limbs, and LEEKS, and shatter'd Armour strew'd.
> Eager Pursuit all Day the *Britons* made,
> 'Till coming Night the bloody Labour stay'd:
> Sounds the Retreat; when all their colours seek,
> And each his Helmet grac'd with *Saxon* LEEK.
> (p. 24)

The next day the Britons process 'With LEEKS adorn'd' (p. 24) as a symbol of the Saxon defeat and give thanks to Heaven. The cause for which they fought is '*True Religion, Liberty*, and *Laws!*' (p. 25), and the leek clearly signifies military victory for the Britons and their release from Saxon slavery.

This version of the patron saint is David as 'soldier saint'.[52] In his emphasis on the martial David, Griffith shows the influence of the Welsh prophetic poem *Armes Prydein Vawr* (*c* 900), from the Book of

Taliesin, in his reworking of Welsh tradition and history.[53] As Glanmor Williams notes, *Armes Prydein* 'reveals David in a new and striking light, as a symbol not primarily of Christian virtue but of patriotic pride and warlike prowess'.[54] The poem concerns the possibility of a confederacy of the Danes of Dublin, the Irish, the Cornish, the men of Strathclyde and Brittany, and the Welsh (the Kymry/Cymry) coming together under the leadership of Cynan, Cadwaladr and the banner of Saint David to defeat the Saxons and unite Britain. As E. G. Bowen states, 'In this context Dewi appears as a typical figure of the British Heroic Age, like King Arthur, fighting the Anglo-Saxons and assuring his men of the ultimate victory of their arms.'[55] Such a treatment of British history contains a more oppositional interpretation of the past, which foregrounds Welsh glory and celebrates the triumph over Saxon perfidy. Indeed, the patron Saint played a substantial role in the Glyndŵr bid for Welsh independence in the fifteenth century.[56] Given that the eighteenth-century members of the Society of Ancient Britons make direct links between the Saxons and the English, does Griffith's poem, then, contain seeds of nascent political nationalism? Is the emphasis on avoiding slavery and maintaining liberty a comment on the particular servitude of the Welsh to the English? Does the leek signify resistance to English dominance?

Historically, however, the leek had often signified Welsh fidelity to English kings. In Shakespeare's *Henry V*, the faithful Fluellen refers to the garden of leeks in which the Welsh reportedly showed their bravery in support of 'Edward the Plack Prince of Wales' (IV. vii. 91–2) at Crécy, and which vegetable thereafter is 'an honourable badge of the service' (IV. vii. 99).[57] As Patricia Parker puts it, the mythic garden of leeks becomes an 'emblem of Welsh fidelity to English Kings'.[58] Despite the potential of the use of an ancient prophetic Welsh poetic tradition, such as that found in the *Armes Prydein Vawr*, it would appear that Griffith's early-eighteenth-century rendition of the leek's significance echoes Fluellen's loyalty. Towards the end of the poem, David falls asleep and has a vision of a beautiful virgin called Liberty, who makes a prophetic speech about the future of Britain. Echoing the Angel's prophecy to Cadwaladr in the *History of the Kings of Britain*, Liberty foretells the coming 'intestine Wars' (p. 26) with which 'the *Isle* shall bleed'. Although they rule the whole of 'Loegria', the Saxons suffer invasions and confusion. The Britons, again in Galfridian tradition, fight amongst themselves and are 'self-conquered'. However, despite this, the race of the ancient Britons remains and, importantly, the language survives: 'Nor Time itself their Language e'er consume, / That, uncorrupted till the Day of Doom' (p. 27). Liberty then turns to the more prosperous fortunes of a united Great Britain under the Hanoverian monarchs:

And now, O Saint! The better Prospect view,
See a long Course of golden Years renew!
Thro' the whole *Isle* the Jars at length shall cease,
The Nations all unite in endless Peace:
One Government, not with unequal Rule,
From *Kernaw* shall extend to utmost *Thule*:
Nations distinct no more; but all the same,
And *Britain* the *One* Universal Name!

(p. 27)

In this vision of union, God himself has chosen the monarchs who will rule over these 'happy Lands' and, as a result of their peaceful rule and removal of (Jacobite and Catholic) tyranny, Britain will also achieve economic prosperity. Liberty also foretells the reign of the current Prince of Wales (George II), who will 'perpetuate such a glorious Race' by marrying the superior Princess Caroline, 'the Mother of this greater Line' (p. 28). The auspicious birth of this glorious Princess will, of course, fall on St David's Day, as the poet stresses in his effusive concluding lines:

This Day, O Saint! th'auspicious Birth shall see:
This Day, that still its DAVID's Name shall bear,
And LEEKS adorn in each revolving Year!
Britons shall then be sooth'd from War's Alarms
To mutual Love, by her Celestial Charms.
Exhaustless Blessings from the Fair attend,
And see the Progeny from Heav'n descend!
But most the *Britons* of the Antient Line
Shall date new Joys from the propitious Sign:
This shall yet raise to Triumphs more sublime,
And mark *This Glorious Day* to the last End of Time!

(pp. 28–9)

Leeks, then, appear to serve a double function. On one level, the wearing of the leeks by the Britons signifies fierce national pride against the invading Saxons. Thomas Brereton's dedicatory poem reinforces this view in its focus on the leek as a symbol of national pride against English mockery: he applauds Griffith's ability to 'rectify the LEEK's mistaken Fame, / And turn the *English* Mock'ry to their Shame' (pp. 3–4). Furthermore, St David appears in Griffith's poem as a military hero whose central role is to defend the British cause and further the unification of Britain under British rule. As the *Armes Prydein Vawr* puts it:

Wise men foretell all that will happen:
They will possess all from Manaw to Brittany
From Dyfed to Thanet, it will be theirs;
From the Wall to the Forth, along their estuaries,
Their dominion will spread over Yr Echwydd.
There will be no return for the tribes of the Saxons: . . .
                          (171–6)[59]

Griffith's poem echoes the sentiments of the *Armes Prydein* in its representation of Dewi as 'the leader of our warriors' (196) and its invocation of a united Britain. Again, the dedicatory poems enforce the resistant stance, viewing the poem as a riposte to English criticism. Thomas Griffith's 'Upon the Following Poem' declares:

Too long have Britons *been the* Saxons' *Scorn,*
And silently the vilest Insults born:
Their Threadbare Jests prophane'd great DAVID's *Name,*
And crude Burlesque eclips'd the Prophet's Fame:
Till You, O GRIFFITH! *Saw our Patron's Wrong,*
And did him Justice in immortal Song.
                          (1–6)

However, the poem's final message could be seen to reverse the politically charged implication of the prophetic tradition. Indeed, as I have shown, the other function of the leek as a national symbol was to signify Welsh fidelity to the English monarchs. Nehemiah Griffith's poem attempts to make these two opposing meanings compatible. In his effusive concluding lines, Griffith uses the ancient Welsh traditions of prophecy to praise and glorify the Hanoverian monarchy, and the much longed-for union of Britain of Welsh poetic tradition is reconfigured in terms of the Hanoverian succession, as it had been for the Tudors. The prophecies – which originally looked towards the 'return' of the Welsh as rulers of their own land – foretell instead the victorious peace of the Hanoverian British state. With the exception of

those of Moses Williams, the texts produced by the Society of Ancient
Britons, like Griffith's poem, seem also to be attempting to fulfil two
conflicting functions. On one level, the Society represents a loyalist
vision of pro-union, pro-Hanoverian sentiment. From this perspective,
the Welsh could indeed be said to acquiesce in an Anglicisation process
which nevertheless glorifies Welsh culture as part of an inclusive
British polity. Indeed, from the sixteenth century onwards, Welsh
literary traditions and histories had been used to bolster a British
nationalism which included English and Welsh together.[60] As I have
demonstrated, the positive treatment of the Hanoverians by the
Society often echoes representations of the Tudor succession as a gain
for Wales. In a similar vein, eighteenth-century Welsh writers could
celebrate post-1707 British unity as inclusive of all the constituent
parts of the kingdom in equal proportion. As Thomas Brereton
suggests in his poem to Griffith: '*Now shall the* Rose, *the* Thistle, *and
the* LEEK, *Each a due Mixture in one Garland seek*' (29–30).

Nevertheless, integration often leads to appropriation, and 'unified
Britishness' more often than not served 'the interests of the English
rather more than the Welsh'.[61] In the closing lines of the stanza quoted
above, Thomas Brereton indicates that his vision of equality in unity
might be simply wishful thinking: he is only imagining a future in
which the Welsh will have the same political clout as the English:

> *And who can tell but our AUGUSTUS may,*
> *In Honour of the Saint's and her lov'd Day* [Caroline's birthday],
> *In Time to come an Order too* [*sic*] *compose,*
> *Which shall ennoble This as well as Those?*
>
> (33–6)

Indeed, as Prys Morgan notes, even the much celebrated Tudor Union
did not necessarily strengthen Welsh cultural identity, despite the
Tudors' own emphasis on their Welsh descent:

> In general the Welsh during the sixteenth century saw their myths and
> legends absorbed into English history and tradition, taken over for the
> purposes of the vigorously expanding English state, or discredited and
> dismissed as fairy-stories by English antiquaries or Renaissance scholars.
> The Welsh ceased to have an independent history.[62]

There are comparable dangers for Welsh identity in an eighteenth-
century context resulting from this cultural appropriation, what Philip

Schwyzer terms 'neutralization' and Kirsti Bohata, more strongly, 'cultural robbery'.[63] In making the old traditions serve the purposes of glorifying the Hanoverian monarchs, are Welsh writers themselves willingly handing over their culture for English assimilation? Despite the tensions I have highlighted, do these Welsh clerics and poets, as Moses Williams suspected, play a role in their own cultural neutralisation?

In answer to these questions I would argue that in the concentration on the Welsh as the original Britons, the heartfelt attacks on Saxon perfidy, the invocations of Welsh poetry of prophecy, the particular use made of the martial tradition of St David and, most importantly, the insistence upon the continued existence and vitality of the Welsh language, these texts do offer resistance to Anglo-British assimilation. In some senses, this resistance is a continuation of what Schwyzer identifies as 'the Welsh paradox'.[64] In the early eighteenth century, there are similar processes at work in constructions of Britishness, but with important qualifications. Unlike their Tudor predecessors, eighteenth-century English writers could draw on an alternative source of national pride which was much more specifically English: Saxonism.[65] Many of these English writers draw on both the tropes of Saxonism and the rhetoric of the 'old' British nationalism, either together or at different times, for a variety of political purposes and with no apparent sense of contradiction.[66] In contrast, the Anglo-Welsh writers I have focused on here express nothing positive about the Saxons at all. If, as Christine Gerrard argues, 'it was impossible to ignore the associations between the German House of Hanover and the Gothic Germanic past', this is nevertheless precisely what these Welsh commentators succeed in doing in their depiction of the Saxons as perfidious conquerors and vile betrayers.[67] While English and Welsh writers continued to share broader aspects of the British nationalism of previous ages (the Arthurian myth would be a case in point), the myths and traditions on which a specifically Welsh identity relied were increasingly disregarded (as in the case of the Galfridian tradition), reinterpreted to fit different political contexts, or simply replaced by narratives of Britishness which were increasingly English in focus.

Notwithstanding the increasing dominance of Saxon-identified versions of national identity, the Hanoverian monarchs (especially Caroline) were keen to construct a British lineage for themselves rather than focus on a constitutional (Saxon) right to rule, as the next chapter will demonstrate.[68] However, given the fact that the staples of Tudor

British nationalism were grafted on to Stuart (and eventually Jacobite) myth-making and propaganda, the old sense of nationalism rooted in the Welsh traditions became increasingly untenable for describing post-1707 Hanoverian Britishness.[69] This was not necessarily bad news for Wales. In a Welsh context, the widespread discrediting of the old myths of British nationalism could be seen as an opportunity to re-appropriate the associated rhetoric and narratives for a more specifically Welsh identity and, indeed, to create new traditions and histories. In this sense we could reverse Linda Colley's thesis in *Britons* to argue that 1707 marks the beginning, not of a more unified sense of Britishness, but instead of a growing sense of national distinctiveness between the two nations of Wales and England, as a more Anglo-centred 'Britishness' begins to emerge. In effect, the 'Welsh paradox' continues in a different context and begins to take new directions.

2

The Cambrian Muse: Gender, Welsh Identity and Hanoverian Loyalty in the Poems of Jane Brereton (1685–1740)

How shall a *Cambrian Muse*, obscure, and mean,
The lowest, latest of the tuneful Train,
Too weak her Wings, too tardy in her Flight,
Amongst their Sterling Coin, dare to present her Mite?
(Jane Brereton, 'The Royal Hermitage', 1733)

Despite the range of views expressed by the Society of Ancient Britons regarding Welsh identity, the fact remains that, like other antiquarian societies in the eighteenth century, all the members were men. The poetry of Jane Brereton therefore provides an alternative testing-ground for exploring aspects of the relationship of Wales to Britain in the early eighteenth century from the perspective of a woman poet. Brereton's work demonstrates a strong sense of Welsh identity as well as a firm commitment to the Hanoverian succession. In her poetry she is constantly striving to carve a niche for herself as a Welsh woman poet at the same time as she asserts her right to speak on behalf of the British nation. Brereton was born Jane Hughes in Bryn-Griffith, near Mold, north-east Wales, in 1685. She began her literary career in the 1710s while living in London and, after returning to Wales and settling in Wrexham, she contributed some lively verse to the *Gentleman's Magazine* in the mid 1730s. Brereton's poetry and her life were commemorated in 1744 when Edward Cave published a posthumous subscription edition of her *Poems on Several Occasions*, complete with a biographical account of the author.[1] She married Thomas Brereton, a member of a prominent, yet impoverished, Chester family, in 1717, and spent her early married life in London, where she published two poems: *The 5th ODE of the 4th Book of Horace, imitated, and apply'd to the King* (1716) and *An* Epistle *to Sir* RICHARD STEELE; *On the*

Death of Mr Addison (1720).[2] According to the 1744 biographical account, Brereton separated from her husband around 1721 because of his increasingly violent behaviour towards her. She and her two daughters (Lucy and Charlotte) moved back to north-east Wales, from where she continued to write poetry.[3]

Although Jane Brereton has received some brief notice in histories of Anglo-Welsh writing, on the few occasions when she has been discussed from an eighteenth-century perspective her Welsh identity has not been a point of significant comment.[4] By contrast, this chapter uses Brereton's Welsh identity as the starting point for an analysis of her poetry. I explore what a Welsh identity might mean for an Anglo-oriented, English-speaking woman who was born in Wales, but who had lived in London and spent the majority of her later years in Wrexham, an area historically more Anglicised than north-west and west Wales. In the light of her specific regional identity I consider the following questions: how does Brereton's Welshness inform her poetry and her writing identity? What kinds of Welsh identities does she construct? What are we to make of her strong allegiance to the Hanoverian succession, her praise of Queen Caroline, and her seemingly Anglocentric interpretation of Welsh and English history? From what kind of contexts, historical, literary and cultural, can we start to understand these seemingly conflicting loyalties? And on a wider scale, what can Brereton's work tell us about the place of Wales in the construction of a British identity in the early eighteenth century?

As this initial assessment suggests, much of Brereton's poetry appears to be riddled with contradiction and marked by compromise. Although these elements in her poetry could be said to stem in part from the personal strain involved in balancing conflicting national loyalties, historically one aspect of Wales's relation to England had always been marked by a paradox. Anglo-Welsh relations from the sixteenth century to the mid eighteenth century are characterised by a high level of political ease between the two countries, which may seem surprising, given the divergent cultural and linguistic history of each. As Philip Jenkins explains,

> For the social historian, it is remarkable to find that radical cultural dissimilarity can coexist with political stability. Seventeenth-century Wales presents a curious paradox, being perhaps the most thoroughly 'other' and Celtic society in the British Isles, yet one so assimilated in political terms as to be essentially indistinguishable from any English region.[5]

Various reasons have been given for this situation. One major reason was, of course, that by focusing on the Welsh language and the bardic heritage as the primary markers of 'difference', the Welsh had always defined their nationality in cultural rather than political terms. Indeed, language and poetry could be said to represent an alternative form of independence for Wales which worked on another level than a striving for political autonomy. I discuss this issue more fully in the next chapter in the context of 'bardic nationalism' and the work of Evan Evans. Historians have also suggested that the physical geography of Wales created an internal division, which helps to explain the lack of a capital city and attendant national institutions which might have been a focus for the articulation of political dissent.[6] Another explanation for this apparent paradox is the centrality of British history to conceptions of Wales in the early eighteenth century. Even before the Tudor Union in 1536, the fortunes of Wales and Welsh identity had been bound up with the conception of a broader British identity, gleaned first and foremost from the identification of the Welsh with the Ancient Britons, and of the Welsh language with the ancient 'British tongue'.[7] In effect, as the previous chapter indicated, the Welsh insistence on identification with the Ancient Britons did not necessarily encourage political dissent to the Union, but could serve to underline the dynastic claims of the Tudors. As a result, it has been argued that 'Wales and Welsh identity emerged from the imperial programme of the Tudors strengthened rather than undermined'.[8] From this context, it could be argued that Brereton's commitment to the dynastic claims of the Hanoverian monarchs does not so much detract from her Welsh identity, but rather refracts this identity through a lens of 'Britishness' familiar to Welsh writers since Tudor times at least.

Nevertheless, it is clearly the case that Anglo-Welsh writers like Jane Brereton were more likely to write in English and orient their work to an English-language culture. These writers were historically more likely to use the term 'Cambro-Briton' than 'Welsh' to signify their national identity. For example, in the late Tudor period, many Anglo-Welsh writers 'as self-styled "Cambro-Britons" (such as John Dee), made their careers in England and addressed an international audience'.[9] A similar trend can be observed on the accession of James I, which was celebrated by 'Cambro-British' writers as an endorsement of Merlin's prophecies.[10] However, although a 'Cambro-British' identity impacted directly on the author's treatment of national allegiance, this was not always straightforward. The term 'Cambro-British' points to further tensions that result from attempting to align political integration with cultural difference. As Peter Roberts notes, 'In addressing a readership wider than their own countrymen, these authors strained to compensate for the loss of a dynasty of Welsh extraction by engaging in the redefinition of "Britishness" which was occasioned by the union of crowns.'[11] As in the work of her predecessors, therefore, we might also expect that Brereton's poetry would show signs of the strenuous effort involved to achieve an acceptable compromise between Welsh and British interests.

On first inspection, however, Brereton's use of her Welsh background is straightforward, although her romanticisation of the Welsh landscape is prescient rather than typical of early eighteenth-century perceptions of Wales. Throughout her poetry Brereton invokes the Welsh landscape of her home. In an early poem, 'Verses on the Loss of a Friend' (1709), probably written from London, Brereton's construction of her homeland is nostalgic, both for the company of the friend and for the beauties of her native land:

> Thro' smiling Meads, there, *Alyn* gently glides,
> And paints with fragrant Pride its fertile Sides;
> In wild *meanders* runs its wanton Maze,
> Winding its Streams a thousand various Ways.
> Oft have I sate, and in the cooling Shade,
> Sung to the Murmurs which its Waters made.
> *Tagus, Pactolus* too, I thought to be,
> Meer Puddles, *Alyn*! when compar'd with Thee!
> That celebrated *Heliconian* Spring,
> The sacred Fountain where the Muses sing,
> Could not appear more pleasing to my Sight,
> Than chrystal *Alyn*!
>   (9–27)

Employing conventional notions of the Welsh exile's longing for her native land, Brereton also uses the Welsh landscape as the basis for her poetic inspiration.[12] She humorously compares the size of the major Spanish and Portuguese river Tagus with that of the river Alyn in Mold. Likewise, the river Pactolus, famous for the gold washed from its shores in Ancient Lydia, is dismissed in favour of the enchanting Alyn. Even the fountains of Helicon cannot outshine the glories of Brereton's native river. For Brereton, the river Alyn, symbol of her native land, becomes her creative reference point and stands in for the more usual invocations of Greek classical culture.[13] It could be argued that, through her use of the classical genre of topographical pastoral favoured by English poets, Brereton, in a manner similar to that of her predecessor Henry Vaughan, is attempting primarily to align herself with dominant Anglicised poetic models: in her case, the eighteenth-century Augustan poetic tradition of English letters.[14] Like Vaughan again, it could also be argued that she is constructing herself as 'a native who has returned to the provinces as no mere provincial', but as a poet conversant with classical tradition and contemporary poetic trends.[15] Nevertheless, Wales is clearly the subject of, and inspiration for, her poetry. Therefore, Brereton can also be said to present Wales as a proper object for creative attention, a topic I explore more fully in chapter 4. Furthermore, as a native, Brereton is uniquely placed to depict the fair and fertile land with which she has been so familiar and is therefore able to authorise her poetic voice through descriptions of her native country.

In her poems which evoke the Welsh landscape, Brereton again uses Wales as a theme for her writing, but also as a trope for a further and more familiar construction of her writing identity: the retiring woman poet. In 'Verses on the Loss of a Friend', for example, Brereton alludes to the Horatian poetic persona, who longs for the country life as an imagined escape from the pressures of an urban existence:

AH! Happy Solitude, thrice blest the Day!
When in thy Shades I pass'd my Hours away;
Exempt from Cares, retir'd from public Noise,
Nought to prevent, or interrupt my Joys: . . .
                    (1–4)

One enabling aspect of this Horatian model for women writers was the rhetorical rejection of ambition embedded in many retirement poems.[16] As women mostly did not have access to power or business, this genre offered woman an accepted set of conventions for expressing their sense of exclusion from public life. In 'Epistle *to Mrs* Anne Griffiths. *Written from* London, *in* 1718', Brereton includes a conventional invocation of the 'beatus ille' theme, but she also figures herself as aspiring to this ideal through her desire to be with a female friend, Anne Griffiths. This friendship is directly linked to the specificities of Brereton's region in Wales and contrasts directly with the hubbub of the metropolis:

Oh, how I long with you to pass the Day,
Sedately cheerful, innocently gay!
Where *Alyn* glides, to breathe my native Air,
To view our pleasant Hills, and dear *Molgaer.**
          (*A mountain in Denbighshire)
                    (95–6)

Brereton constructs rural Wales as a place where she can fulfil her role as a poet in the Horatian mode. The connected tropes of rural retreat and female friendship have a particular gendered force for Brereton. In addition to describing the Denbighshire landscape as a place of innocent pleasure, Brereton, like many of her female predecessors and contemporaries, offers her poetry as private verses exchanged between female friends. Brereton authorises herself by constructing her poetic persona in the context of an idealised view of the Welsh countryside, and compounds this association of the woman poet and innocence by stressing that her poetry is written for the private entertainment and amusement of a female counterpart who, unlike the speaker, is happy in full possession of the sweets of the Welsh countryside.

If Brereton's use of her Welsh identity ended with such idealised invocations of her native land she could be incorporated as an early example of the later eighteenth-century sentimental, and also picturesque (as opposed to sublime), appropriations of the Welsh countryside. However, her longing for Wales from an exiled position in London could also define her writing as archetypally Anglo-Welsh; the fact that she does not seem to have known Welsh adds weight to this assessment. In both the poems discussed so far, Brereton can be seen to align her poetic voice, and the themes of her poetry, with an ability to describe the particular, yet generalised, pastoral beauties of Wales. In terms of constructions of female authorship in the period, Brereton's self-fashioning here can be read as an attempt to create herself in the mould of the amateur woman poet who eschews the commercial world of literary London and associates her authorial persona with specifically feminine virtues of retirement, innocence and lack of ambition. However, Brereton does not fit easily into either of these two frameworks. As is clear from her two poems published while she was living in London, she did not confine herself to private epistles to distant female friends. Her poem on the death of Addison is an attempt to associate herself with an important and influential literary figure of high public renown.

Furthermore, even after she had moved to Wrexham, she was not in cultural isolation, but part of a literary and antiquarian-minded circle focused on Mary Myddelton at Croesnewydd, as well as on close terms with the Mellers and Yorkes of nearby Erthig.[17] Brereton has been called the 'poet laureate of Croesnewydd', and indeed the subscription list and the dedicatees of many of her poems demonstrate her involvement with Mary Myddelton's household and acquaintances.[18] This group also included the lexicographer Revd Thomas Lloyd (Miss Myddelton's chaplain), who provided Brereton with connections to some of the main antiquarian concerns of the day, a pursuit usually exclusively male. One of Lloyd's acquaintances was Revd Humphrey Foulkes, a correspondent of the famous antiquary and author of *Archæologia Britannica* (1707), Edward Lhuyd. As Mary Burdett-Jones notes, 'Thus by belonging to Madame Myddelton's circle Jane Brereton got to read Humphrey Foulkes's dissertations on antiquities in manuscript and was inspired to write an ode'.[19] I discuss this ode in detail at a later stage in the present chapter, but the fact of Brereton's access to such antiquarian documents shows that she directly benefited as a writer from literary circles within Wales. As such, Brereton's invocations of 'solitary' Wales are shown to be mostly rhetorical.

The image of the woman writer distanced from worldly affairs which Brereton promulgates in her Welsh verse is mitigated further by the political inflection of some of her poetry. In one early poem, *The 5th ODE of the 4th Book of Horace, imitated, and apply'd to the King*, Brereton makes a clear attempt to align herself with London Court culture and position herself as a writer in relation to a Whig-inflected glorification of Hanoverian rule. As the last clause indicates, the poem is an overtly political panegyric on George I. Written in 1716, it makes no mention of Brereton's Welsh identity. Nevertheless, the poem is significant for its articulation of the Hanoverian bias which epitomises her work. The poem is a blatant exercise in panegyric to George I and views the Hanoverian succession as restoring the glories of ancient Britain:

> O Thou! Whom Heav'n's propitious Pow'r
>   Ordain'd to do fair *Britain* Right,
> Her ancient Lustre to restore,
>   Return! and glad her longing Sight: . . .
>   (I, 1–4)

Brereton's invocation refers to the fact that George left England in the summer of 1716 to visit Hanover, the first visit since his accession. The context of the Hanover visit was the King's growing concerns about the Northern War, and Baltic affairs in general, as well as his wish to alienate the Pretender and French interest even further by negotiating a banishment of the former from the court in Avignon (established after the failure of the '15 Rebellion) to Italy.[20] Brereton's use of the Horatian ode – especially the fourth book – as the chosen form for her patriotic sentiments is typical of the age. As Dustin Griffin has recently shown, and as I explore in chapter 4, unabashed patriotic odes of an occasional (and ephemeral) nature were widespread in the first half of the eighteenth century, and although many were, like Brereton's poem, rather crude in execution, they constituted a recognisable poetic genre dedicated to national sentiment and celebration of military victories.[21] In this instance, the King's absence in defence of the nation provides Brereton with her theme, and she makes it clear that his mission is vital to national security and peaceful affluence. Containment of Stuart resistance was also a particularly pressing concern for the King at the beginning of his reign, in the light of the Jacobite uprising of 1715. In stanza V, Brereton brings together all the internal and external threats to Britain (the French, Catholics, the Jacobites and Swedes), which will be neutralised by the King's defence of the nation:

> Who fears the false rapacious *Scot*?
>   The *French*? The *Swede*'s romantick Pride?
> Who dreads what tripple Mitres plot?
>   While *George* and Heav'n espouse our Side: . . .
>   (V, 1–4)

As well as providing an interesting example of a female poet attempting to express overtly patriotic sentiments in her poetry, Brereton's stance in this poem could be seen to support Linda Colley's argument concerning the Protestant foundation of post-1707 Britain. In Colley's terms, older national and regional allegiances were superseded in part by a more general adherence to Protestantism and internal coherence in the face of outside intimidation from continental Europe, specifically Catholic France. As she explains,

> More than anything else, it was this shared religious allegiance combined
> with recurrent wars that permitted a sense of British national identity to

emerge alongside of, and not necessarily in competition with older, more organic attachments to England, Wales or Scotland, or to country or village . . . an uncompromising Protestantism was the foundation on which their state was explicitly and unapologetically based.[22]

Jane Brereton's poem certainly demonstrates that Catholicism is the major threat to British security and declares her patriotism by stating that King George and Heaven will fight together on behalf of the Protestant British: 'Who dreads what tripple Mitres plot? / While *George* and Heav'n espouse our Side'. She shows no Celtic connection with the Scots, who are perceived solely in terms of the Jacobite threat posed in the years following 1715.[23] In another sense, therefore, her poetry evinces the continuing internal divisions within Britain, a situation emphasised by critics such as Murray Pittock, who are keen to point out complexities which are possibly overlooked in Colley's claim for a monolithic 'Protestant solidarity as the basis for unitary British identity'.[24] In order for Britain to be secure, Brereton suggests, dangers must be dealt with from within as well as outside, and she is firmly on the side of the Hanoverian monarchs. In contrast to the present day, when there is a sense of Celtic solidarity between Wales, Scotland and Ireland, Brereton's poetry dramatises a close relationship between Wales and England in a vision of Britishness which perceives Scotland as a threat. Such a stance does suggest that, contra Colley, British identities were shaped as much by issues arising from domestic division as they were by anxieties about external forces.

As I have hinted, what is also significant about Brereton's version of what was, by the early 1700s, a recognisably Whiggish poetic agenda, is her explicitly feminine take on the conventional tropes of pro-Hanoverian rhetoric. Brereton has carefully selected her Horatian precedent by choosing an ode which incorporates a sense of female perspective: Horace's image of the nation as a mother calling for her absent sons is an enabling motif for Brereton as it provides her with a domestic framework in which to express her political sentiments. Brereton figures the ladies of Great Britain sending grateful thanks to the King as they adorn themselves in the morning and sip their tea in the evening. Such peaceful occupations and domestic security, it is suggested, are made possible by the triumph of the Protestant succession. Britain's present stability and future glory are inextricably connected to the Protestant succession, and Brereton draws a direct line back to William III ('Nassau'):

To Thee our purest Wishes flow,
  To Thee our grateful Songs are due;
Religion, Liberty, we owe
  To great *Nassau*, and greater You!
Long, long may you our Isle adorn,
  While all confess your gentle Sway;
These our Toilet Vows each Morn,
  And these each Ev'ning crown our Tea.
                    (IV, 1–8)

Such visions of domestic activity are directly aligned to agricultural prosperity at home, as well as empire- and trade-building across the seas:

The Lass now jocund milks our Kine,
  Which we securely grazing view;
Our publick Fears we now resign,
  And our domestick Care renew:
The Merchant plows the briny Flood
  To fetch us rich Brocades;
And *Carolina*, great and good,
  To virtuous Life persuades.
                    (III, 1–8)

Caroline, the Princess of Wales, is a royal symbol of British feminine virtue. The prosperity, wealth and security brought to the nation through the Hanoverian succession reform society on a domestic level, and trade is specifically enacted in order to adorn the virtuous British fair: 'The Merchant plows the briny Flood / To fetch us rich Brocades'. Commerce is thus presented as another form of domestic agricultural activity. The image of the merchant ploughing the sea links internal agriculture with foreign trade under the rule of the Hanoverians.[25] Furthermore, the reference to the 'briny Flood' alludes to the biblical story of Noah in Genesis. Just as Noah sent out the raven and then the dove to ascertain dry land, so too do the British (also God's elect) launch their representatives on the seas to further domestic prosperity. Brereton thus moves away from her Horatian template to provide a specifically eighteenth-century British version of national pride and virtue, inflected through gendered representations of national prosperity. Significantly, it is a 'Lass' who milks the 'Kine' so cheerfully and it is the women who watch the herd 'securely grazing'. Overall, Brereton succeeds in linking what was essentially an extremely masculine and aggressively jingoistic set of principles to a feminine mode which emphasises the private domestic virtues resulting from public acts of military endeavour and imperial ambition. This feminine perspective on a traditionally male poetic preserve helps to explain why Brereton was to turn her full attention to Queen Caroline as a female representative of the glories of Hanoverian rule and the British nation.

Jane Brereton's poetry is thus further evidence of what is now being recognised as a robust tradition of women's political verse which extends into the eighteenth century. Carol Barash's influential study of *English Women's Poetry, 1649–1714* (1996) resurrected women poets from the mid seventeenth century to the death of Queen Anne as political writers.[26] However, Barash's persuasive reading of Anne Finch's poetry as a retreat from the public world of state affairs into a private world of solitary and appropriately feminine meditation and contemplation led many scholars to see Finch's work as marking the demise of women's poetic intervention in political affairs. As a Stuart loyalist, Finch would indeed have seen 1688 as the end of active political engagement. Brereton's work complicates these narratives in a number of important ways. Her Whiggish, pro-Hanoverian stance suggests a very different trajectory of women's political poetry from that described by Barash. As I have shown elsewhere, in relation to the Williamite verse of Elizabeth Singer Rowe, post-Revolution culture produced a new style of women's political writing which was staunchly Whig and which, as Kathryn King has recently argued, 'advanced a cultural and political agenda that was Protestant, militaristic, triumphalist and intensely nationalistic'.[27] Brereton's poetic attempt to fuse such an approach with an acknowledgement of her Welsh identity adds a further geographical/national dimension to our sense of the range of women's political engagement. Her use of the Hanoverians, particularly Queen Caroline, as a focus for her patriotism also acts as a corrective to Barash's emphasis on women's use of the Stuart monarchs as a focus for their political engagement. Furthermore, if Whig principles of liberty and freedom encouraged women to think of themselves as political subjects more generally, these values enable Brereton to imagine herself not only as a political poet, but also as a Welsh poet authorised to comment on the matter of Britain itself.[28]

The British History, Melissa and Merlin's Cave
In her ode to George I, Brereton is more concerned to articulate political loyalty to the King and Britain than to express any sense of a

specifically Welsh identity. However, in her post-1727 poems to Queen Caroline, wife of George II, Brereton frequently includes a Welsh emphasis alongside her support of the Hanoverian monarchs. In the mid 1730s, the Queen commissioned a structure to be built in Richmond Park which was popularly known as Merlin's Cave, and which swiftly attracted a huge amount of contemporary commentary, both eulogistic and satiric. Merlin's Cave, completed in 1735, was the second of two ' "associational" pavilions' at Richmond: the first being a Hermitage which contained busts of Newton, Locke, Samuel Clarke, William Wollaston and Robert Boyle.[29] While the Hermitage played on Caroline's religious and scientific interests, the Cave provided the 'political and royal counterpart' to Caroline's image.[30] Inside the Cave (which was in reality a kind of thatched hut) was a series of six waxwork figures representing a range of historical and contemporary figures, including Merlin; his secretary; Henry VII's queen, Elizabeth of York; and her granddaughter, Elizabeth I. Two of the figures in the Cave invited a range of interpretations. One could have been Minerva, Spenser's Britomart, Britannia or Ariosto's Bradamante. The other could have represented Queen Elizabeth's nurse, Spenser's Glaucé, Ariosto's Melissa or the popular prophetess Mother Shipton.[31] By including this range of figures Caroline was presenting the public with a visual allegorical representation of the legitimacy of the Hanoverian succession, or, as Christine Gerrard phrases it, 'a shrine which advertised her dynastic pedigree and her descent from British antiquity'.[32] Such a project was especially important for the Hanoverian monarchs, who, in contrast to the Stuarts, had no natural claim to the British throne and who therefore were compelled to invent a dynastic mythology and legitimacy.[33]

How exactly, then, did Merlin's Cave endorse Caroline's 'dynastic pedigree' and that of the Hanoverian succession overall? The presence of figures representing Henry VII's queen (mother of Prince Arthur Tudor) and Elizabeth I deliberately evokes an Arthurian and Spenserian context through which to read the Cave's political message. Central to this Arthurian appropriation is, of course, the figure of Merlin, whose main prophecy concerned the return of Arthur as King of Britain. This myth had been variously employed by the Tudor monarchs to establish a Welsh-British ancestry which endorsed their claims to the throne. In the *Faerie Queene*, of course, Spenser also used Merlin's prophecies to Britomart in order 'to glorify Elizabeth by tracing her descent from Arthur'.[34] In one reading of the

Faerie Queene, Spenser can be seen to reaffirm 'the historical claim first made by Henry VII and his queen, and thereafter made by Henry VIII, and finally by Elizabeth: that the Welsh monarchs on the throne were the rightful descendants of the fabled kings of ancient Britain'.[35] By including these figures in the Cave and associating herself with Merlin and his prophecies, Caroline was, therefore, in an ideal sense, promoting her own legitimacy to be Queen of Britain in a way that satisfied both Welsh interests and the more recent notion of a united Britain by asserting a common lineage from the Ancient Britons to the House of Hanover.

Jane Brereton was one of the many writers who responded positively to Merlin's Cave.[36] Despite the contemporary popularity and revival of Spenser from the 1730s onwards, however, it was not the Spenserian element of Caroline's pavilion which especially drew her attention. Brereton's pseudonym at this time, and the name under which she contributed to the *Gentleman's Magazine*, was Melissa. The prophetess Melissa, from Ariosto's *Orlando Furioso*, was one possibility for the sixth wax figure in Merlin's Cave. Melissa's role in leading Bradamante to Merlin in canto III of *Orlando Furioso* has an obvious dynastic purpose, as it results in Merlin's prediction of the future success of Bradamante's lineage. Allusions to Spenserian and Ariostan versions of Merlin's prophecy therefore established a double claim on Caroline's behalf for the legitimacy and glory of the Hanoverian monarchs and eighteenth-century Britain. As Christine Gerrard explains:

> Spenser's Merlin envisions the Arthurian line culminating in the Tudors, Ariosto's Merlin foretells the rise of the House of Este. Leibniz, among others, had recently established that it was from the House of Este that the lines of Brunswick and Hanover were descended. Caroline was thus implicitly associating her own royal pedigree with the British Arthurian myth – a double confirmation of the antiquity of the House of Hanover.[37]

In her self-styled role as Melissa, therefore, Brereton fashions herself as both prophet and bard of the Hanoverian succession.[38] But how does Brereton, as Melissa, use Merlin's prophecies to signal her own position within these debates? In 1733 Brereton published a poem on the first of the Queen's pavilions, 'The Royal Hermitage: A Poem', subtitled as '*On the* Bustoes *in the* Royal Hermitage' in the 1744 *Poems*. In the opening stanza, Brereton draws attention to both her Welsh identity and her status as a woman writer:

WHILE to our QUEEN each duteous Bard conveys
The faithful Tribute of exalted Praise;
While Genius, Learning, all their Force combine
To make the Numbers, as the Theme, divine;
How shall a *Cambrian Muse*, obscure, and mean,
The lowest, latest of the tuneful Train,
Too weak her Wings, too tardy in her Flight,
Amongst their Sterling Coin, dare to present her Mite?
(1–8)

In an allusion to her own marital status, Brereton uses the biblical story (Luke 21: 1–4) of the widow's mite to suggest her unsuitability for speaking on political and learned matters. Just as the widow's contribution to the treasury seems meagre when compared to the 'Sterling Coin' of the rich men, Brereton's poem must, she suggests, seem a poor offering in contrast to the 'exalted Praise' offered by other poets. Brereton's modest stance here actually serves to authorise her panegyric to Caroline, however. As a woman herself, Brereton can more easily approach the female representative of monarchy and is able to ask Caroline to 'accept from thy own Sex this artless Strain' (16).[39] In choosing Caroline as the focus of her praise, as opposed to the often absent George II, Brereton also authorises herself further by focusing on Caroline's feminine qualities, as well as her learnedness, and speaks to her as one woman to another:

O *Wife*! More happy in thy Lord alone
Than in the Pow'r, and Splendor, of his Throne.
O *Mother*! blest in your Illustrious Race,
The Guardian Angels of our future Peace.
O *Patroness of Science*! wilt thou deign
T'accept from thy own Sex this artless Strain?
Around the Throne too dazling Glories dwell;
May I, most gracious *Queen*! approach thy Cell?
(11–18)

Brereton's identity as the 'Cambrian Muse' is initially presented as similarly 'obscure', 'mean' and lacking in literary credibility: 'The lowest, latest of the tuneful Train'. However, Brereton turns her geographical obscurity to political advantage. She begins by drawing a parallel between Caroline's rule in Britain and Henry VIII's Welsh policy: '*O Queen*! More learn'd than e'er *Britannia* saw, / Since our fam'd *Tudor* to the Realm gave Law' (9–10). Furthermore, the poem ends with a Merlin-like prophecy which connects the movement of the solar system and the tides with the rule of Caroline and the loyalty of eighteenth-century Britons to the Hanoverian monarchs:

> While plenteous *Thames* flows from its Crystal Urn;
> While ebbing Tides to *Ocean's* Bed return;
> While circling Waves around *Britannia* move;
> While Liberty, and Honour, *Britons* love;
> While the fair *Moon* reflects the solar Ray,
> And guides the Motions of the swelling *Sea*;
> While the bright *Sun* the golden Day shall give,
> With *Caroline's* these *Sages'* Fame will live.
>
> (59–66)

Therefore, although Brereton styles herself as 'low' and 'mean' in her role as the 'Cambrian Muse', in practice she situates herself at the centre of political and national debate. Brereton thus becomes a kind of female poet laureate dedicated to praising the Queen (as one of her own sex) and the present and future success of Hanoverian Britain. It could be argued, therefore, that Jane Brereton is staking a claim for the right of a Welsh woman to intervene in matters of national importance.

These themes are continued in a companion poem on Caroline's second Richmond pavilion. *Merlin: A Poem* was written in 1733, but inscribed to Caroline as 'Queen Guardian' in October 1735, after the completion of the Cave in that year. As the title makes clear, in this poem Brereton makes Merlin and ideas of prophecy central. Here the 'Cambrian Muse' has changed into 'a *British Muse*' (3), who borrows Merlin's authority to endorse her status as a female poet:[40]

> ILLUSTRIOUS QUEEN!
> The loyal Zeal excuse,
> The fond ambition of a *British Muse,*
> Who wou'd, in *Merlin's* Praise, attempt to soar,
> And in his *Cave,* Your Patronage implore:
> Protection seek, beneath Your *Royal Name*;
> And borrow Strength to rise, from *Merlin's* Fame.
>
> (1–7)

Merlin entreats Melissa to speak, and alludes to the demise of the Welsh bardic tradition, which ironically allows Melissa to be heard:

since 'the *Cambrian Bards* neglect the Muse' (46), Merlin declares himself happy to accept *'Melissa*'s humbler Strains' (47). By using Merlin as her poetic voice Brereton authorises herself to speak on dynastic and political issues. Moreover, as Melissa the prophetess, Brereton can stake a claim in foretelling the future prosperity of the House of Hanover. The 'British Muse' ascends a mountain, where she reaches Merlin's Cave and imagines seeing a vision of Merlin beneath 'a venerable *Oak*' (20) brandishing a *'British Harp*' (30) and wearing a robe adorned with *'Angles, and Circles*' (27).[41] Merlin entreats Melissa to speak by drawing on his glorification by Caroline in the Cave and alluding to Brereton's previous poem on the Hermitage:

> Why will *Melissa Merlin*'s Praise decline,
> Distinguish'd now by Royal CAROLINE?
> Believe not *such*, as wou'd asperse my Name;
> But trust those *Authors*, who defend my Fame.
> You, to the Royal *Grotto*, touch'd the Lyre,
> And durst in God-like *Newton*'s Praise aspire.
> Why shou'd not *British Merlin* grace thy Page,
> In *Mathematicks* once esteem'd a Sage?
> (34–41)

Again, Brereton uses Merlin simultaneously to articulate her own sense of unworthiness and to authorise her speech:

> To *Learning*'s *Patroness* my Thanks convey;
> And humbly at her Feet present thy Lay.
> Conscious, how mean, and how unskill'd thy Hand,
> I see thee tremble at my kind Command.
> Let my Persuasion, once, thy Fears beguile;
> The gracious QUEEN will condescend to smile:
> For *Merlin*'s sake, will give *Melissa* Leave
> To touch the Strings in my much honour'd *Cave*.
> (96–103)

At the end of *Merlin* there are two lines which connect this poem with a further piece called *Merlin's Prophecy*. In a seemingly unconnected statement Merlin ends the poem by stating 'And *Wallia*'s gen'rous Prince will not disdain / What I foretell; – tho' low, thy Lyrick Strain' (104–5). *Merlin's Prophecy* is duly inscribed to his Royal Highness, the Prince of Wales, and begins by claiming Frederick as the rightful inheritor of the throne of Britain, in keeping with Merlin's traditional role as a prophet of future dynasties:

ROYAL *FREDERICK*! *Britain*'s Pride!
  Prince, for future Safety giv'n;
    For Thee's decree'd a Virtuous *Bride*,
  Choicest *Gift* of bounteous Heav'n.
    To reward thy filial Duty,
  To perpetuate *Brunswick*'s Race,
    Wit, and Learning, Youth, and Beauty,
  Heav'n prepares for thy Embrace.
                          (1–8)

Brereton is referring here to Frederick's recent engagement to Augusta of Saxe Gotha and, as Colton suggests, the Cave may have been part of an attempt by Caroline to heal the rift between her son and his parents. More broadly, Merlin's prophecy is used by Brereton to underline further the future success of the Brunswick line, in terms very similar to Brereton's earlier praise of George I; hence the use of the phrase 'gentle Sway', which is repeated verbatim:

  And lo! I see a *glorious Race*,
Successive rising to Renown!
  Decree'd *Britannia*'s Throne to grace;
And give new Lustre to a Crown.
  Ordain'd to wield the Sceptre Royal,
With righteous Pow'r, and gentle Sway;
  And rule o'er *Britons*, Brave, and Loyal,
'Till Heav'n, and Earth, shall melt away.
                          (25–32)

Merlin's presence in Brereton's two poems goes some way to explaining Christine Gerrard's sense that in her linking together of a very Druidic Merlin (in *Merlin* he appears beneath an oak sprouting mistletoe) with a celebration of Newton's astronomical discoveries, Brereton is making a 'strange' connection.[42] But when read in relation to the 'Bustoes' poem it is clear that Brereton is making a point about the connection between the two pavilions which, at first, does indeed seem paradoxical. In *Merlin*, Brereton makes Merlin speak of his magical powers (moving the stones from Ireland to Stonehenge) and his study of nature as well as his prophecy. But despite his powers, Brereton implies, even Merlin has to bow to Newton's greater feats. Before the reign of Caroline all was mere superstition, as Merlin recounts:

> Oft to PLINLIMON have I took my Way,
> Rose with the *Sun*, toil'd up th' Ascent all Day;
> But scarce could reach the Mountain's tow'ring Height,
> Ere radiant *Vesper* usher'd in the Night.
> The Summit gain'd, I sought with naked Eye
> To penetrate the Wonders of the Sky.
> No telescopic Glass known in that Age
> T'assist the Optics of the curious Sage.
> Tho' lov'd *Astronomy* oft charm'd my Mind,
> I now erroneous all my Notions find.
> I thought bright *Sol* around our *Globe* had run,
> Nor knew Earth's Motion, nor the central *Sun*.
> And had I known; could I Belief have gain'd,
> When Ignorance, and Superstition reign'd?
>   (64–77)

Brereton is trying to do two things here. On the one hand, she is favourably contrasting present enlightenment, symbolised by the patronage of Newton by Caroline, with past 'Ignorance'. In these terms, as Merlin's pronouncements make clear, this is a new age of reason, as opposed to the dark ages of superstition. On the other hand, by making Merlin himself speak these sentiments, Brereton is also aligning Caroline and the Hanoverian monarchs with the ancient British line and to Merlin's traditional role of singing to his 'Harp prophetick' (63). Merlin's prophecy here incorporates a sense of Caroline's particular achievements in the realms of science and endorses her rule as one of reason and enlightenment. Brereton thus makes the connection between the two different, yet related, meanings of the two pavilions.[43] At the same time as she praises Caroline as patroness of science and representative of a new age of reason and reformed religion, by using Merlin as her poetic speaker Brereton also endorses the Hanoverian claims to be the true inheritors of the British throne in the same way that the Tudors legitimised their own rule. This is shown when Merlin flies over his 'native Isle' and sees Hanoverian Britain as a place 'Where Arts improve, and Peace and Plenty smile' (89).

The poems of Jane Brereton clearly fit into a recognisable, and predominantly male, Whig literary tradition which used Arthurian material, particularly Merlin's prophecy, to eulogise and legitimise the Protestant succession.[44] What is different about Brereton is her self-fashioning both as Melissa the prophetess and as the Cambrian bard. In order to authorise her poetic voice and national sentiments, she carefully frames her commentary within gendered expectations of feminine modesty, but also draws on a long-politicised tradition of female prophecy. As Merlin's Melissa, Brereton can figure herself as the spokeswoman for the present and future successes of the Hanoverian dynasty. Furthermore, in her bardic incarnation, Brereton also alludes to the traditionally masculine vaticinatory role of the Welsh bards and appropriates this position to authorise her poetic speech. The 'Cambrian Muse', she suggests, is uniquely placed to predict a future for Britain which is loyal, peaceful and prosperous. As such, it could be argued that Brereton stakes a claim for the place of Wales within early eighteenth-century conceptions of Britain based on economic success, Hanoverian loyalty and Protestant faith. By using the Tudor Union as an implicit model for a post-1707 Britain, Brereton can simultaneously legitimise the House of Hanover through allusions to Britannic mythology and present the Welsh–English alliance as an example of peaceful integration. In this sense, it can be argued that the 'Cambrian Muse' has a truly British dimension and that Brereton succeeded in making her country central to the conceptualisation of Britain as a unified nation in the early eighteenth century. However, Brereton's stance in relation to Wales is, perhaps, more complicated than is indicated by this initial assessment.

Hanoverian Loyalty and the Cambro-Briton

In the ode which she addressed to the antiquarian Humphrey Foulkes, *On Reading some Dissertations, in the Reverend Dr Foulkes's Modern Antiquities*, Brereton begins by styling herself as a 'Cambro-Briton' who has taken pleasure in reading the history of her people.[45] But far from upholding a sense of loss about the demise of ancient British power and independence, Brereton instead praises Heaven that the Welsh have been saved from themselves, first by the Romans, and subsequently by Edward I:

> A *Cambro-Briton* must with Pleasure trace
> The Means which Heav'n ordain'd to save our Race.
> Tho', in the Fight, our warlike Fathers prov'd
> Fierce as Wolves, and as our Rocks unmov'd;
> Yet Heav'n be prais'd that here, the Eagles flew,

And *Roman* Arts that Fierceness cou'd subdue;
That Laws prevail'd, which their just Rights maintain'd;
And but from savage Liberty restrain'd!
(11–18)

The Roman invasion of Britain is seen as wholly positive. Although the Britons are styled as fierce and martial, they are also seen as 'savage' and uncivilised until the welcome influence of Roman culture in the form of 'Arts', 'Laws' and 'Rights'. Likewise, instead of appearing in his better-known incarnation as usurper of Welsh freedom and perpetrator of bardicide, Edward I, of 'great and glorious Name' (20), is not only lauded for getting rid of the 'inferior' Welsh law of the tenth-century king 'Howel Dda' ('And own his Laws, our *Howel Dda*'s excel!'), but praised for his championing of the female sex, particularly widows:[46]

Still honour'd by our Sex, still dear to Fame,
Be the first *Edward*'s great, and glorious Name!
Who abrogated that unrighteous Power,
By which our Sex enjoy'd nor Land nor Dower.
(19–22)

In total, Brereton represents the 'savage Liberty' of her ancestors as thankfully overcome by the 'Superior Blessings' (29) of a rational Christianity based on forgiveness and tolerance: 'pure Religion' (30) clears away the 'Mist of Superstition' (31), and blesses the Britons with 'equal Laws, and Gospel Light' (39). As Katie Gramich and Catherine Brennan note, she 'is no Welsh nationalist heroine'.[47] For Brereton, the loss of Welsh freedom results in the survival of the race of the Britons, not in their annihilation. Brereton's 'Cambro-Britishness' could be seen, then, as capitulation to what she perceived as superior English rationality, albeit couched in terms of Christian salvation and a vision of a unified Britain: '"Love one another," the blest Saviour said: / O *Britons*! Let the Mandate be obey'd' (51–2).

Brereton's ode is interesting not only for what it reveals about her own sense of national identity, but also for what it shows us about the views of the literary and antiquarian circle she was part of at Croesnewydd. Indeed, as the title of the poem indicates, Brereton is writing in direct response to some recent reading-matter, specifically Foulkes's 'A dissertation on the Welsh Laws, and some of the customs of the Welsh that are mentioned in them', extracted from the 'Welsh Laws' published by William Wotton and Moses Williams.[48] If Brereton's ode is read alongside the dissertation it is clear where she found the rationale for her poetic sentiments, and also notable that as a widow she would have been particularly interested in the content of Foulkes's work. Indeed, he focuses particularly on the legal position of women, and in the following lines we can see the exact inspiration for Brereton's lines: 'The women had but hard usage before our Union in Edwd 1$^{st.}$ For the wife had no share of the lands of her husband, in thirds or joynture, except the Princes daughter. The widow carried onely half of the personal Estate' (pp. 211–12). As well as detailing various aspects of Welsh law, Foulkes frequently inserts commentary on his subject and points the very Whiggish moral about improvement through progress:

> But I must not forget here before I close this dissertation to acquaint the reader that the true use we ought to make of the foregoing reflections upon the government and laws of the Antient Britains, as well as of the History therewith printed: is to wean us from the vulgar Error, that the former days of our Ancestors were better than these; and to thank providence, that we have been reserved for these latter and better times. . . . We are improved we see by every Conquest made of us. We were most obliged to the Romans even when they were Heathens; and not a little to the Saxons when they were civilized themselves. (pp. 208–9)

Despite Foulkes's clear antiquarian interest in the history of Wales, it is equally clear that his views are far from resistant to union with England. On the contrary, he views conquest as an essential civilising process. Significantly for Brereton, in this dissertation Foulkes draws attention to the better position of women as a result of union. He ends his text by stating:

> I thought fit to let the woemen [sic] understand thus much of the old laws and customs amongst their Ancestors; whereby they might see that these days are much better to them especially, than the antient; not onely as to their cloathing and furniture, and other conveniences of life: but also in their rights and priviledges [sic]; And all these advantages they enjoy, are owing to our happy Union with the English, and to the improving genius of the modern times. (pp. 216–17)

When the very specific context of Brereton's ode is revealed, the power of contemporary opinion makes its presence felt. As a woman commenting on the work of a male antiquarian, Brereton must have felt compelled to endorse his opinions. At the beginning of the poem she presents her poems to 'the Province of judicious Friends' (9), and pre-empts criticism by stating that although some will 'blame' her 'When to these Lines they see a Woman's name' (1–2), as it might 'prejudice the Cause', she is only expressing the 'pleasure' she gained from reading Foulkes's work. Might it be the case, then, that in her 'Ode' to Dr Foulkes, Brereton's views are fundamentally shaped by her gendered need to express pleasure in the work of a man?[49] To phrase it another way, are Brereton's national sentiments limited by the constraints of gender? For example, in another poem addressed to a male acquaintance, Mr Hinchliffe, who had praised her ode on the King in a poem of his own, Brereton connects loyalty to George 'the Fire of *British* Kings' (V, 1) with a sense of feminine virtue and propriety. For a woman, to oppose the Hanoverian succession is tantamount to a loss of virtue:

> While female Rebels plague our Isle,
>   Quite lost to Virtue, Sense, or Shame;
> While these the best of Kings revile,
>   My Loyalty I'll thus proclaim . . .
>   (II, 1–2) [50]

'*To Miss W——ms, Maid of Honour to the late* Queen' is a poem in praise of a Welsh member of the Queen's household.[51] In contrast to the poem to Foulkes, here Brereton's sentiments do appear to be a straightforward enunciation of a proud Welsh heritage, with Miss Williams as a symbol of the independent spirit of Wales. The poem begins by praising Miss Williams for her grace and charm, but it is her identity as a Welshwoman which enables Brereton to move on to discuss Welsh history in a different way. Williams is the 'Descendant of a glorious Race, / Who oft the *British* Crown did grace' (9–10). The poem continues by offering a less positive view of the Roman invasion and Saxon dominance than the previous poem, despite the hint of a civilising influence in the choice of the word 'Arts' (similarly deployed in the previous poem):

> Ere here the conqu'ring Eagles flew,
> Ere Roman Arms or Arts we knew;
> Long they maintain'd their Country free,
> Nor yielded but to Fate's Decree.
> Subdu'd at last the Homage paid,
> And *Saxon* Kings and Laws obey'd; . . .
>   (11–16)

Here the Saxons are figured as conquering the Welsh and reducing the nation to a state of servitude. The choice of the word 'Homage' reinforces this point, as in this context it places the Welsh people in the position of vassals declaring allegiance and binding themselves in service to a race of 'superior' rank.[52] In this instance, therefore, Brereton appears to lament the falling of the 'glorious Race' after the Saxon conquest.

The appearance of 'a Bard from *Merlin* sprung' (17) who 'to his Harp prophetick sung' (18) marks a shift in emphasis. The bard's prophecy concerns the presence of a Welshwoman at the Court of George II:

"From *Cambrian* Race a Nymph shall rise,
"Bright as yon *Venus* of the Skies;
"Whence *Romulus* or *Brutus* came,
"Who gave to *Rome* and *Britain* Name:
"As *Pallas* wise, as *Cynthia* chaste,
"With sparkling Bloom like *Hebe* grac'd;
"She in the *British* Court shall shine,
"In Beauty next the *Brunswick* Line,
"To that Great Queen Attendance pay,
"Whose Birth shall honour **David's* Day
         (*The first of *March*, St *David*, the Patron of *Wales*)
"This Nymph our Glory shall retrieve,
"Receive that Homage which we give,
"They us subdued by Arms and Arts;
"She'll make Reprisals on their Hearts.
         (19–32)

On one level, Brereton again appears to be endorsing an unproblematic view of history which, in keeping with Welsh enthusiasm for Geoffrey of Monmouth's *History of the Kings of Britain*, subscribes to the Galfridian narrative of the origins of the British race as stemming from Brutus. The Cambrian nymph is a direct descendant of this illustrious line and she is destined to 'shine' in the '*British* Court' of the Hanoverians, where she is compared to figures from Greek mythology: the gods and goddesses of Wisdom, Chastity and Youth respectively. In relation to Williams's position as maid of honour to Caroline, Brereton reworks her previous lines concerning the Romans and the Saxons. She plays on the additional meaning of 'homage' by suggesting that in the homage paid to the superior beauty of Miss Williams the more negative payment of homage as an acknowledgement of servitude is reversed, and the former 'Glory' of the '*Cambrian* Race' will be restored. Even though 'they' (presumably the Saxons) conquered the Britons, Miss Williams, representative of Cambria, will 'make Reprisals on their Hearts'. Again Brereton chooses her vocabulary carefully, as a 'reprisal', in its specific sense, is the forcible retrieval of property or persons from another nation which has been responsible for the initial 'theft'.[53] Miss Williams will charm by her feminine appeal in a way that will compensate for the glory of Wales lost by 'Arms and Arts'. As a maid of honour, she is constructed as penetrating the centre of power and standing in as a symbol of the glories of the Welsh race. Through the figure of Miss Williams and conventional representations of feminine beauty Brereton makes an attempt at redressing the balance of power between England and Wales. The poem therefore reveals a stronger sense of Welsh national pride than she has been credited with so far. After the death of Caroline (and indeed Foulkes) in 1737, did Brereton feel freer to express a stronger sense of an independent Welsh identity than hitherto? Does concentrating on a female figure free Brereton further from gendered expectations of female literary propriety?

Ostensibly, the poem operates in praise of 'that Great Queen' Caroline and serves to express Brereton's pro-Hanoverian sympathies. The maid of honour is worthy of such praise not only because she is Welsh, but also because she is so close to the centre of power and associated so directly with the Queen: 'She in the *British* Court shall shine'. Brereton thus adroitly turns praise of the noble race of the Britons into recognition of the current reign of the Hanoverians. The '*Brunswick* Line', it is suggested, stems from and continues the illustrious line of Britons, just as the Tudors were seen to restore the British line to the throne in the sixteenth century. Here Brereton continues the themes of her Merlin poems. The use of a Welsh context to authorise the Hanoverian succession is further endorsed by the play upon the fact that Caroline's public birthday was 1 March, St David's Day. Caroline thus becomes a symbol of Welsh loyalty to the Hanoverian succession, at the same time as Brereton is more covertly positing a notion of an illustrious Welsh past: the true race of Britons. However, as in all of Brereton's poems, her stance is not straightforward. Her use of 'Saxons' is a case in point. On one level it could be argued that she is hinting covertly at the German link between the Hanoverians and Saxons: Williams will make reprisals on the hearts of those at Court, who are implicitly linked to the Saxon conquerors.

On the other hand, it would seem that Brereton is sidestepping or neutralising the Saxon problem. Indeed, the Saxons often presented difficulties for Anglo-Welsh literary negotiations of a unified Britain because of their association with the English, whom Welsh writers do not want overtly to criticise.[54]

In the context of early eighteenth-century poetry by other Anglo-Welsh writers, Brereton's seemingly contradictory position is not exceptional. In his article, 'Some Anglo-Welsh poems in honour of George III, Queen Charlotte and the Prince of Wales', Roger Stephens Jones discusses a range of poems in English written 'by Welshmen or men with Welsh connections' on the marriage of George III to Sophia Charlotte and in response to the birth of their son, George Frederick Augustus.[55] Focusing particularly on the birthday poems which commemorate the arrival of a new Prince of Wales, Jones concludes that: 'The birthday poets are men suffering from internal conflict, unable to commit themselves entirely to either of two principles and two nations and unable to achieve a satisfactory compromise.'[56] In Jones's terms, then, Anglo-Welshness is a state which reveals 'a degree of schizophrenia': an impossible position, whereby the poets attempt, and fail, to reconcile commitment to Wales on the one hand and to England on the other.[57] One particular area that Jones pinpoints as revealing tension is the treatment of the Welsh past, a past based on liberty and freedom, but one which is rejected in favour of a vision of eighteenth-century England's commercially successful imperialism, embodied in the figure of George III. The majority of poetry produced by the Society of Ancient Britons reveals very similar political sentiments and conflicts. As we saw in the previous chapter, Nehemiah Griffith's *The Leek* is a case in point. From evidence in her *Poems* and in *The Leek*'s dedicatory verse, it is apparent that Brereton knew Griffith. *Merlin* opens with a quotation from *The Leek*, and she also wrote an entire poem in his honour: '*To* Nehemiah Griffith, *Esq; Author of the Leek*'.[58] In this poem, Brereton represents herself as responding to the history of Wales by typically feminine expressions of sighs, tears and tenderness:

> WHEN you, O *Briton*! our pass'd Woes relate,
> My Soul grows anxious for my Country's Fate;
> Sighs rend my Breast, my Eyes dissolve in Tears,
> And all the Woman's Tenderness appears.
>
> (1–4)

Brereton's womanly fears are then appeased, as Griffith shifts 'the melancholy Scene' to 'shew us happy under *George*'s Reign' (5–6) and to sing the praises of Caroline. She ends the poem with the declaration: 'What more could *Wales* desire, or Heav'n allow, / Than She our *Princess*! and our Poet *Thou*?' (19–20).

Griffith's poem, and the fact that we know it was read by Brereton, is useful for making absolutely explicit the negotiations needed to prop up her position as a Cambrian panegyrist of a united Britain. Griffith's poem performs many functions simultaneously: it is a celebration of Saint David (the patron saint of Wales), a history of Britain, a panegyric on the Hanoverian success, and an acknowledgement of the role which could be played by the Ancient British (the Welsh) in the creative imagining of a post-1707 Great Britain. It is this last point which is the most pertinent for thinking through the seeming incompatibility of all these different functions. Griffith's claim that the Ancient Britons will most of all 'date new Joys' from the Hanoverian succession is representative of a broader mythologising process, concerning what Tony Conran terms 'a series of Welsh messiahs' who will return to liberate the Welsh from oppression.[59] This mythologising could work to imagine Welsh independence, as in the case of Cadwaladr or Owain Glyndŵr, but also, as in the case of Arthur, serve to enforce British unity through English–Welsh alliance. This last approach underpinned positive Anglo-Welsh attitudes to the Tudor Union. As Conran points out, if Henry VII's eldest son Arthur

> had not died before his father, it would have been King Arthur who passed the Act of Union and so fulfilled Arthur's traditional role of uniting the Welsh and the English under a British king. . . . For the Welsh, Arthur is the major myth of Britishness, a perpetual invitation to look beyond the needs of Wales and to regard Britain as a whole as the promised land of the Welsh people.[60]

As the poetry of Brereton and Griffith demonstrates, in the early eighteenth century such mythologising is tailored by Anglo-Welsh or Cambro-British writers to suit the contemporary situation. For Brereton, Merlin's prophecies, as spoken by 'Melissa', both foretell and narrate the success of the Hanoverian reign in terms of a broader British interest. For Griffith, the Hanoverian succession is the fulfilment of a vision of a united Britain which is particularly gratifying to the Welsh, as it confirms their status as the 'original' British race.

A knowledge of the broader patterns of Anglo-Welsh relations, Anglo-Welsh poetry and the views of certain Cambro-British coteries in the early eighteenth century allows us to read through the contradictions of Brereton's ostensibly 'paradoxical' use of history and to understand how her 'Cambro-Britishness' actually helps to bolster a sense of identity which is integral to a new sense of Britishness in the period – an identity based on Protestantism and support of the Hanoverian monarchs, and therefore one which stakes a claim to be central, not marginal, to a post-1707 Britain. Brereton's poetry can thus be read not just as a series of failed attempts at an impossible reconciliation, but as part of an ongoing process of integration and therefore increased political power for Wales. On a less positive note, it could be argued that Jane Brereton and other Anglo-Welsh writers of the early eighteenth century are simply a product of an ongoing process of Anglicisation in Wales, whereby the gentry and middling class were more likely to be Anglo-oriented and English-speaking. From this perspective, Brereton's pro-Hanoverian sentiments could be read as either self-advancement or capitulation to English power. By positioning herself as the bard and prophet for the Hanoverian dynasty, it may be the case that Brereton is more interested in her own fame than in that of her fellow countrymen. Similarly, by turning her 'Cambrian Muse' into a 'British Muse', Brereton could be seen to subsume her Welsh identity under the name of (post-1707) Briton.

The similarities between Brereton, Griffith and their circle point to a less ambitiously craven motive behind her writing, however, and suggest that her views are representative of a certain cultural group rather than idiosyncratic. As I suggested at the start of this chapter, traditionally the old British history had often been used to bolster both a Welsh and an English identity, especially since the Tudor Union. As P. R. Roberts notes of the years after the Union, 'The Welsh sense of nationality was preserved at the same time, and with much the same argument, as the English national destiny was being expounded in a Protestant ideology naturalized, as it were, in a British tradition.'[61] From this perspective, the formal union with England was not seen as the loss of independence for Wales, but as the recovering 'of a previous British unity'.[62] The tensions in Brereton's poetry between her Welsh identity and her (post-1707) British allegiance can, therefore, be seen to stem from an 'inherent ambiguity in the claims that both the English and the Welsh were the heirs of the British tradition'.[63] These claims for a joint British heritage help to explain the stance adopted by

Brereton in her bid to support the Hanoverian monarchy yet also to maintain a sense of the importance of Wales in British culture.[64] As such, Brereton is very much a product of her time and place. She is also a typical example of her class and language group. As an anglophone, middle-class, London-oriented Court Whig, it is very unlikely that Brereton would score highly as a Welsh nationalist heroine. Nevertheless, her poetry clearly dramatises a strong sense of Welsh identity. Moreover, the fact that this identity was based on ideas of British unity, rather than Welsh independence, does not negate Brereton's Welsh pride, nor does it undermine her attempts to put Wales, her native land, on the poetic map of Great Britain.

3

'Gray's Pale Spectre': Evan Evans, Translation and the Rise of Welsh Bardic Nationalism

From the very beginning, Welsh–English translation has been embedded in the nexus of ideologies associated with the relationship between Wales and England. Indeed, 'Welsh-language literature' itself could in one important sense be said to have first appeared in English translation. Or, to put it less provocatively, Wales was in part awakened to the national distinctiveness of its ancient literary culture partly by viewing it through the eyes of England. It is, of course, a classic colonial situation.[1]

The mid eighteenth century was a period of extremely fruitful interchange between English and Welsh literary scholars. Paradoxically, this was also a period when Wales began to assert its rich bardic heritage in ways which strengthened a distinctive and potentially oppositional national literary revival, spearheaded by the ground-breaking publications of the scholar-poet Evan Evans (1731–88).[2] Evans (also known as Ieuan Brydydd Hir [Ieuan the Tall Poet] or by his bardic name, Ieuan Fardd) was a fiery Welsh patriot who, as Geraint H. Jenkins has noted, 'was preoccupied by two issues of critical importance in eighteenth-century Wales': 'the Anglicization of the church in Wales' and 'the sorry plight of Welsh culture'.[3] Evans's services to Welsh literary scholarship included the transcription of numerous important manuscripts. His published version of these transcripts, *Some Specimens of the Poetry of the Antient Welsh Bards* (1764), was arguably the most influential Welsh antiquarian work of the eighteenth century, representing the 'most extensive early examples of Welsh–English literary translation'.[4] The *Specimens* were a ground-breaking collection of ten examples of Welsh poetry, ranging from the work of the *Cynfeirdd* (the 'first or earliest' bards, such as Aneirin and Taliesin) to the *Gogynfeirdd* (the 'not so early' bards).[5] Evans can indeed be credited with, as he states in the preface, drawing the work of the Welsh bards 'out of that state of obscurity, in which they have hitherto been buried, and in which they run great risque of mouldering away'.[6] Through his antiquarian researches, Evans was, along with other Welsh scholars such as Lewis Morris, participating in the pan-European 'search for origins which became a key aspect of the modern process of nation building and which involved the attempt to define a nation as an ancient, established, historically rooted "fact"'.[7] As Charlotte Johnson states, 'Evan Evans was a poet and a scholar, but more than both he was a patriot. His love of his country and of its antiquities was a prime motive for publishing the *Specimens*.'[8]

Despite Evans's clear patriotic motives, scholars of eighteenth-century Welsh literary history have suggested that Evans's translations were mostly executed for this English audience, and have viewed the *Specimens* project as symptomatic of a typical 'equivocating Welsh response' to eighteenth-century constructions of 'British ideology'.[9] M. Wynn Thomas has argued, for example, that by recovering and reprinting the works of the ancient Welsh bards, Evans can without doubt be seen as engaged in a patriotic or 'foundationalist' act of 'nation-building'. However, he also suggests that Evans nevertheless displays 'a carefully depoliticized cultural nationalism' and 'a commitment to contributionism: in other words, a dutiful emphasis on what Wales could offer Britain'.[10] From this perspective, as Thomas suggests, antiquarian recovery of the kind practised by Evans – translating ancient Welsh texts into contemporary English – can be interpreted in colonial terms, with the sense that 'Wales was in part awakened to the national distinctiveness of its ancient literary culture partly by viewing it through the eyes of England'.[11] Or, as M. Wynn Thomas and S. Rhian Reynolds put it,

> The dominant motive of Evans, and of most of the others active in Welsh–English translation during the eighteenth and nineteenth centuries, was to prove to even the most sceptical of the powerful English that Wales had a literary heritage and culture of great wealth and antiquity. They sought the approbation of the colonizer in an attempt to restore national self-respect and to assert an element of autonomy.[12]

From this perspective, translations such as those by Evans are 'tributary offerings', whose function is to contribute to wider British glories.[13]

As Thomas goes on to note, however, Evans's texts 'remain to be closely studied both in themselves and in the context of our new understanding of the way a British ideology was being constructed during this period'.[14] In response to Thomas's suggestion, I will argue that, when read in the light of recent reconsiderations of bardic nationalism and readings of anti-colonial sentiment, Evans's work can be seen to resist this notion of British contributionism. Katie Trumpener, in her use of the phrase 'bardic nationalism' and Jane Aaron, in her coining of the correlative term 'bardic anti-colonialism', both imply a more combative motive for antiquarian recovery and memory. Trumpener identifies the way in which the recuperative work of eighteenth-century nationalist antiquaries from Ireland, Scotland and Wales 'represents a groundbreaking attempt to describe literature as the product of specific cultural institutions and to understand literary form as a product of a particular national history'.[15] Aaron makes the point that, in the eyes of various post-colonial critics, such as Homi K. Bhabha, 'for a colonized people to claim a literature as their own, and label it "national", is fighting talk; the discovery of such literature constitutes a vital step towards their freedom'.[16] Indeed, for Evans, 'It was to the glory of his country and to the honour of her language that his scholarship was dedicated'.[17] In terms of motive, Evans is considerably more outspoken about his patriotism in the Welsh preface to *Specimens*, 'At y Cymry' ('To the Welsh People'). Here he states to his 'Fellow Countrymen', or 'Cydwladwyr', that the *Specimens* are a direct riposte to English attacks: 'as the English claimed, that we do not possess any Poetry worth showing off, I did my best to translate this small Anthology, in order to cast off, if possible, that slur'.[18]

In relation to Evans's antiquarian publications these broader national issues are bound up with what we might term 'the politics of translation'.[19] To begin with, in terms of audience the issues are considerably more complicated than the view that Evans capitulated to English readers and tastes simply by the *act* of translation. Indeed, his translations were criticised precisely for the fact that they did not embellish the originals or make them palatable to eighteenth-century poetic tastes. As Charlotte Johnson has noted, English reviewers were 'disappointed at the literalness of Evans' translations'.[20] However, this refusal to adapt the original poems to contemporary Anglicised and/or metropolitan literary expectations can be read as a political choice, rather than simply as inadequate translation skills. Furthermore, by printing the poems in Welsh, including a Latin dissertation, *Dissertatio de Bardis* (which provided selections of the poetry in the original Welsh alongside Latin translations), and offering a preface in Welsh, in addition to his English preface and translations, it is clear that Evans was also anticipating an international and a scholarly Welsh audience, as well as anglophone readers. In this respect, the composite nature of *Specimens* makes it a remarkably multilingual text.[21]

In the mid eighteenth century, translation was a hot topic and one which, as now, had clear national implications. In the 1760s, of course, the focus for such debates was the publication of James Macpherson's Ossian poems.[22] In his English preface, Evans suggests that it was spurious 'translations' of the fake Erse poet which prompted him to publish a Welsh riposte to Scottish claims for an ancient literary tradition. As Mary-Ann Constantine has noted with regard to the *Specimens*, 'Ossian haunts its pages from the preface'.[23] Evans presents his selections as proof of the excellence, antiquity and, in a side glance at Macpherson, *authenticity* of the literature of Wales.[24] He stresses that his translations are not to be seen as 'in competition' with Ossian, and is at pains to point out that his project 'was first thought of, and encouraged some years before the name of Ossian was know in England' (p. i). In some ways, however, Evans deliberately presents the *Specimens* in the context of Ossian, proving to an English audience that Wales had more of authenticity to offer than Scotland.[25] In a typical 'foundationalist' move, he emphasises the antiquity of his own national history: 'I had long been convinced, that no nation in Europe possesses greater remains of antient and genuine pieces of this kind than the Welsh; and therefore was inclined, in honour to my country, to give a specimen of them in the English language' (pp. i–ii).[26] It could be argued here that Evans is indeed presenting his work in a contributionist manner to prove to the English that Wales has as much, if not more, to offer in this line than Scotland. Despite the obvious Welsh pride, it could also be suggested that there is a clear sense of a wider English-speaking, Ossian-loving audience whom Evans wants to impress with his *authentic* cultural documents.

However, the relationship with Macpherson is more complex than this pro-contributionist analysis allows for. Indeed, the debate about the authenticity of the Ossian poems is bound up with issues of translatability, or rather 'untranslatability'.[27] Evans's work is full of barbed asides which centre on this question of 'genuineness'. In relation to his Welsh examples, Evans writes:

> As to the genuineness of these poems, I think there can be no doubt; but though we may vie with the Scottish nation in this particular, yet there is another point, in which we must yield to them undoubtedly. The language

of their oldest poets, it seems, is still perfectly intelligible, which is by no means our case. (p. ii)

Intelligibility is a sign of inauthenticity. As Constantine goes on to suggest, 'Time and again the intractability and obscurity of the early medieval Welsh, and the corresponding awkwardness of the translation, is juxtaposed with the suspicious "smoothness" of Macpherson's texts'.[28] Such intractability directly affects translation practices. In the closing lines of the preface Evans admits that 'I have been obliged to leave blanks in some places, where I did not understand the meaning in the original, as I have but one copy by me, which might be faulty' (p. v). He expresses the hope – later extended to projected plans for future scholars – that he will have the chance to compare his transcriptions with other manuscript sources.

The difficulty of translating becomes especially prominent in relation to the early poetry of Taliesin and Aneirin. In his prefatory account to Taliesin's poem to Elphin ('Dyhuddiant Elphin/Elphin's Consolation'), Evans admits that his process of selection was guided very simply by the fact that this was the only one of the poems ('above fifty of them') which 'I could thoroughly understand' (p. 53). He adds: 'This should be a caveat to the English reader concerning the great antiquity of the poems that go under the name of Ossian, the son of Fingal, lately published by Mr. Mackpherson' (p. 54). Similarly, in relation to the *Gododdin*, extracts from which he translated into Latin in the *Dissertatio*, Evans again comments on the obscurity of the language (again he says this is partly due to his having seen only one manuscript): 'I thought I would include here some extracts from the *Gododdin* of Aneurin [*sic*], even though they may be completely obscure because of their antiquity and the unfamiliar dialect in which they are written' (p. 78). In 'At y Cymry', Evans compares the untranslatability of Aneirin to Macpherson's seamless productions:

The work of our Bards, which date from a hundred years after that [Ossian], are incomprehensible to the wisest and most skilled Men in the old language of Britain. Who of us could take the Gododin [*sic*], the work of *Aneurin* [*sic*] *Gwawdrydd, Fychdeyrn Beirdd*, and make such a brilliant translation as the one by the translator of *Fingal and Temora*? I don't think there is anyone who would make so bold as to undertake such a masterpiece. I was hardly able to interpret some of its verses here and there, which can be seen in the Latin essay concerning the Bards. (p. 105)

Evans's comments give a clear picture of the difficulties facing a scholar in the mid eighteenth century. Manuscripts and books were not readily available in public libraries, and private collections, such as those at Hengwrt and Mostyn, were difficult to access. It is from this context, as well as the comparisons with Ossian, that Evans's motives and translation practices must be understood. In the preface, Evans admits of his copy texts that 'it is an arduous task to bring them to make any tolerable figure in a prose translation' (p. iv). Yet his refusal to embellish the poems beyond his knowledge points to his resistance to the pressure both of Ossianic example and of English taste:

> As to the translation, I have endeavoured to render the sense of the Bards faithfully, without confining myself to too servile a version; nor have I, on the other hand, taken liberty to wander much from the originals; unless I saw it absolutely necessary, on account of the different phraseology and idiom of language. (p. iv)

Here Evans confronts the untranslatability of his source texts, not just in terms of the obscurity of particular words, but also in terms of its inherent strangeness or distance. Due to the obscurity of the language, Evans admits he has difficulty not only translating, in a literal sense, the poetry of the Welsh bards, but also interpreting the poetry, in the wider sense of making the past intelligible to the present. It is this resistance to give up the intransigence of the past, and its function as a nation's history, which makes Evans's translations more politically charged than a contributionist reading of *Specimens* allows for. Whereas Macpherson (and, it could be argued, Thomas Gray) make the ancient British past easily intelligible, not only to the present, but also to a metropolitan English audience, Evans insists on its difference, its untranslatability, its resistance to easy assimilation. Untranslatability is therefore a political gesture as well as an editorial problem. Whereas Nick Groom characterises Evans's translations as 'unthreatening', due to their prosaic nature, I would suggest that by refusing to 'Ossianise' his source texts Evans is demonstrating the resistance of Welsh culture to English assimilation.[29] He is also subtly emphasising English gullibility in being duped by the 'exquisite' yet spurious translations of Ossian. Indeed, although 'At y Cymry' states that part of his motive in translating the *Specimens* was to counter English claims that 'we do not possess any Poetry worth showing off' (p. 104), he also makes a much stronger statement in this essay (as Constantine also notes) against Ossian's status as the genuine article skilfully translated. Although the 'volumes are held in high esteem by learned English gentry' and are 'exquisitely translated', Evans adds, 'I'm afraid that the Scot is pulling the wool over our eyes' (p. 104).

Edward I and the Massacre of the Bards

Just as translation style and choices are not devoid of politics, Evans's editorial decisions, his framing commentary and his running footnotes also have a political import.[30] Evans's extensive footnotes are fascinating in this respect. Ostensibly serving to fill in historical facts and details about bardic traditions, the notes are actually full of barbed references to the English and pointed comments about the invading Saxons. One particularly politically charged tradition is that concerning Edward I's massacre of the Welsh bards, upon his conquest of the nation in 1282. The fact that Evans's 'mouldering' manuscripts still exist to copy is all the more remarkable, he suggests, given the attempt of Edward I to eradicate the bards altogether. Of his copy text he writes:

> This is a noble treasure, and very rare to be met with; for Edward the first ordered all our Bards, and their works, to be destroyed, as is attested by Sir John Wynn of Gwydir, in the history he compiled of his ancestors at Carnarvon. (pp. iii–iv)

As Evans indicates, the seventeenth-century source for the story of the massacre of the bards is John Wynn's *History of the Gwedir Family*, which was not published until 1770 but could be consulted in manuscript in Mostyn library. Wynn's study was the source for the more readily available treatment of the episode in the second volume of Thomas Carte's *A General History of England* (1747–55; 1750), which, as is well known, was the source used by Thomas Gray in his famous ode, *The Bard*.[31] On the title-page Carte styles himself 'an Englishman', and it is from an English perspective that he tells the story of the massacre. His treatment of Edward is correspondingly sympathetic and positive. The King is described as 'the greatest and wisest of our *English* monarchs' (Book VIII, p. 195), who 'acted with great prudence and circumspection in all his affairs' (p. 190). The representation of the Welsh as unruly and uncivilised means that Edward's conquest of Wales can be depicted in terms of colonial necessity. The English are described as 'civilizing the *Welsh*' (p. 191), a process which is only hindered by 'the unreasonable obstinacy of the *Welsh* in adhering to their ancient customs' (p. 191). In Carte's terms, Edward is betrayed by the Welsh, and therefore his resolution 'to make an entire conquest of a country, which had ever served for a place of retreat to a turbulent nobility' (p. 191) is seen as politically expedient as well as prudent. Despite his positive treatment of Edward, Carte does admit that the bards – but only the bards – received harsh treatment:

> The onely set of men among the *Welsh*, that had reason to complain of *Edward*'s severity, were the *Bards*, who used to put those remains of the antient *Britains* in mind of the valiant deeds of their ancestors: he ordered them all to be hanged, as inciters of the people to sedition. Politicks in this point got the better of the king's natural lenity: and those, who were afterwards entrusted with the government of the country, following his example, the profession became dangerous, gradually declined, and, in a little time, that sort of men was utterly destroyed. (p. 196)

On one level, Carte's interpretation of the political role of the bards could be seen as the same as that of the Welsh antiquarians. In fact, when relating the account of the massacre Carte often uses the exact phrasing of his Welsh source. In both cases, the bards are not only poets, but also play a politically oppositional and dangerous role, directly stirring up 'the people to sedition' (the exact phrase used in the original) by bolstering Welsh pride in their ancient culture; a culture which was effectively annihilated by Edward's actions in killing those who were its custodians. However, whereas from a Welsh perspective it is precisely the bards' function as 'inciters of the people to sedition' which constitutes their value, Carte views these 'seditious' actions as negative and obstructive to successful union with England. He comments that whatever method Edward took – conciliation or force – he could not make the Welsh loyal to an English king: 'They liked no prince or ruler, but one of their own nation: and still harped upon this string, whenever the King talked with them on this subject' (p. 197). The view of the massacre of the bards episode in Carte's influential account therefore frames Edward's actions in terms of his frustration with an unruly and proudly independent Wales. The killing of the bards is seen as part of a Welsh–English power struggle rather than, for example, a British–Norman conflict. The enemy of Welsh liberty and Welsh culture is here clearly England. It is no surprise, then, that for the Welsh the figure of Edward could be symbolic of the cultural and military oppression of the Welsh by the English, as well as a figure of tyrannical monarchy in general. As Geraint H. Jenkins notes, among

Welsh commentators 'It became fashionable to pillory the name of Edward', even to the extent that by the 1790s 'Some of the wilder democrats in London-Welsh circles found it hard to resist the temptation to urinate on Edward I's grave at Westminster'.[32]

The historical connection between the massacre of the bards and the conquest of Wales could be seen as making explicit the threat that colonial invasion posed, not only to the nation as a political construct, but also in terms of cultural heritage and literary tradition. In this respect, the figure of Edward I could usefully serve as an appropriate focus for Welsh resistance to post-1707 ideas of British integration as well as a target for republican anti-monarchal sentiment. Eighteenth-century interest in the historical period and events represented by Edward I also reveals an antagonistic history between England and Wales which challenges the common perception that, in contrast to Ireland and Scotland, eighteenth-century Wales was peacefully annexed to its more powerful neighbour. Furthermore, it is no coincidence that in a period which was marked by a dramatic increase in antiquarian activity, a historical event which represented the loss of, or threat to, the very traditions that were now being recovered gained particular prominence. Indeed, a typical result of conquest is that the conquered nation discovers 'a new unity under the experience of foreign rule'.[33] However, it remains to be seen if eighteenth-century Anglo-Welsh writers did, in fact, utilise the political potential of the tradition of the massacre of the bards and the Edwardian conquest to challenge dominant notions of British inclusiveness.

By presenting his *Specimens* in the context of the Edwardian massacre, Evans makes his project work simultaneously as an act of antiquarian recovery and of cultural patriotism. The choice of poetic specimens Evans includes is continually framed by reference to the Edwardian conquest and the act of bardicide. For example, Poem IX, 'Ode of the Months' by Gwilym Ddu of Arfon (*fl.* 1280–1320) to his patron Sir Gruffudd Llwyd, is described as one bard's lament for 'the decay'd state of his country', which Sir Gruffudd had attempted unsuccessfully to rescue from 'slavery' (p. 45). In his introductory remarks to this poem, Evans foregrounds Edward I, that 'cruel tyrant', in order to contextualise the poem that follows. He states: 'It will not be amiss to give a short account of that inhuman massacre of the Bards made by that cruel tyrant Edward the First' (p. 45). To compound his position, he quotes from the manuscript copy of Wynn's *History* to authenticate his remarks, selecting the section where Wynn mentions Edward as the king 'who caused our Bards all to be hanged by martial law, as stirrers of the people to sedition' (p. 46). In relation to Gwilym Ddu, Evans adds that 'it is not improbable that our Bard might have been one of those who suffered in the cause of his country, though he had the good luck to escape Edward's fury' (p. 46).

'Ode of the Months' is a lament both for the plight of the court poets and for the fate of Wales. Yet, as Evans remarks, despite the dominant elegiac note, the poem is also a commemoration and celebration of Welsh bardic and heroic culture: 'the following poem remains not only as a monument of the heroe's [sic] bravery, but of the Bard's genius' (p. 47). Gwilym Ddu declares that since the capture and imprisonment of Gruffudd due to 'the unjust oppression of the land of the Angles . . . the office of the Bard is but a vain and empty name' (p. 48). He continues in elegiac vein:

> The world droops since thou are lost. There are no entertainments or mirth. Bards are no longer honoured: The palaces are no longer open, strangers are neglected, there are no caparisoned steeds, no trusty endearing friendship. No, our country mourns, and wears the aspect of Lent. (p. 50)

Yet even as the bard sings about the end of poetry, he and his poem attest its survival. In its utilisation of what Katie Trumpener has termed a 'survival in destruction' motif, this particular 'specimen' epitomises Evans's project in relation to the tradition of Edward I and the alleged massacre.[34] The poem may end with a despairing description of the fate of a conquered country at the hands of 'Angles', whom Evans makes quite clear in a footnote are the English:[35] 'We must now renounce all consolation. We are confined in a close prison by a merciless unrelenting enemy; and what avails a bloody and brave contest for liberty' (p. 50). Yet what the poem presents overall is a damning picture of English oppression, which cannot, however, overcome the resilience and resistance of Wales and Welsh bardic culture.[36] By choosing this poem for inclusion, and by using the editorial frame of Edward I's massacre, Evans is making a political point not only about the superior quality of Welsh literary traditions, but also about the loss of Welsh liberty at the hands of English colonial power. There is a clear understanding here of a colonial situation whereby cultural resilience is silenced by military force.

In the *Dissertatio*, Evans turns again to the subject of Edward I. In contrast to Thomas Carte's account, Edward is not seen as a judicious and civilising influence over the 'unruly' Welsh, but as 'savage' and 'barbarous' in the extent of his 'revenge' on Llewelyn and David:

> When Edward the First conquered Wales, he acted like a tyrant towards the Bards, and had many of them hanged. Not really surprising when you think of the barbarous way in which he treated prince Llewelyn himself, and his brother David. But Edward had been put to flight once by Llewelyn, and so could not pardon him or his followers. He took a savage revenge. (p. 88) [37]

Evans outlines the role of the bards and their function as patriotic defenders of their country's independence, responding in particular to John Wynn's assertion, in *The History of the Gwedir Family*, that they stirred up the people to rebellion:

> The Bards were accused of inciting the people to rebellion, and the charge was true, because they used to urge their countrymen to regain the freedom which their forefathers had once enjoyed. For the Bards were to the Welsh what the orators had been to the Athenians, and these Philip of Macedon wanted to be handed over to him, so he could reduce Greece to slavery. The magistrates of England after Edward followed his example in Wales, and made the Bards everywhere subject to iniquitous laws; this is why they practically disappear from that time until the year 1400. (p. 88)

A positive spin is placed on the bards' role 'of inciting the people to rebellion'. Evans presents the bards as heroic freedom fighters, justly urging 'their countrymen to regain their freedom'. A classical context is also constructed for the bardic order: Edward is compared to Philip of Macedon in his wish to enslave the Welsh by removing their equivalent of the Athenian orators.[38] The bards are thus assigned the role of the poet as legislator, a role which included extensive political power and influence. Therefore, although they function as recorders of loss and defeat, their bardic songs are also testimony to a national struggle for survival against English oppression.

In relation to the treatment of the Edwardian conquest, Evans's use of history can be said to reveal a stance which is resistant to assimilation to English norms. Central to Evans's conception of the bardic function is that the bards were also historians. Therefore, to recuperate the work of the bards is to reinstate a national history for Wales. This distinct history is in danger of being lost, according to Evans, by the interventions of more recent English historians, such as William Camden. He complains that 'We do not have any history concerning our Ancestors written by our own Authors, but instead only what has come down to us from the Bards' (p. 101). In the *Dissertatio* he stresses the important function of the bards as custodians of national history: 'The works of those Bards who were historians are our sole means of tracing the genuine, the authentic history of Britain, and yet these works are in grave danger of disappearing altogether, as they have been for a long time now' (p. 90). To rescue the bards from oblivion is also to save a nation from historical obliteration. The importance of Geoffrey of Monmouth's *History of the Kings of Britain* for this separate Welsh history is emphasised by Evans, as it was by many an eighteenth-century Welsh patriot. In 'At y Cymry', in order to uphold the authenticity of the Galfridian tradition, Evans argues that Geoffrey did use a legitimate source for his work, Tysilio's *Brut y Brenhinedd* or *The Chronicle of the Kings of Britain*, and traces a direct line from the bards through Tysilio to Geoffrey of Monmouth:

> It was the Bards . . . who kept the genealogies of the Kings and recorded their magnificent deeds, and, certainly, it is from them that Tysilio the son of Brochwel Ysgythrog, the prince of Powys came to write the History which now goes under the title *Brut y Brenhinoedd*, which Galfrid ap Arthur from Aber Mynwy [Geoffrey of Monmouth], translated from the Breton language in Latin and from Breton into Welsh, as he himself admits in several old parchment copies which have yet to be seen in Wales. (pp. 101–2)[39]

Although he does admit that Geoffrey embellished his 'sources', he also declares that his work 'does not entirely deserve the defamatory treatment the English have given it since Camden's time', due to the fact that, according to Evans, Nennius' *Historia Britonum* (*c*.830) preceded Geoffrey by 300 years and 'provides the same History concerning our Beginnings' (p. 102). Part of Evans's plans for future research included an edition of Nennius which would presumably add further fuel to the Galfridian version of the illustrious (and traceable) origins of the Britons, and therefore the Welsh. In the English Appendix (No. 1) he comes back to this idea of future research, undertaken by an imaginary Welsh scholar who, under the auspices of an antiquarian society (the Cymmrodorion), would follow in the footsteps of Edward Lhuyd and provide a glossary of words in the old manuscripts. Of his ideal scholar, Evans writes: 'For who would be better qualified than such a person to decide the controversy about the genuineness of the British History, by Tyssilio [*sic*]' (p. 156). The recuperation of the Welsh language and the understanding of the bards are firmly connected to a correct understanding of the national past.

In 'At y Cymry', Evans stresses that, due to their lack of proficiency in the Welsh language, it is not the place of English historians to perform these acts of national recuperation. Even Camden, claims Evans, 'can only ramble on' about matters of importance to Wales, due to his insufficient knowledge of the language. These attitudes are in keeping with those of Evans's supporter Lewis Morris, who was also suspicious of English historians, especially those who, as Geraint H. Jenkins phrases it, 'committed the cardinal sin of denying the authenticity of the "British History"'. Like Evans, Morris 'was convinced that a large element of truth was embedded in Geoffrey of Monmouth's tale and insisted (wrongly as it turned out) that the chronicle known as *Brut Tysilio* or *Brut y Brenhinedd* was the Welsh source which Geoffrey claimed to have translated'.[40] Lewis Morris also defended ancient Welsh history against those English historians who denied Geoffrey's authenticity, and, as Lewis's protégé, Evans is very much of the same mind.[41] Evans insists again that an understanding of the bards is a prerequisite for an understanding of the Welsh national past, but he also makes a firm distinction between different types of bardic culture. In 'At y Cymry' he asks: 'Perhaps some of you may be asking Why I have not translated the works of some of the splendid more recent Bards who were writing following the revision of the old *cynghanedd?*' (p. 106). In an interesting take on eighteenth-century notions of the role of the poet, Evans argues that his choice was dictated by the nature of the bards themselves and the topics they addressed. The more recent bards 'were flatterers of the nobility', and although they claimed to be engaged in military endeavours, they were, in fact, 'sleeping in their beds' (p. 106). By contrast:

> At the time of the Princes, however, the contrary was the case, the Bards were witnesses to the courage and greatness of their Princes, and they themselves were brave warriors. . . . Apart from this, the Princes were victorious in their wars with the English and this caused the Bards to wear themselves out, to immortalise their splendid deeds, and to praise their valour in such a commendable cause as the defence of their Land and their Freedom against a foreign Nation who had deprived them of the Heritage of their Ancestors. These were certainly subjects worthy of the Bards, and a suitable means of making their Subjects respect and honour them. (p. 106)

For all the lip-service Evans may have paid to English readers, his recovery of the British past through the bards as freedom fighters against the English can be read as a defiance of post-1707 British political consensus. This is bardic nationalism in its most literal form. As with the treatment of Edward I, the endangered history of the Welsh is the history of the bards writing in defiance of English incursions on Welsh freedom. The fact that the poems which Evans recovers relate mostly to heroic Welsh resistance to the tyrannical English oppression symbolised by Edward I suggests that to recover this past is implicitly to prove to the English that, in the event, Wales and its literary traditions could not be destroyed. For Evans, Edward I represents the loss of Welsh liberty and independence, as well as the eradication of a rich bardic culture which upheld that freedom and liberty. In this context, to recover the work of the bards is to undo the oppression of Edward and the English nation by acts of scholarly defiance which are not necessarily de-politicised. My interpretation of Evans's antiquarian work provides further evidence of eighteenth-century Welsh 'bardic nationalism', where antiquarian cultural recovery translates into a political stance which articulates 'resistance not only to the military conquest of Wales but also to the arrogant assumption of the English that other cultures are there to be absorbed into their own'.[42] This sense that bardic nationalism could conjoin 'a cultural nationalism with a nationalism of more clearly articulated political, perhaps even revolutionary goals' produces a very different reading of Evans's antiquarian activities than one which sees his work as mere contributionism.[43] Indeed, unlike English interpretations of the bard and minstrel as isolated individuals, for Evans and his fellow antiquaries in Ireland and Scotland the figure of the bard is inherently politicised as well as historically and culturally rooted, functioning as 'the mouthpiece for a whole society, articulating its values, chronicling its history, and mourning the inconsolable tragedy of its collapse'.[44]

Evans and Thomas Gray

Yet the most famous representation of the massacre of the Welsh bards was not, of course, from the pen of a Welsh man or woman but, rather ironically, was the work of a poet who has been seen as quintessentially English: Thomas Gray. Gray's dramatic presentation of the vengeful Bard proved memorable and provided the inspiration for a number of artists and writers:

On a rock, whose haughty brow
Frowns o'er old Conway's foaming flood,
Robed in the sable garb of woe,
With haggard eyes the poet stood;
(Loose his beard and hoary hair
Streamed, like a meteor, to the troubled air)
And, with a master's hand and prophet's fire,
Struck the deep sorrows of his lyre.

(I, 2, 15–22)[45]

Although Evans had begun collecting manuscript copies for his *Specimens* (1764) well before the publication of *The Bard* in 1757, it was Gray's powerful and influential ode which kick-started interest in the massacre myth among Welsh scholars and initiated a vogue for literary representations of the Edwardian conquest.[46] Gray was genuinely and profoundly interested in Welsh literary culture. In addition to *The Bard*, his Common Place Book includes an essay on Anglo-Welsh history – 'Cambri' – and in poems such as 'The Triumphs of Owen' (based on 'Arwyain Owain Gwynedd') and 'The Death of Hoël' (from the *Gododdin*), he used Evans's Latin translations of Welsh poetry from the *Dissertatio de Bardis* as his source.[47] For some commentators, the relationship between Evans and Gray (and other members of their Anglo-Welsh circle, such as Daines Barrington, Thomas Percy and the Morris brothers) epitomises a particularly fruitful episode in Welsh–English literary relations which can be described under the broad umbrella of 'Celticism'. As Ffion Llywelyn Jenkins comments:

> At no other time during the eighteenth century does the connection between Welsh and English literature have such a profound reciprocal effect. . . . Celticism provides us also with a rare instance of Welsh literature gaining widespread recognition in England, being acknowledged as authentically ancient, of international stature and even as a forerunner of the modern English literary tradition. [48]

However, given that it was not a Welsh poem or work of scholarship which achieved the most widespread and enduring literary fame, but Thomas Gray's *The Bard*, it could be argued that, for the Welsh side of the equation, the 'Celtic' movement is another example of 'contributionism', whereby Welsh traditions are important only in relation to what they can offer England and English poetry. Or to put it more strongly, the English fashion for all things Celtic is an example of cultural assimilation, whereby Welsh traditions are reused and repackaged by English writers in a way that not only wrenches Welsh literature out of its original contexts, but also empties it of any historical and political force.[49] For example, the tradition of the Edwardian massacre is conventionally seen as significant because it provides the basis of a poem seen to epitomise an identifiably inclusive 'British' literary tradition: Gray's *The Bard* (1757).[50] From a Welsh angle, as I have shown, the Edwardian conquest means something quite different: the end of a dream of 'a united Welsh polity' and, as such, 'a national conquest and a national disaster'.[51]

In relation to *The Bard*, does the popular treatment of the Edwardian massacre by an English poet result, then, in the political neutralisation of its specifically Welsh significance? Did the English enthusiasm for bardism endanger 'the bardic tradition in a new way, as English poets tried to impersonate the bardic voice and to imitate bardic material, without grasping their historical and cultural significance'?[52] Moreover, by making Welsh traditions serve a wider British ideology, are English writers in fact Anglicising Welsh culture by diluting it to suit Anglo-British tastes? Or, does Gray's representation of the loss of nation and culture at the hands of a usurping power invigorate the recuperative efforts of Welsh antiquarians, such as Evan Evans, to reaffirm the resilience and richness of their cultural and historical heritage?

In recent years, Gray's poem has most often been read in the context of the developing ideology of Britishness in the eighteenth century. Howard Weinbrot views Gray's ode as a very 'British' poem which, in keeping with his overall thesis concerning the heterogeneous nature of British literary culture, offers readers a 'national ode', a poem 'about national identity'.[53] For Weinbrot, *The Bard* demonstrates the triumph of native British literary culture over Greek literary form, with Gray succeeding in turning the Pindaric into a vehicle for 'his nation's needs'.[54] In this reading of the poem, Gray emerges as a 'cultural patriot', a defender of 'native culture' and 'Britishness'.[55] In response to Wienbrot's thesis, Dustin Griffin rejects 'the idea of Gray as a crypto-oppositional voice', arguing instead that *The Bard* and its sister poem, *The Progress of Poetry*, are dealing with the question of the political efficacy, or otherwise, of English poetry in the eighteenth century.[56] Both poems are expressions of Gray's ambivalent views regarding the role of the poet as political commentator and national voice. Tellingly, Griffin argues, *The Bard* refers only vaguely to any poet writing after

Milton and can evoke only Elizabeth I (and the flowering of literature in her reign) as a monarch worthy of praise. By a similar token, Paul Odney draws attention to the English bias in Gray's 'British' poem, noting that 'In celebrating Elizabeth, Gray connects the Celtic past with one of the most mythical reigns in *English* history' (my italics).[57] Overall, however, Odney reads *The Bard* as authorising an act of 'British cultural historiography' in which 'Gray's Bard becomes the symbolic figure of Britain's poetic genius, establishing the origins of native poetic tradition and reasserting the national role of the poet-hero'.[58]

Despite different emphases, most critics view *The Bard* as a poem which utilises 'native' British history as a way of redefining poetic and national identity. Indeed, in the use made of bardic prophecy, of Welsh scenery and place-names as well as Tudor lineage, the poem undoubtedly engages with some recognisably Ancient British tropes. What is surprising, however, is that none of these commentators asks what it might mean for eighteenth-century Welsh readers to read about a Welsh bard's denunciation of a 'ruthless' *English* king. Despite the fact that Odney states that the poem 'celebrates a Welsh resistance',[59] he does not consider that, *ipso facto*, this resistance must be against England, which could therefore puncture the Britishness which Gray is elsewhere seen as constructing. Furthermore, none of these readings takes into account either the Anglocentric nature of eighteenth-century Britishness or the particular symbolic significance for Wales of the Edwardian massacre.[60] Katie Trumpener's welcome focus on the Welshness of *The Bard* is surprisingly rare. Although she suggests that *The Bard* popularised bardism in England, and therefore perhaps contributed to the dilution of its cultural force, she also reads the poem as commemorating 'forever the injustice of the English', through the depiction of the bard's final act of suicide and his curse on Edward and his line:

> 'Enough for me: with joy I see
> 'The different doom our fates assign.
> 'Be thine despair and sceptred care;
> 'To triumph, and to die, are mine.'
> He spoke, and headlong from the mountain's height
> Deep in the roaring tide he plunged to endless night.
>   (III, 3, 139–44)

In this context, Gray's poem contributes to a Welsh national vision which stands in opposition to co-option with England. Such a view suggests that the poem might offer a quite different vision of literary history from the inclusive Britishness with which it is usually associated.[61]

When read from a Welsh perspective it is clear that *The Bard* has patriotic potential. Welsh scholars and poets responded extremely positively to Gray's popularisation of the tradition of bardicide and did not ostensibly view the ode as a form of cultural appropriation or political neutralisation. Indeed, Gray's use of the Tudors to bolster a British identity is a particularly Welsh historiographical trope. As the previous chapter indicated, numerous Welsh poets and scholars from the sixteenth century onwards view the Tudor succession as fulfilling the ancient prophecies which predicted that Welsh monarchs would rule over a united Britain.[62] In his patriotic poem, *The Love of Our Country* (1772), discussed more fully in the next chapter, Evans himself lauds the Tudors as taking away 'the English galling yoke' and restoring liberty to the British people:

> THE day of liberty, by heaven design'd,
> At last arose – benevolent and kind –
> The Tudor race, from ancient heroes sprung,
> Of whom prophetic Bards so long had sung,
> Beyond our warmest hopes, the sceptre bore,
> And brought us blessings never known before;
> The English galling yoke they took away,
> And govern'd Britons with the mildest sway.[63]

As we also saw in the views of the Society of Ancient Britons and the poetry of Jane Brereton, the Tudors do not represent 'English' history. They are the true – Welsh – fulfilments of the ancient bardic prophecies which sang of future glory for the Welsh as leaders of a united Britain. In this sense, the Britishness constructed by Gray in *The Bard* could be seen to correspond closely with Welsh constructions of the Ancient British past.

However, this is not to say that the relation between Welsh tradition and English poetry was either simple or straightforward. Indeed, the use made of the 'British' Tudors could be seen as yet another example of English appropriation of Welsh myths and traditions which are then subsumed under the umbrella of Great Britain. Such a view has been expressed in relation to Thomas Gray's poetry. Alok Yadav notes, for example, that 'many English writers of the late seventeenth and early eighteenth centuries understood the ancient Britons as their ancestors, a notion central to the Tudor self-conception and evident . . . in the lineage for English poetry constructed in Thomas Gray's *The Bard*.[64] In many ways, then, as I have been suggesting throughout this study, eighteenth-century notions of the way in which Wales features in the creation of a British national identity are remarkably similar to those identified by Philip Schwyzer as existing in the 1500s. Many sixteenth-century Welsh scholars 'provided the raw materials for the construction of a British national ideology which was ultimately hostile to a separate sense of Welshness'.[65] In a similar way, it could be argued, Gray's poem incorporates the Welsh tradition of the massacre of the bards into a poem which offers a version of Anglo-Britishness that ultimately dilutes the original nationalist force of the myth. In Gray's terms, it could be argued that the Tudors symbolise the flowering of 'native' English literature, not the return of the Welsh to their rightful inheritance.

Nevertheless, in a variety of work by eighteenth-century Welsh scholars, Gray's ode is generally discussed in glowing terms. In *Specimens*, for example, Evans's discussion of 'that inhuman massacre' is followed by his remark that Edward's actions 'gave occasion to a very fine Ode by Mr. Grey' (p. 45). Immediately, the loss of bardic culture as a result of the massacre is offset by Gray's 'fine' performance. It is as if Gray's poem ameliorates the tragic actions of Edward. In his dissertation on ancient Welsh music, *Musical and Poetical Relicks of the Welsh Bards* (1784), Edward Jones makes a similar claim, but takes this idea of compensation in loss one step further. Referring to the act of bardicide, Jones remarks that

> This lamentable event has given birth to one of the noblest Lyric compositions in the English language: a poem of such fire and beauty as to remove . . . our regret of the occasion, and to compensate for the loss. But in heightening our regret consists the great merit of this admirable ode: and without bestowing on it any such extravagant praise, I may boldly affirm that the *Polyolbion of Drayton's* and the *Bard of Gray*, have contributed no less to the reputation of their authors than to the glory of Wales, and are the only modern productions worthy to alleviate the loss we sustained, in so immense a waste of literary treasures, and such irreparable ruin of genius.[66]

Gray's ode is singled out, alongside Michael Drayton's chorographical poem, *Poly-Olbion* (1612), as compensating for the cultural loss caused by Edward I's extermination of the bards.[67] In this sense, *The Bard* represents the rebirth of poetry after destruction. The 'survival in destruction' motif used by Evans throughout his presentation of the authentic works of the Welsh bards is here used by Jones in relation to Gray. *The Bard* simultaneously increases the sense of loss in restaging the massacre, and yet also works to alleviate the pain suffered by a nation which has experienced 'so immense a waste of literary treasures, and such irreparable ruin of genius'.[68]

On one level, then, Gray's ode fills a positive space in Welsh tradition, in that it makes up for the losses experienced as a result of the massacre and presents, as a form of compensation, the glories of Wales to a wide audience. The danger is, however, that Gray's poem might start to stand in for the authentic Welsh examples. Just as 'the genuine work of the Welsh *Cynfeirdd* did not please as much as Macpherson's fakeries', *The Bard* and Gray's poetic adaptations of extracts from the *Gododdin* were seen by some to surpass the examples offered by Evans in *Specimens*.[69] The complicated relationship between Evans and Gray epitomises the fraught yet often productive interchanges between Wales and England in the eighteenth century which I am tracing in this study overall. Such complications also reveal some of the tensions involved in constructing a coherent British identity in this period. On the one hand, the relationship between Evans and Gray was 'mutually beneficial'.[70] The antiquarian recovery of ancient Welsh literature provided English poets with fresh inspiration, such as 'the image of the poet as priest and as warrior'.[71] As a result of this appreciation, Welsh scholars and poets regained a 'sense of importance and self-esteem'.[72] On the other hand, a relationship between two countries of unequal power always risks the danger that the less powerful culture will be subsumed by the dominant nation. In their dealings with the English, Welsh writers historically had to chart a difficult and precarious course between 'the risks of utter oblivion and of total co-optation'.[73] In relation to Evans and his use of the massacre of the bards, I have been suggesting that this remains true in the eighteenth century. In the case of Gray's *The Bard*, however, was the image reflected back to Wales of itself too alluring to resist? By allowing Gray to speak for the nation and to compensate for its losses, did Welsh writers unwittingly silence their own voices and lose themselves again to English dominance?

Evans's undated and posthumously published poem 'A Paraphrase of the 137th Psalm, Alluding to the Captivity and Treatment of the Welsh Bards by King Edward I' is fascinating in the light of the above questions. The poem is one of the few of Evans's poems written in English and appeared as part of some 'Selections' of his poetry and correspondence in an edition of *Specimens* published in 1862.[74] Not only is it an example of a Welsh poet taking Edward's act of bardicide as his central theme, the poem is also an eighteenth-century interpretation of and direct response to Gray's famous ode *The Bard*. The poem opens with the Welsh people (exiled in England) collectively lamenting the loss of their native country and culture at the hands of Edward I. Here the Thames, usually a symbol of Britain's imperial and commercial strength, is a symbol of Saxon oppression, an 'inhospitable flood':

> Sad near the willowy Thames we stood,
> And curs'd the inhospitable flood;
> Tears such as patients weep, 'gan flow,
> The silent eloquence of woe,
> When Cambria rushed into our mind,
> And pity with just vengeance joined;
> Vengeance to injured Cambria due,
> And pity, O ye Bards, to you.
>   (1–8)[75]

Evans has chosen his biblical text carefully. The paraphrase of one of David's psalms allows him to make a parallel between the Welsh and the Israelites: both victims of enforced diaspora, both God's chosen people. Indeed, it has been argued that this poem inaugurates a 'new' nationalist literary agenda, in that

> Evans's adaptation of David's psalm becomes a manifesto for a new nationalist literature, as it links a latter-day cultural nationalism to a sanctified biblical precedent, to invest the Welsh with the Israelites' self-confidence as a chosen people and to raise cultural self-preservation to the status of a religious duty.[76]

Furthermore, for all of the Celtic nations the general appropriation and popularity of bardic poetry by the English could be seen as 'a repetition of the cultural subjugation of Wales, Ireland, and Scotland, a restaging of the scene of Babylonian captivity, in which the exiled and imprisoned bards were ordered to sing for their new masters'.[77]

This emphasis on this collective sense of cultural grievance is certainly apparent in Evans's poem where the Saxon conquerors charge

the weeping Cambrians to take up their silent harps again to sing for
their captors: "'Resume your harps," the Saxons cry, / "And change
your grief to songs of joy'" (15–16). The Welsh refuse to sing 'songs of
joy'. Instead, they sing songs which rehearse (as Evans's own poem
does) the wrongs dealt to Wales by the Saxon conquerors:

> What! ? shall the Saxons hear us sing,
> Or their dull vales with Cambrian music ring?
> No – let old Conway cease to flow,
> Back to her source Sabrina go:
> Let huge Plinlimmon hide his head,
> Or let the tyrant strike me dead,
> If I attempt to raise a song
> Unmindful of my country's wrong.
> What! ? shall a haughty king command
> Cambrians' free strain on Saxon land?
> May this right arm first wither'd be,
> Ere I may touch one string to thee,
> Proud monarch; nay, may instant death
> Arrest my tongue and stop my breath,
> If I attempt to weave a song,
> Regardless of my country's wrong!
>   (21–36)

As is apparent in the above lines, the poem is riddled with allusions to
Gray's *The Bard*. Like Gray, Evans draws on topographical and fluvial
references to make the connection between cultural and national
resistance.[78] Whereas in *The Bard* Modred's 'magic song' used
to make 'huge Plinlimmon bow his cloud-topped head', here
Evans imagines 'huge Plinlimmon' hiding in disgust if the poet were to
sing in praise of the conquerors. Adapting Gray's image of the river
Conway as a 'foaming flood', Evans imagines the river stopping
altogether, while 'Sabrina' – the river Severn – returns to its source at
Plinlimmon in horrified response to the vision of England ringing
'with Cambrian music'. Given the symbolic significance of both these
rivers – the Conway straddled by one of Edward I's castles and the
Severn as a marker of the border between Wales and England – it is
clear that Evans is infusing the geography of Wales, and his poem,
with political meaning.[79]

The poem ends with a direct quotation from Gray, in a vision of the
deserted and haunted location of Llewelyn's former court:

On Conway's banks, and Menai's streams
The solitary bittern screams;
And, where was erst Llewelyn's court,
Ill-omened birds and wolves resort.
There oft at midnight's silent hour,
Near yon ivy-mantled tower,
By the glow-worm's twinkling fire,
Tuning his romantic lyre,
Gray's pale spectre seems to sing,
'Ruin seize thee, ruthless King.'
                    (65–74)

Trumpener reads this conclusion to Evans's poem as a straightforward response to Gray, arguing that the poem ends with 'a virtual paraphrase of Gray and with the symbolic suicide of the "last poet", who swears vengeance with his death'.[80] I would suggest that Evans responds to Gray in more subtle ways. In the first instance, the poem is not necessarily narrated by the bards, as Trumpener suggests elsewhere. It is ambiguous as to who is speaking and where. The poem opens with the plural – 'Sad near the willowy Thames we stood' (1) – but directs the attention *to* the bards; the lines are not spoken by the bards themselves. The poem in fact opens with the fate of the Welsh collectively. The Cambrians are lamenting their servitude and the loss of bardic poetry, which sustained and celebrated Welsh independence and military prowess as well as safeguarded national, cultural and literary institutions. Evans is here not only appealing to the Bards themselves, but also elegising the fate of the entire Cambrian nation, who all refuse to sing in praise of their captors. This helps to explain the use of the first-person poetic voice halfway through the poem, where the poet himself, in writing the poem we are reading, is demonstrating his defiance in refusing to sing 'songs of joy' for his new masters. Nevertheless, Trumpener's sense that this poem recasts the traditional role of the bard as celebrant of his native land is accurate. Indeed, instead of being annihilated, the Welsh poets (not just the bards, but modern-day poets like Evans) exchange songs of praise for 'new poems of execration against the conquerors'.[81] In this context, Evans's consistent use of the word 'weave' to refer to the songs he will compose in retaliation to Saxon dominance alludes to Gray's 'grisly band' of avengers in *The Bard*, who foretell the downfall of Edward's line: 'Weave the warp and weave the woof, / The winding-sheet of Edward's race' (49–50). By using the word 'weave', Evans is not only alluding to Gray, but also aligning his own poetry with the ancient Welsh traditions of prophecy and, therefore, adding further political potency to his writing.

Furthermore, although the poem is written in dialogue with Gray's ode and ends with a direct quotation from Gray, it does not conclude with a paraphrase of Gray's vision of the bard hurling himself off the mountain top 'to endless night'. In fact, Evans ends his biblical paraphrase with the gothic vision of the ruins of Llewelyn's court, and it is 'Gray's pale spectre' who 'seems to sing' the opening line of Gray's ode, which is also the closing line of Evans's poem: 'Ruin seize thee, ruthless King!' 'Gray's pale spectre' hints at the ghostly echoes of *The Bard* in Evans's poem, although it is ambiguous as to whether the 'spectre' refers to the 'ghost' of Gray himself or whether the presence refers to the ghost of the last bard, as imagined by Gray. Evans's bard may repeat words of vengeance straight from Gray, but the effect is that of an echo of the original poem: the spectre is so pale and shadowy that he only *'seems* [my italics] to sing' the curse of Gray's bard. In effect, Evans ends where Gray began. Instead of ending with the suicide of the last bard, where, in Gray's terms, triumph can only be achieved through self-inflicted death, Evans suggests that the initial execration – 'Ruin seize thee ruthless King' – is renewed in the poem he has just written. The political force of the original curse is repeated throughout Evans's poem, just as it echoes throughout the ruins of Llewelyn's court.

The relationship between Gray and Evans encapsulates the complicated dual processes of reciprocal influence and antagonistic distrust which I am suggesting typify Anglo-Welsh relations at this time and which complicate any easy notion of post-1707 British unity. Indeed, what does it mean for Evans to echo the words of an Englishman in an English-medium poem which elsewhere dramatises the refusal of the Cambrian bards to sing for their 'Saxon' masters? [82] For all Gray's services to Welsh scholarship, it could be argued that the original act of cultural obliteration is strangely re-enacted – both in Evans's poem and in the preference for Gray's ode over the actual productions of the bards – by 'Gray's pale spectre'. Does Evans, quite literally in this instance, let Gray have the last word? In conclusion, I suggest that although Evans was profoundly influenced by Gray's poetry, this influence does not efface Evans's national pride or dilute the force of his patriotism. [83] Evans's description of Llewelyn's ruined court is generally inspired by the gothic 'graveyard' or 'melancholy' school of poetry popularised by Gray and other poets, such as Edward Young. However, in the use of the lines 'Near yon ivy-mantled tower', Evans makes a further, more unexpected, inter-textual link to Gray's famous *Elegy Written in a Country Churchyard*, through a direct echo of its ninth line:

> Save that from yonder ivy-mantled tower
> The moping owl does to the moon complain
> Of such as, wandering near her secret bower,
> Molest her ancient solitary reign.
> (9–12)

Despite the more obvious connections between *The Bard* and Evans's own work, it is this allusion to Gray's *Elegy* which might provide the key to reassessing Welsh 'bardic' resistance to British incorporation in the eighteenth century. Indeed, what is crucial about the last section of the *Paraphrase* is the precise locating of the conventions of graveyard poetry in the Welsh landscape. Not only does Evans invoke specifically Welsh place-names – Mona, Conway, Menai – in a manner similar to that of Gray in *The Bard*, he also places 'Gray's pale spectre' at the centre of the ruined court of Prince Llewelyn, the last Prince of Wales, who was defeated and slain by Edward I. As such, Evans reanimates the politics of the bardic massacre by lamenting the decline of Welsh culture in the context of the loss of political autonomy. Moreover, while Gray may be contemplating the role of the poet in more general terms in both the *Elegy* and *The Bard*, what Evans does is re-politicise the role of the bard by placing it back in the original Welsh context of patronage, allegiance and eisteddfodic culture; Evans's reference to the 'silver harp' being won on 'Arvon's shore' constructs the last context.[84] By doing so, Evans can be said to graft the English school of graveyard poetry on to a nationalistic Welsh agenda and to return poetry to its original bardic function of singing the glory and lamenting the demise of noble patrons and national leaders.

Furthermore, whereas Gray uses the graveyard mode to explore the role of the poet as an isolated outsider or marginal figure, Evans politicises the genre to refer to the lament of the bards for their lost political leaders and the loss of their country. The conventional 'ruins' are not just for poetic effect, but are a political symbol of the past glory of Wales. Evans's famous poems in Welsh and English on Ivor Hael (*fl.* 1340–60), patron of the renowned Welsh poet Dafydd ap Gwilym (*fl.*

1315/20–1350/70), epitomise this nationalisation of the gothic mode. Like Gray's *Elegy*, the English version – 'On Seeing the Ruins of Ivor Hael's Palace, near Tredegar, in Monmouthshire' – critiques the vanity of human pride and pomp by focusing on the decaying ruins of the once noble palace:

> Amidst its alders Ivor's palace lies
> In heaps of ruins to my wondering eyes;
> Where greatness dwelt in pomp, now thistles reign,
> And prickly thorns assert their wide domain.[85]

However, the core of the poem focuses specifically on the loss of the bards and the decline of patronage: 'No longer Bards inspired thy tables grace' (5). The ruins thus signify not just a generalised human vanity, but the loss of a specifically Welsh culture and tradition.[86] In this named location – near Tredegar, in Monmouthshire – it is not 'Gray's pale spectre' who sings, but Dafydd ap Gwilym, whose poems lament the loss of patron and implicitly of country:

> In plaintive verse his Ivor, Gwilym moans,
> His patron lost, the pensive poet groans:
> What mighty loss, that Ivor's lofty hall
> Should now with screeching owls rehearse its fall!
> (9–12)

In his bardic re-politicisation of Gray's poetry Evans exhibits a much stronger resistance to British incorporation than he has been given credit for. However, his work also suggests that the relation between Wales and England in the eighteenth century was more poetically fruitful – as well as more fraught – than has previously been acknowledged. The mutual influence, indeed interdependence, of the poetry of Gray and Evans points to a much more complicated 'archipelagic' vision of eighteenth-century Britishness than an exclusive emphasis on either assimilation or rejection allows for. Indeed, while 'Gray's pale spectre' seems to have haunted the minds of many literary-minded eighteenth-century Welsh patriots, this is certainly not to say that either Gray or English culture had the last word. Indeed, it is worth remembering that most of Evans's poetry is in Welsh, and therefore that Evans is continuing and performing the bardic function through his own work, not just alluding to an annihilated past. Evans is himself proof of the continuing vitality of

Welsh poetic tradition. Furthermore, as the striking opening lines of the Welsh version make clear, Evans's *englynion* has a poetic (as well as a politico-cultural) force lacking in the couplets of the English equivalent:

> LLYS Ifor Hael! gwael yw'r gwedd, — yn garnau
> Mewn gwerni mae'n gorwedd;
> Drain ac ysgall mall a'i medd,
> Mieri, lle bu mawredd.
>
> (1–4)[87]

4

'Cambria Triumphans': Patriotic Poems of Eighteenth-Century Wales

Shall a regard
For bravest heroes, and a land renown'd
Of old for noblest deeds, contract the frown
Of quaint DERISION?
　　(Richard Rolt, *Cambria*, 1749)

What theme more noble could the Muse have thought,
Than those who bravely for this COUNTRY fought?
　　(Evan Evans, *The Love of Our Country*, 1772)

This chapter explores four 'Cambria' poems, two by English writers and two by Welsh writers, in the context of patriotic poetry in eighteenth-century Britain. As the above quotations from two of these poems suggest, the connection of the Muse with themes of a patriotic nature was viewed as an inherently 'noble' undertaking which celebrated the 'brave' past of the nation. Yet in both these poems there is also an anxiety about whether the theme is valid. Rolt worries that his choice of topic – Cambria – may be sneered at, despite the heroic deeds of her ancient heroes. Like Rolt, Evans frames his patriotism in terms of a rhetorical question, as if to anticipate the need to defend his subject: Wales. Evans and Rolt were not alone in feeling defensive about expressing patriotic sentiment in poetry, but their anticipatory defensiveness was no doubt heightened by the fact that the subject of their poems was not Britain, but Wales. Indeed, although patriotic British feeling and national sentiment featured prominently in the poetry of writers such as Mark Akenside, James Thomson, Thomas Gray, John Dyer and William Collins, as well as informing a vast array of ephemeral and topical verse, the nature of eighteenth-century patriotism itself and the forms it should take were much-debated issues.[1] In recent accounts, patriotism in eighteenth-century English poetry has been seen to have a distinctly British flavour, epitomised by Thomson's 'Rule Britannia' (1740).[2] In contrast, little has been said on either the complicated role played by Wales in constructions of eighteenth-century British patriot identity or how a distinctive Welsh patriotism might differ substantially from that produced in an Anglo-British context with England as its main focus.[3]

In this chapter I aim to draw out the main characteristics of what I term 'Cambria poetry' in order to complicate the view that eighteenth-century poets employed the patriotic muse in the service of a unified British national identity, which included Wales in an unproblematic fashion. Even at first glance, there are some clear differences between English and Welsh negotiations of patriot loyalty to one's country. Whereas Anglo-British poets, for example, frequently glorify recent military or naval victories, and the double-edged success of commercial and global expansion, Welsh writers, as I shall show, rarely address these issues, choosing instead to locate their patriotism in the glory of Wales's bardic past and the resilience of the Welsh language.[4] The quotation from Evans with which I began this chapter does not, for example, refer to those who fought in the service of eighteenth-century Britain, but to the historical clashes between Ancient Briton and Saxon. For many Welsh patriots the 'Other' was not France, but England. Furthermore, despite Rolt's and Evans's defensiveness, Welsh writers were much more familiar with the idea that poetry was a suitable medium for nationalistic feeling. The notion of the poet as a public patriotic voice for the nation is central to Welsh poetic tradition and persists into the twenty-first century. The figure of the Welsh bard had always been as a communal spokesman, committed to political commentary and patriotic loyalty. However, I am not concerned here simply to draw out contrasts between Anglo-British and Welsh patriotic poetry, although this broader context is of course relevant. Rather, my aim is to explore the poetic treatment of 'Cambria' itself as a focus for national sentiment. My broader purpose in doing so is to elucidate further both the position of Wales in eighteenth-century Britain and the status of 'British' values in eighteenth-century Wales.

One of the main objectives of all the poems discussed here, both Welsh and English, is to prove that, contrary to the opinions of English satirists, Wales is not only worthy of patriotic panegyric, but is also the source of a rich poetic tradition and culture. In their different ways, all these 'Cambria' poets are aiming to explain and defend Wales and the Welsh to an English audience for whom Wales appears to be a strange and foreign land, not a familiar neighbour. The perceived 'strangeness' of Wales to the English is an important point to remember when assessing claims for 'unified Britishness' in the eighteenth century. By aiming to recuperate the poetic fortunes of Wales and refute English stereotypes of the country, these poems connect the poetic and the patriotic projects together. As Evans makes clear in *The Love of Our Country*, this is part of a broader attempt to wrest the representation of Wales and Welsh history away from 'Saxon' writers, who are inevitably partial and biased (as well as inaccurate), and to place the task of writing Wales in the hands of the Welsh.

The most well-known of these satirical accounts was *Wallography; or, the Briton describ'd: being a pleasant relation of a journey into Wales* (1682) by William Richards.[5] At the end of the 'Epistle Dedicatory' the author makes the following derogatory remarks and praises England at the expense of Wales:

> If there are any *Good Things* in *Wales*, the enjoyment whereof is worth the wishing you, I pray Heaven to crown you with the Fruition of them: But possibly it may be a Province not much *crowded* with Blessings; may you therefore Flourish in the Affluence of good *English* Mercies; may you always possess good *English* riches, Health and Honours, and all other Happinesses and Prosperities of our own Nation! (6 [no pag.])

The Welsh are described as 'a pretty *odd sort* of Mortals', a 'Taphy' is 'a *Trickish* Animal' and every Welshman is 'a *Jest* . . . a Living *Pun*, a walking *Conundrum*, and a breathing *Witticism*' (5 [no pag.]).

The resilience of such views of Wales is suggested by the fact that *Wallography* was still being reprinted into the 1750s. Yet, as the editor of the 1753 edition remarks, despite the sentiments in the Epistle, the work does contain satire against the English too: it is not until we are almost halfway through the book that the author reaches Wales. What comes before this is more a satire on 'the rural People of ENGLAND' (p. 37). As such, the editor states that 'This matchless Piece of Nonsense should have been divided into two Parts', the first section being 'ANGLOGRAPHY, or *The* ENGLISHMAN Described'. Nevertheless, the satire on Wales is more fiercely crude and certainly more tied to national characteristics. Whereas the satire on rural degeneracy in England sits apart from the praise of the English nation in the Epistle Dedicatory, the Welsh nation and people are damned together. The Welsh are described as bestial and their land as a

'*Wilderness*' (p. 39). The people are characterised as savage and uncivilised; they are 'a *rude* People' whose savagery stems from and reflects the wild '*Deserts* and Mountains' (p. 38) in which they live. The Welsh are barely human, it is implied, 'so far from being *Men*, that they can scarce be advanc'd into *Living* Creatures' (p. 39). In short, Wales is 'the very *testicles* of the Nation' (p. 39). The usual satirical suspects are also all on display here in crude form: every Welshman thinks himself a gentleman, and the main diet is cheese and leeks in a land only fit 'to breed a Famine in' (pp. 43–4). The Welsh are also deemed to be barely literate – 'a writer of his Name is term'd a *Rabbi*' (p. 45) – and the famous bards are termed '*Meter-mongers*' (p. 46).

However, although the Welsh language is described as 'Native *Gibberish*' (p. 59), there is a grudging respect for its '*Virginity*' which was 'not deflowr'd by the mixture of any other Dialect', in contrast to Latin, which was 'debauch'd by the *Vandals*' (p. 58). The Welsh, although elsewhere characterised as desperate to leave Wales, are said to be 'passionately fond' of their language, with a correspondingly passionate hatred of English: the declaration '*Dim saissonick, i. e.* no *English*' (p. 59) is seen as evidence of this hatred, rather than as the natural reaction of a monoglot Welsh-speaker to an Englishman. On the other hand, to speak English is seen as a mark of distinction: those who are 'above the ordinary *Scum*, do begin to despise' the Welsh language and 'fancy themselves above their Tongue' (p. 59). In some houses, we are told, no Welsh is spoken at all and the children are taught in English. This process of Anglicisation is seen as a desirable process, yet there is also the suggestion that it is English which is playing the role of the barbarous incomer destroying native culture. The English language in Wales plays the same role as the influx of the barbarian Goths into Rome, which contributed to the fall of the Roman Empire: 'So that (if the Stars prove lucky) there may be some *glimmering* hopes that the Brittish *Lingua* may be quite extinct, and may be *English'd* out of *Wales*, as *Latin* was barbarously *Goth'd* out of *Italy*' (p. 59).

Finally, the Cambro-Briton's admiration for heroic actions is exemplified in the canonisation of 'Bishop *David*', who is characterised as 'a pert fight[er]' who '*basted* and swadled [his] Foes'. We are told that David is now consecrated by the '*Trophy* of a Leek' (p. 59) on St David's Day, but '*smells* as rank of Renown from that Vegetable *Preservative* that Embalms his Fame, as they do of a *Scallion* that carry it about for his Glory' (pp. 59–60).

A Trip to North-Wales: Being a Description of that Country and People, by Ned [Edward] Ward (1701), is in the same satirical travel-writing vein as *Wallography* and is clearly heavily indebted to the earlier text for its anti-Welsh satire (many of the phrases and descriptions are identical).[6] Here again we find the characterisation of the Welsh as dirty, semi-literate, poor, obsessed with genealogy, leeks and cheese. However, this text lacks even the very grudging respect of its predecessor. The Welsh language is said to be 'inarticulate and guttural, and sounds more like the Gobling of Geese, or Turkeys, than the Speech of Rational Creatures' (p. 3). North Wales is described in the following derogatory fashion: 'The Country looks like the fag end of the Creation; the very Rubbish of *Noah*'s Flood; and will (if any thing) serve to confirm an Epicurean in his Creed, That the World was made by Chance' (p. 2).

In both these texts there is a sense of the otherness of Wales which calls into question the peaceful harmony often suggested of Wales's integration with England and her role as a pacific Anglo-centred partner since the Tudor Union. *A Trip to North-Wales* is similar again to *Wallography* in its description of the savage and uncivilised aspects of Welsh geography:

> I had no sooner passed the River *Dee*, but I began to grow sensible that I was not in *England*; for the Country I was got into, look'd no more like it, than if a Man had been in America, or the most uninhabited parts of *Arabia*. There was a savage Air in the Face of every body I met, that plainly told me, These must be Descended from *Brutus*, the Nephew of *Virgil*'s Heroe. (p. 7)

This colonially inflected view of the strangeness of north Wales to an English eye is also raised in the 'Epistle Dedicatory', where Ward declares that a description of the area might be of interest to readers,

> Especially, when I consider, that (tho' it be a part of this Island of *Great Britain*) it is (in a manner) as much unknown to us, that live in the Centre of the Nation, as *Newfoundland* to a Country Vicar, or *Ultima Thule* to a primitive Geographer.

Wales is presented as being on the periphery of civilisation, on the extreme margins of the 'Centre of the Nation', as remote as Newfoundland or the unknown *Ultima Thule*. The only knowledge the English have of Wales, it is suggested, comes from William Camden's

Britannia and the work of the historian and cartographer John Speed.[7] In a view of Gerald of Wales which (ironically) chimes with that of Evan Evans, William Camden is said to have gleaned his information from 'a parcel of Old Moth-eaten Records, very little to the purpose, and that Eternally Voluminous Romancer, *Giraldus Cambrensis*', while Speed's information comes only from 'Traditional Legends, of equal Authority with *Rabelais's Gargantua*, and *Beards Theatre*'.[8] Rather than Wales being viewed as a comfortable neighbour created in England's image, the view here is of a fierce and threatening strange land of savagery. It is a classic colonial view, but also radically revises the notion that Wales was a familiar part of the English imagination in this period. The unfamiliarity of Wales to an eighteenth-century English audience again needs to be kept in mind when assessing the scale of the task facing those writers who were attempting to place Wales in a more prestigious position on the collective mental map of Great Britain.

Cambria Triumphans, or, A Panegyrick Upon Wales (1702)[9]

Cambria Triumphans is a rare early example of an English 'defence' of Wales, printed in London and marketed for an English audience. Written by one Ezekiel Polsted, 'Gent.', the poem has two aims, as stated in the preface 'To the Reader'. First, it seeks to express gratitude (for what, specifically, it is not clear) '*to that* Principality, *whose Civilities were multiplied*, not only beyond all Merit, *but*, even beyond all Expression'. Secondly, Polsted wishes to defend Wales specifically against the aspersions cast in the satirical anti-Welsh 'travel narrative', *Wallography*:

> *My last* Reason *was, that the World might be no longer imposed upon by the* Scurilous Wallography: *And therefore cannot but tell the Author (if Living) or his Admirers (which with the Ignorant, are Numerous) that wrongs always being wrote in Marble, Vicissitude of time can hardly scratch them out; the whole being a* Gallimauphry of Spleen and Rancour, *and an* Hodge-Podge of Falshood and Ignorance.

Although Polsted states that 'Wales *suffers not a Diminution, by the Excursion of a Scabby Pen*', he positions himself as her champion, in view of the fact that conquerors rarely 'put their Laurels on their own Heads'.

This chivalrous defence is couched in terms of Wales as the inspiration for literary and cultural eminence, as triumphant in the contest for 'the monopoly of Wit' (I, 22). The poem functions as a version of the seventeenth-century genre of 'the competition for the bays in which Apollo is depicted judging the pretensions of a number of competitors'.[10] What is particularly fascinating about this aspect of the defence, given that her Welsh identity is rarely a source of sustained comment, is the role played by 'the matchless Orinda' – Katherine Philips (1632–64) – and Wales itself, as inspirer of the Muses. By the start of the eighteenth century, Philips had already featured in a number of poems contesting the male 'monopoly of wit', usually named with, or as a chaste alternative to, the playwright Aphra Behn.[11] Here Philips is footnoted as '*The inimitable Poetess of* Cardigan', and her existence is due to the remarkable paradise that is Wales:

> Matchless *Orinda*! sure no Common Earth
> > Could give thee Birth?
> If once a Denison below
> The Miracle to *Wales* we ow [*sic*];
> Which seems Triumphantly to fit.
> And govern the Monopoly of Wit;
> > As if for the chast Muses Court design'd,
> And from the gloomy fogs of other Earth refin'd.
> > > (p. 2)

In the presence of the chaste Orinda, who owes her genius to her connection to Wales, Apollo and the nine Muses 'Their Pow'r resign' to one in whom reposes all 'Witts treasury' (p. 2). Orinda herself then becomes the Muse (of the present poet) and representative of the poetic spirit of Wales, acting as a more divine inspiration than the more usual aid to poetic composition of '*Bacchanalian Juice*'. The Heliconian Muses are forced eventually to admit Wales's superiority as 'Orinda, the *Aonian* May[d]es, suceeds [*sic*]' (p. 7). Apollo explains to the weeping superseded Muses that '*One* Woman the *Nine Goddesses* excel!' (p. 9). A tradition of Welsh writing in English is being adumbrated here with a woman poet as its figurehead, in direct contrast to the exclusively masculine bardic tradition. Just as women could aspire to the throne of wit, despite traditional disadvantages and gender restrictions, Wales too, the poem suggests, can challenge conventional expectations of literary excellence.

Poetic creativity is directly linked to the landscape of Wales, which has nurtured Orinda's genius. The country is presented as a 'Transplanted Paradice! . . . / Where wanton *Harps* do captivate the

Ears, / Able to force the Envy of the Spheres' (p. 5). The 'aspiring Rocks', 'th'angry Sea' and 'the Flow'r Enamell'd Land' (p. 5) all combine to make a

> Joyful *Elysium*! Where *Parnassus* reigns
> An *Helicon* each humble *Vale* contains,
>   The *First*, we know
> To be on ev'ry *Hill*, the *last, below.*
>   (p. 6)[12]

Wales becomes the new Helicon; Apollo is defeated, and Cambria is triumphant in the war of wit by joining the forces of Philips and, in another canon-forming gesture, the Welsh epigrammatist John Owen ('The British Martial'), who 'ascends the Skyes, / And Great *Appollo's* Abdicated Throne Supplies' (p. 7).[13] In response to this outrage, Jove, Hercules, Vulcan and Mars swear revenge, until Rodrick the Great, 'The *Cambrian Mars*' (p. 11), defeats and disperses them.

The triumph of Wales over the '*Deities of Wit and War*' (p. 12) lead Polsted towards the more familiar ways of delineating Welsh identity, which I have discussed in previous chapters: the Tudors, St David, Protestantism, early Christianity in Wales, resistance to Saxon invasion and preservation of language. The Welsh are praised for withstanding the force of the Saxons and for accepting English rule only until they had a '*Prince of their own Blood*, viz. Henry 7'. The view that the Welsh were the first to introduce Christianity is added to the list of virtues – 'You first took Arms in truths defence' (p. 13) – as is Welsh support for the Reformation (perhaps to be expected of an admirer of the anti-Catholic John Owen):

> When an *Egyptian Darkness*, seiz'd the Age
> You the Oppressing Shakles, disengage; . . .
>   (p. 15)

The integrity of the Welsh is also suggested by the way in which they are 'Absolute' in the use of their '*Lofty Language*', which preserves intact and entire '*Pristine Fame*' and '*Hereditary Glory*' (p. 19). St David's Day is crowned by '*Triumphant Liverys*' (p. 20) – leeks – and the martial version of the patron saint David, discussed in chapter 1, is emphasised by the foregrounding of his defence of Wales against 'Th' *Insulting Saxons*' (p. 21). In its articulation of the staples of a nascent Welsh nationalism in a literary context the poem provides a useful starting-point for beginning to distinguish between a specifically Welsh patriotic vision in the eighteenth century and one that is broadly Anglo-British. Indeed, when compared to the central tropes of British patriotism – Gothic/Saxon liberties, Crécy, Agincourt, Elizabeth I, '"Revolution principles", commerce and the British navy'[14] – it is already clear that a very different definition of patriotic loyalty to one's country would be needed for Wales.

Although crude in execution, *Cambria Triumphans* is significant in its imagining of Wales not only as a subject for contemporary poetry, but also as a rival to the classics. In its relocation of Helicon to Britain, the poem is an early example of what was to become a popular genre in the eighteenth century: the progress poem. Epitomised by Thomas Gray's *The Progress of Poetry* (1757), poems in this genre trace the movement of the Muses from Greece to Rome, and then to Albion.[15] Critical treatment of this genre has mainly been concerned with English poetry (also Gray's real concern, it could be argued), and it is usually read in the context of expressions of patriotic sentiments about Britain. Typically, the Muse leaves Greece and Rome in search of freedom and liberty which, since the decline of those classical civilisations, she can find only on British shores. The genre relies on an implicit parallel between British and classical culture and also, as Richard Terry notes, 'proposes the political and literary supremacy of the English over national rivals like the French'.[16] What is significant here, of course, is that it is Cambria who wins the war of wit, and it is Cambria, therefore, which becomes the new home of the Muses, a Welsh Helicon. The poem is a very early example of what was to become a more widespread interest in 'literary primitivism', an 'appreciation both that poetry had been native to early cultures and that primitive poetry possessed merits comparable with the more refined verse of modern ages'.[17] The Welsh bards, particularly Taliesin, were soon to be appropriated as evidence of such a phenomenon, as John Husbands declared in 1731: 'I have been told by a gentleman of a very good taste, who understands that tongue, that the Welsh odes of Taliesin are equal to anything in antiquity. It is indeed very certain that the ancient Britains [*sic*] gave great encouragement to the Muses'.[18] *Cambria Trumphans* is clearly adumbrating these ideas in a Welsh context at an early stage in their development. However, what is different about this poem is that it does not stop at claiming native superiority over classical cultures; it also attempts to construct a canon of Welsh writing of more recent origin than the ancient Welsh bards, one which even, in the invocation to Katherine Philips, includes a woman.

Cambria: A Poem in Three Books (1749)[19]

> Yet let not the grave CENSOR deem my theme
> The song of FOLLY, nor with brow austere
> Condemn these trivial inoffensive lines:
> For say, ye rigid CYNICS, is the praise
> Of FREEDOM your contempt?
> (Book III, p. 66)

Richard Rolt is another example of an Englishman taking up the pen in slightly anxious defence of the Cambrian cause. At the beginning of Book II he explains the rationale for a project which he suspects might be deemed foolish or trivial, as the lines above suggest. His comments reinforce, although not here for satirical purposes, the sense of Wales as existing on the margins of British national consciousness, as he explains that he chose to write in poetry, rather than prose,

> As that alone may possibly invite a great number of British subjects to gather a little information of so material a tract of their native island, of which the general part of the kingdom seem as entirely ignorant as they are of the late Russian discoveries in the Tartarian sea. (p. 25)

Like Polsted, Rolt begins by lamenting the fact that Wales is not usually the subject of poetry and then declaring that he will rectify the situation:

> SHALL other climes incite poetic strains,
> With scarce a city, mountain, vale, or stream
> Unsung; and CAMBRIA, thou! unnoted pass
> By the PIËRIAN train? Forbid it heav'n,
> This blest asylum, thro' the depths of time
> Mark'd out for sacred freedom, should in vain
> Attract the MUSES' aid!
>
> (p. 5)

The obscurity of Wales is turned into its strongest characteristic as a 'blest asylum' where 'sacred freedom' encourages the Muses. Wales is presented here as a form of the 'still sylvan heart of the country' which Dustin Griffin identifies in English patriotic poetry as a common trope, pitting English rural innocence against the 'dangers of commerce and overseas expansion'.[20] Rolt also draws on the patriotism inherent in progress-of-poetry poems, where the fate of a nation is directly tied to its literary fortunes, a trope also apparent in *Cambria Triumphans*. As I have mentioned previously, the patriotic concepts of freedom and liberty are crucial to this construction. What is different, of course, about Rolt's poem, as in *Cambria Triumphans*, is that the Muse relocates to Cambria after her escape from the cultural ruins of once glorious Greece and Rome. In one of the songs from his 'opera' *Eliza* (1754), Rolt employs this idea in more conventional ways: the Muses leave Greece and Rome as the 'Gothic mantle' encroaches and make their way to 'this blest isle', the place of virtue and freedom (England).[21] In *Cambria*, however, Rolt relocates the tropes of British-identified patriotism by imagining Wales as the locus for freedom, liberty and, thereby, poetic expression. Moreover, in the final lines of the poem the Muse is directly identified as Welsh, 'ambitious to applaud / Her natal country' (p. 66).

Rolt was baptised in Shrewsbury in 1724 and attended Shrewsbury Grammar School. This close proximity to and connection with Wales (Shrewsbury could be referred to as the capital of Wales) partly explains why he chose Cambria for the theme of his three-book poem.[22] Rolt was also well known for his historical writing, an interest clearly apparent in his examination of Welsh history in *Cambria* and the extensive historical footnotes accompanying the poem. Although not published until 1749, Rolt's poem also needs to be read in the specific context of the so-called 'Patriot' Whig Opposition to Walpole which formed a counter-Court around Frederick, Prince of Wales, in the 1730s, a circle which latterly also included Rolt.[23] The poem is dedicated to Prince George – Frederick's son and the future George III – and is clearly couched in Opposition terms. Rolt makes a direct link between support of the Brunswick line and Wales, which plays on the fact of Frederick's status as Prince of Wales:

> Illustrious PRINCE! Long may our CAMBRIA boast
> The ROYAL BRUNSWICK LINE, they long enjoy
> CARNAVON'S honours, nor the baleful breath
> Of foul sedition fear.
>
> (p. 6)

The Welsh are figured as particularly loyal subjects despite, or because of, being 'remote' from 'polish'd cities' (p. 6). Rolt assures Frederick that the hills of Wales will 'smile beneath thy care' (p. 6) and the rocks grow smooth under his protection. The symbolic value of Wales and Frederick's status as a Cambrian prince in patriotic rhetoric has been touched on by Christine Gerrard.[24] Although she does not discuss *Cambria* directly in her study, the key themes of the Patriot poetry of Opposition she identifies provide a template for reading much of Rolt's work, as I will demonstrate in this section. Nevertheless, the poem's specifically Welsh framework shifts the treatment of patriotism and demonstrates some different ways Wales could figure in the eighteenth-century national imagination as a symbol of British identity. More specifically, Rolt's work provides a further example of how the old British myths and narratives of nationalism were revived and reconfigured to suit different contexts and allegiances.

Cambria works in the tradition of historically framed poetic panegyrics on Wales, as shown in Nehemiah Griffith's earlier poem *The Leek* (1717) and discussed in chapters 1 and 2. The first book covers British history from the Ancient Britons up to the Union of Wales with England. The second and third books are chorographical in scope and present a historically inflected 'tour' of the nation, which includes discussion of the Welsh language and various descriptions of natural landscape. Book I especially is part of a broader scheme of Patriot Opposition myth-making, what Gerrard has called the Patriot Opposition's 'most effective contribution to the prevailing spirit of patriotism', namely 'its recourse to, and recovery of, British history'.[25] Rolt takes a sceptical view of 'the fabulous assertions of Geoffrey of Monmouth', preferring instead, and following William Camden's 'Gomerian thesis' in *Britannia*, to stress the Gomerian/Celtic origins of the first Britons. He asks rhetorically if it is more reasonable to believe that 'this island was first peopled by the numerous, warlike, and enterprising Gomerians, rather than by a fugitive band of dispirited Trojans?' (note to page 6). However, ultimately Rolt suggests that it does not really matter what the exact origins of the Britons were; what is important is that they represent ancient liberty and freedom:

> If CIMBRIAN GOMER from the CELTIC shore,
> Or heav'n-descended BRUTUS, first explor'd
> The fertile borders of the swelling THAMES,
> Imports not; BRITONS! 'tis enough you boast
> A race of heroes, antient as the pen
> Of time; whose love of freedom, honour truth,
> Disdain of servile ease, and glorious toil
> For liberty, be your sublimest praise.
>   (pp. 6–7)

The ancient Britons in their simplicity and valour epitomise that patriot watchword 'Liberty', which is juxtaposed with the dissipation of 'Imperial ROME' (p. 120). In typical Opposition fashion, Caesar is figured as a tyrant and Brutus represents Liberty: 'AMBITIOUS CAESAR! Soon thy glories fade, / And LIBERTY her chosen BRUTUS sends / To strip the fading laurels from thy brow' (p. 12). Similarly, and predictably, the republican Cato is described as 'godlike' (p. 131). Those Britons who refuse to bow to Caesar and flee with 'Vanoc' to 'the hills of CANTREDMAUR' (p. 16) are described as living secure and content, 'Among these desert rocks, to breathe the pure / Unsully'd air of liberty divine' (p. 16). In their defiance of Roman power, the Ancient Britons are precursors of one version of mid-eighteenth-century Patriot Britons: 'Fir'd with heroic zeal, and high contempt / Of slavish life' (p. 17).

As in the poetry of Jane Brereton, discussed in chapter 2, Rolt acknowledges the civilising forces of Roman culture. Yet he laments the loss of innocent British independence to the 'luxuries of ROME' (p. 19) in much stronger terms than Brereton: 'CURSE on the LATIAN modes! For they deprav'd / Our honest plain integrity' (p. 19) and, most of all, deprived Britons of their 'FREEDOM' (p. 20). This sterner attitude towards the Romans is echoed in Book III, where the decline of Isca epitomises the fall of the Roman Empire and the futility of human grandeur in the face of time: 'Down rush imperial fabricks' . . . 'Thus ISCA crumbled into nothing' (p. 45). After being expelled from the majority of Britain by the Romans, the Britons see their 'mother land' (p. 20) successively overtaken by Saxons, Caledonians, Danes and, lastly, the Normans. The Cambrians in 'their distant mountain tops . . . struggled hard, And bravely held an independent state' (p. 20) until the downfall of 'LLEWELLIN' at the hand of Edward I, which, Rolt adds in a note, 'terminated the long and fatal period of antient British liberty' (p. 21). This is a very Welsh construction of liberty in its anti-Roman imagery and its pre-Gray focus on Edward I and Llewelyn. In his relative sympathy for the loss of Ancient British independence under the Romans, Rolt engages with what Rosemary Sweet has called the 'fundamental paradigm' underlying British patriotism and national identity in the eighteenth century: the binary opposition of the 'civilised' Romans versus the 'barbaric' Ancient Britons. As Sweet notes, although the dominant view was that the Romans were a civilising force, this often 'sat somewhat uneasily with the elevation of what was essentially a foreign Roman culture and Roman conquest' of a native British tradition. As a result, in the work of antiquarians, there was a 'tension between celebrating Roman dominance over Britain and establishing a genealogy of British liberty, independence and civilisation'.[26] These tensions seep into the poetry of the period. For many Welsh writers, these tensions were irreconcilable, given the much more direct associations of the Welsh with the Ancient Britons and native historical traditions.[27] It is wholly appropriate in a poem taking Wales as its theme, then, that Rolt should glorify the Ancient Britons and vilify the Romans as usurpers and as symbolic of overreaching imperial ambition. In an eighteenth-century context, given the widespread currency of parallels between the Roman and British empires, anti-Roman sentiment could also figure as a critique of present imperial drives and, in a Welsh context, expose further tensions between Wales and her hegemonic neighbour, England. At this point in the poem Rolt's treatment of his theme seems to prefer a Welsh patriotic vision over the British.

Despite the ostensible lament for the loss of British liberty, however, and in stark contrast to most Welsh writers (excluding Jane Brereton), Edward I is treated relatively sympathetically, as 'mildly' cementing 'the BRITISH nations' (p. 22), while still treating the Cambrians as 'aliens' who were 'excluded from the benefit of the laws of England' (note to line 278, p. 22). This partly neutralises Rolt's anti-Roman stance, as the Edwardian conquest was often viewed by English commentators as performing the same civilising process as the Roman invasion: in the Edwardian defeat of Wales 'the English saw themselves as completing the conquest which had eluded the Romans'.[28] However, like his Welsh counterparts, Rolt views the Tudor Union as ending the feud between the Welsh and the English, although he stops short of identifying the Tudors as Welsh. The first book ends by praising the Tudor race and the happy union of Wales and England:

THE royal NORMAN, mildly to his pow'r
Cements the BRITISH nations; yet prolong'd
The grand alliance, till on ENGLAND's throne
The race of TUDOR rose; untied then
The kindred states with filial love embrac'd.
And thus indissolubly firm, not all
A leaguing world, can quell the gen'rous sparks
Of FREEDOM planted in our infant souls;
Tenacious of those ever sacred rights,
For which our heroes bled, our patriots plann'd.
(p. 22)[29]

Patriots and heroes are now shared by both nations –'our heroes', 'our patriots' – and the best traits of the Welsh are merged with the English to provide a basis for 'indissolubly firm' British unity, dedicated to fighting corruption and maintaining freedom.

As I shall discuss in a moment, despite Rolt's use of some recognisably Welsh national tropes and his sympathetic stance towards Wales, his simultaneous employment of a poetic rhetoric more closely aligned to Anglo-identified expressions of Britishness creates tensions, contradictions even, in his poetic vision. Like his Welsh counterparts, Rolt foregrounds the importance of the Welsh language as a key constitutive factor of a particularly British liberty. Book II begins by asking the question:

> AUSPICIOUS heav'n! why this peculiar grace
> Conferr'd on Britons? How have they preserv'd
> A speech invariable?
>   (p. 25)

Rolt focuses on the preservation of the Welsh language as a marker of the resilience of the plain British spirit in contrast to the great, yet vanished, culture and language of 'Imperial ROME'. Although Rome possessed a language 'fit for angels', the Romans have lost 'their native tongue divine' (p. 26). In contrast, 'uncorrupted, the GOMERIAN speech / Remains as in anterior ages, strong / Deep-cadenc'd, nervous, unimpair'd by time' (pp. 26–7). In a similar vein to the satires, but used positively here, the Welsh language is seen as being in a virgin state, uncorrupted by outside influence, despite the many attempts (especially by the Normans) to eradicate it. Rolt does not dwell on the preservation of the Welsh language, but uses it as an introduction to the ways in which Cambria and her language – representative of true Britishness – are more resilient than Roman culture. Italy may have 'olives, vineyards, and perennial spring', but Cambria has 'More useful blessings' such as sheep and wool, and 'welch frize' (note to line 29, p. 27), well known to the Shrewsbury merchants. This national superiority extends to the far reaches of the globe: India may boast diamonds, but Wales produces coal to warm the hearth. Similarly, the orange groves of India are 'trivial' when 'Compar'd with gnarled oaks, whose aged trunks / Thick spread the CAMBRIAN soil, to rib our fleets / And bear BRITANNIA's thunders round the globe' (p. 28). The 'wholesome air' of Cambria represents 'kind humanity' (p. 28), but also serves to back up Britain's imperial expansion and naval supremacy. Wales is depicted by Rolt as a paradise of 'wholesome' nature, which adds a moral dimension to the pursuit of empire, epitomised by the gardens at Powys Castle, described as a Welsh version of 'ELISIAN STOWE' (p. 31). By its simplicity and symbolic value as a rural Horatian retreat, Wales purifies the pursuit of empire and dissociates modern Britons from the taint of Roman luxury: 'Happy the man, approv'd, and blest by heav'n, / That in the sylvan shade shakes from his breast / The bait of folly, and the sting of vice' (p. 33). As noted earlier, this emphasis on 'the sylvan shade' of the nation was popular in Anglo-British patriotic verse, and as Rolt moves more firmly into Opposition territory the poem becomes more closely aligned with British patriotic poetic traditions, although still approved and bolstered by Welsh examples and precedents. It could be argued that, in parts of Rolt's poem, Wales serves to make modern Britons feel better about the state of the nation, as it represents the first and last innocent retreat from luxury and corruption. Although he appears to reject the most obvious model for British imperial ambition, the Roman Empire, through the focus on the liberty-loving Ancient Britons, Rolt nevertheless constructs an alternative defence of British empire based on (ironically enough) a view of Cambria as a place of virtuous Horatian simplicity.

The tensions inherent in trying to superimpose an eighteenth-century version of patriotic Britishness on a description of Wales, or, to put it another way, of using Wales as a context for delineating emerging Britishness, surface again in the closing lines of Book II when the poet arrives in Menevia: St David's, in Pembrokeshire. The notes here acknowledge the importance of the city and the connection to 'the tutelary saint of Wales' (p. 38), but the real significance at this juncture is the connection to Admiral Vernon:

Here glorious VERNON to his natal land
Returning, on the rocky coast was dash'd.
In that sad moment pale BRITANNIA shed
A copious flood of tears.
(p. 38)

Although he is now an obscure figure, Vernon is described by Dustin Griffin as 'probably the most popular English admiral in the eighteenth century before Nelson'.[30] After his decisive victory over the Spanish at Porto Bello in 1739 he was 'hailed as a national hero and British patriot', and was lauded as such in an outpouring of poems in his praise.[31] Vernon's success at Porto Bello and subsequent criticism of

Walpole's foreign policy 'ensured Vernon's rise as a symbol of liberty and patriotic whig opposition'.[32] Furthermore, 'His determined defence of liberty, country politics, and blue-water strategy [was] a neat encapsulation of whig patriotism'.[33] As Rolt's poem demonstrates elsewhere, Roman 'Patriot-heroes', such as Brutus and Cato, were extremely popular as figures through which to articulate national pride. However,

> these legendary classical figures were joined by other heroes long enshrined in British legend and resurrected in response to the demands of the 1730s [and in turn] the images of the naval heroes Ralegh, Drake and Blake were superimposed on to the figure of Admiral Edward Vernon.[34]

We see a clear example of this in Rolt's poem as the figure of Britannia prays to the 'GOD of ocean', asking him to save Vernon, and framing him in relation to Drake and Raleigh:

> "See there my dearest BRITON, ah! Behold
> "The gallant HERO, whose victorious arm
> "Laid low the bulwarks of imperious SPAIN;
> "Brave as my DRAKE, and as my RALEIGH great.
>   (p. 39)

The god answers Britannia's prayers and bids the storm be still, and Vernon sails speedily to port. Initially, this may seem an odd note on which to end a section of a poem on Wales. Rolt is obviously valorising present-day Britain through reference to successful Elizabethan trade- and empire-building. Britishness is here inflected through a staunchly anti-Catholic and anti-Spanish stance in relation to the lauding of Drake and Raleigh as brave Protestant heroes.

Rolt's rather belated (in 1749) poetic use of Vernon and previous naval heroes might be typical of British patriotic rhetoric, but it does sit awkwardly in a poem on Wales and unsettles his attempt to build a composite poetic vision of inclusive Britishness. Rolt may be trying to situate Wales at the heart of the nation, but he is only partially successful thus far. The contradictions with which Rolt grapples are the fundamentally different national histories belonging to England and to Wales. I have already mentioned the way in which tensions between Roman and Ancient British versions of the past could parallel Welsh–English antagonism. The problems he faces later in the poem also highlight the ideological strain of cohering two differing national narratives into a single British patriotism. Bluntly put, in the Welsh historical imagination the main enemies to Welsh freedom were the Saxons: the English. Furthermore, despite poetic attempts to assert equality between the two nations, eighteenth-century Wales was seen by the English as marginal to mainstream 'British' interests and still, as I have shown, an object of bemused derision to many an English writer. Moreover, while English writers interested in Welsh history might glorify the Welsh language as a residual symbol of Ancient British independence, few outside Wales showed any practical interest in its present or future state.[35] The last book of *Cambria* makes a final attempt to resolve these contradictions by focusing on the figure of Sir Watkin Williams Wynn (third baronet, 1693?–1749) as an ideal Welsh-British patriot.

After a poetic tour of Wales, taking in its main towns, such as Aberystwyth, Bangor and Carmarthen, Rolt finally brings the poem to a close. At the end of Book III he appears to return to themes of a specifically, albeit stereotypically, Welsh provenance and collects all the most prominent aspects of Ancient British identity together: in the vale of 'Cluyd' 'bluff yeomen' drink to Arthur accompanied by the strains of 'the BRITISH harp'; 'fam'd MENEVIA's priest' (St David) tells his army of Britons to wear leeks in their hats to distinguish themselves from the Saxon enemy; forsaking his throne, Cadwaladr is warned by angels and retires to Rome, 'The last of BRITISH kings' (pp. 62–4). There is then a kind of impasse as Rolt struggles to find a way of connecting the past to the present. As a way of resolving this problem, the poem ends with a eulogy to Sir Watkin Williams Wynn, who is figured as a prince coming home to a perfect microcosm of the nation (Wynnstay), framed by codes of hospitality and virtuous leadership:

> WYNNSTAY exceeds
> The princely palace throng'd by sordid tribes
> With venal adulation insincere:
> Here mild BENEFICENCE unfolds the gates,
> And in the vestibule fair VIRTUE stands
> With cheerful aspect; with extended hands
> Conduct each welcome guest, proud to complete
> The board of hospitality, and WYNN.
> Look down ye sceptred monarchs from your thrones,
> See honour'd WILLIAMS circled by his friends.
>   (p. 65)

A contrast is drawn here between the model of hospitable beneficence and virtue, represented by Wynn, and a debased ideal of monarchy where the prince is surrounded by sycophancy and the king is a lonely figure unconnected to the people. It is as if at the end of the poem Rolt's patriotic loyalty to Frederick falters when compared to the more familiar virtues of Wynn, who is pictured returning to Wales accompanied by the 'hoarse huzza's' (p. 66) of his people, from the lords to the shepherds. The section on Wynn ends with a parallel between the eighteenth-century baronet and the Theban general Epaminondas (c.418–362 BC), who was known for freeing the Thebans from Spartan control and raising their profile within Ancient Greece. Epaminondas appears to be a rather obscure as well as an ambivalent model for a ruler. Although he was successful in leading the Thebans in revolt, in the long term his policies weakened the much-admired Greek city-states, contributing to their eventual decline. It would seem that Rolt employs Epaminondas here to suggest the reawakening of a small nation in heroic resistance against a dominant power, and to figure its leader as a man of the people, a champion of the oppressed:

> So when EPAMINONDAS, thro' the throng
> Of joyful Thebans, high-applauded past;
> The chief, the guardian of his country, found
> His merit grac'd with universal love.
>   (p. 66)

If we are to follow this parallel and compare the Welsh and the Thebans, it would seem that Wynn is being applauded here for distancing himself from an English hegemony to be the figurehead for a more independent (and virtuous) country free from English control. Wynnstay itself, which 'straddled at least five Welsh counties and extended into Shropshire', could almost be imagined as a version of the Greek city-state or as a symbolic substitute for the whole of Wales.[36] As such, Rolt's vision of British unity could be said to collapse completely at this point in favour of Welsh separatism.

A Poem Sacred to the Memory of the Late Sir Watkin Williams Wynne (1749) consolidates this representation, describing Wynn as a 'Friend to thy country, liberty and truth!'who stood up in the name of freedom against 'ministerial wiles' (p. 10). In similar language used in *Cambria*, Wynn is representative of 'all the glories of the British race' (p. 10) against 'Imperial Rome':

A race that check'd victorious Caesar, aw'd
Imperial Rome, and forc'd mankind to own
Superior virtues Britons only knew,
Or only practis'd; for they nobly dar'd
To face oppression; and where freedom finds
Her aid invok'd, there will the goddess fly.
(p. 6)

The Britons, like Epaminondas, are daring in the face of oppression. We then make the same leap from Rome to Edward I to be found in *Cambria*, and again we see the Muses flee to Britain as a place of freedom and virtue. Wynn is now the 'soul of Cambria' (p. 19) and the reincarnation of Llewelyn, the last Prince of Wales. Rolt's treatment of Edward I is markedly less admiring in this context:

For Cambria, in Llewelyn, saw her last
Of princely race expire; yet proud of WYNNE,
She paid him voluntary honours, such
As monarchs seldom share, honours deny'd
The royal Norman.
(p. 20)

Wynn is the epitome of what a perfect monarch/prince should be (and most often is not): 'A father, patron, benefactor, friend' (p. 21). The honours bestowed on Wynn include a Pan-like (he is referred to as 'Pan' on p. 22) fusion of him with the Welsh landscape, and it is rural Wales (associated in *Cambria* with political virtue) that mourns Wynn the most. In response to his death, the streams dry up, the lambs stop playing and the birds cease to sing. Overall, Rolt's poems are a dizzying and often contradictory mix of different nationalistic tropes, centring on Opposition rhetoric of patriotism and liberty, which he attempts to cohere around the figure of Sir Watkin Williams Wynn as Welsh figurehead and champion of freedom and political virtue. It must be noted, however, that Rolt's seemingly effusive brand of eulogy seems typical of responses to Wynn's death, and it is clear that the baronet was held in 'high regard . . . within Wales'.[37] Appropriately (albeit mockingly), Horace Walpole called Wynn the 'Prince of Wales', which became the 'unofficial title' of the 'master of Wynnstay until the nineteenth century'.[38] The poetry of opposition centring on Frederick often created a series of parallels with historical princes associated with crucial moments in English nation-building and identity-formation. Rolt's own poem, *A Monody, On the Death of His Royal Highness Frederick-Louis Prince of Wales* (1751), encapsulates this in the parallels it draws between the Black Prince, 'Steuart Henry' and Frederick (pp. 4–5).[39] However, *Cambria* pointedly does not end with Frederick and the Brunswicks in any of their reincarnations, but with Sir Watkin Williams Wynn coming home to the arms of his wife as the whole of Wales rejoices at their happiness. I want to suggest that, for Rolt, Wynn stands in for Frederick as a real *Welsh* ruler, not just a titular Prince of Wales, and that, as such, he is creating an alternative vision of Britishness which has Wales at its heart. If we were to push this reading one step further, it might even seem that, despite his lip-service to contemporary notions of Britishness, Rolt's poem gestures towards imagining Wales as an independent nation.

There remains, however, the question of Rolt's and Wynn's Jacobitism, and how this informs the representation of Wynn in *Cambria*. Wynn was allied with the Opposition Whigs in the 1730s and 40s (he also acted as a patron of Bolingbroke's *The Craftsman*), and after the 1747 general election he aligned himself with Frederick, Prince of Wales.[40] Although Wynn was 'an archetypal tory of the Hanoverian era', in that he was in continual opposition to the Whig ministry, he also had Jacobite sympathies. These different political positions point to a split in his political identity: 'That between the conventional opponent of government at Westminster and the secret Jacobite plotter'.[41] In these ways he encapsulates what J. C. D. Clark has called 'the politics of the excluded' in the eighteenth century: the Tory, the Patriot Whigs and the Jacobites.[42] From the perspective of Rolt's *Cambria*, we can add a fourth identity which also fits that of the politically marginal: the Welshman. Rolt also seems to have toyed with Jacobitism. Betty Rizzo relates the anecdote that in 1745 Rolt rode out to meet and join Charles Edward Stuart, although he claimed only to want 'to see history in the making'.[43] Taking all these connections (or coincidences) into account, is it then possible to read *Cambria* as a crypto-Jacobite poem? This question may not be as far-fetched as it initially sounds. As Christine Gerrard notes in her reading of 1730s poetry, Opposition rhetoric could be the last resort for the Jacobite sympathiser. Of one example, William Somervile's *The Chace* (1735), she writes: 'The prophetic hopes centred on the future glories of Frederick's reign, rather than the current blessings of George's, make this an opposition Whig poem written in a Tory-Stuart idiom'.[44] Similarly, Richard Powney's *The Stag Chace in Windsor Forest* (1739)

celebrates Frederick as 'a Cambro-British Prince of Wales' . . .
'crowned by some rather Stuart-like Windsor royal oak invested with
the antiquity of mystic Druids'.[45] Further questions are raised here. Is
Cambria an 'opposition Whig poem written in a Tory-Stuart idiom' set
in Wales with a Welsh hero? If Frederick is the 'legitimate "substitute"
for Tory Stuart loyalty' in Somervile's and Powney's poems, then does
Wynn perform the same function in *Cambria*?[46] The best answer is,
maybe. Indeed, any focus on the Prince of Wales, whoever he may be
at the time, is predicated on a hope for the future king, and as such has
echoes of the 'Mab Darogan/Son of Prophecy' – Arthur, Owain
Glyndŵr, Henry VII – who will return as deliverer to his native land.
The appeal of such an idiom – the nostalgic yearning for a monarch –
for both a Welsh and a Jacobite identity is clear, but its appropriateness
as a defining element of patriotism dedicated to the present unity of
the Hanoverian British nation is manifestly limited. Yet again, Rolt's
attempt to construct a British patriotism in a Welsh context encounters
irreconcilable contradictions, and ultimately his poem on Cambria is
incompatible with mainstream patriotic loyalty.

The Love of Our Country (1772)

> BUT it may be, with propriety asked, What have I, who am a Welshman,
> to do with English poetry? I answer, That the ill usage our country has of
> late years received from English writers, will both warrant and justify any,
> the very dullest retainer of the muses, to stand up in its defence.
> (Preface 'To the Reader', p. 131)[47]

The Love of Our County is the first and longest of the few poems Evans
wrote in English. Although Evans states that his purpose in writing the
poem was 'chiefly, to inculcate the love of our country, to men of
learning and fortune in Wales' (p. 131), as the opening quotation
illustrates, he also chose English as his medium in order to defend Wales
against the attacks it has 'of late years received from English writers' (p.
131). Although the primary audience may indeed have been Welsh,
Evans's aim in writing was also to defend his country and to expose the
'Anglo-Welch prelates' who 'confer Welsh benefices on parsons that do
not understand the Welsh language'.[48] Evans is aware of the stance he
is taking by writing in English and gives a clear motive for eschewing
Welsh as the medium for this production: 'I have done it in English
verse, in order that men of learning, in both nations, may understand it'

(p. 132). The preface ends with a spirited riposte to those who attack Wales: 'I HOPE it will convince such malevolent writers, for the future, that we can upon occasion retort, and that we do not want either spirit or abilities to shew a becoming resentment on receiving ill usage, let it come from what quarter it will' (p. 132).

History is a battleground for fighting modern-day quarrels between Wales and England. In order to defend his country, Evans is concerned to set the record straight, placing due emphasis on the heroic past of the Welsh, which of course necessitates focusing on the Saxon–Celtic conflict. In his preface, Evans attacks the use of Giraldus Cambrensis (Gerald of Wales) as a major source for English historians, specifically Lord Lyttelton.[49] He argues that Giraldus was Anglo-Norman in sympathy and traduced his countrymen (on his mother's side) in order to curry favour with the English. Evans advises Lyttelton that in order to write a proper history of the Welsh he must use better sources:

> if his lordship had a mind to do us justice as an historian, he might have been supplied with materials in abundance from Hengwrt library and elsewhere in Wales, and have saved his credit as a writer as well as a nobleman, by doing justice to a brave and injur'd people. (p. 132)

In the poem itself, Evans reiterates this point and connects the present-day historians with the Saxons. Although Evans states that he would expect attacks from 'such despicable scribblers, as the author of the letters from Snowdon', it is surprising that someone such as Lyttelton 'should shew so much low partiality':[50]

> The false Historians of a polish'd age,
> Shew that the Saxon has not lost his rage,
> Tho' tam'd by arts, his rancour still remains,
> Beware of Saxons still, ye Cambrian swains.
>   (p. 139)

What Evans is suggesting here is that 'polish'd' productions, such as those by Lyttelton, are more pernicious than open satire or direct abuse. Posing as objective truth, the histories written by Englishmen inadvertently perhaps display the real views of Welsh 'inferiority'. In a footnote, Evans remarks that in his *History of Henry II* Lyttelton's 'favourite Epithet' for the Welsh people is 'barbarous', despite his seeming objectivity.[51] Evans adds caustically that by this action Lyttelton 'has remarkably verified the British Proverb, "Calon y Sais at y Cymro'" (p. 138). In a manuscript poem entitled 'Verses addressed to Mr Vaughan of Hengwrt requesting leave to peruse his *MSS* in order to do justice to our country, which has lately been much abused by Lord Lyttleton and other English writers', which must have been written at a similar time to *The Love of Our Country*, Evans reiterates these sentiments:

> When Scribblers of the Saxon brood
> Take up their pens to draw our blood
> It ought to warm each Cambrian Heart,
> And make them for their folly smart.[52]

Only Vaughan can save the reputation of the Cambrians:

> Tis your's alone, our country's stain
> To wipe and make us shine again;
> O may one spark of generous fire
> Strike your own breast from the great fire
> That Anglia's sons may see the light
> And hide themselves in shades of night.[53]

The battle is now over representation: who controls the interpretation and presentation of Cambria's past, and who defends her future. In his address to the reader, Evans made the connection between history, antiquarian recovery and patriotism clear: 'I must fairly own that I prefer the ancient British bards before the best English poets, and the ancient British verse as more manly and heroic than the wretched rhimes of the English' (p. 132). In the poem itself, Evans calls on the Muse to help his national defence – 'to sing my Country's Love' (p. 133) – and adds: 'For what more just than to embrace that earth, / That like a second mother gave us birth?' (p. 134). Evans's version of patriotism is firmly aligned with the defence of one's natal land:

> Hence first the hero and patriot came,
> Whose names are listed in the rolls of fame;
> Who bravely struggled in their COUNTRY's cause,
> Who form'd its manners, and who plann'd its laws.
> (p. 134)

The role of poetry, in true bardic fashion, is a patriotic one, but it also proves the process of civilisation in Wales, as heroic deeds become poetic subjects:

THIS noble principle, at length refin'd,
Invented arts to polish rude mankind;
And Poetry the first of all the train,
That sung brave actions in immortal strain.
What theme more noble could the Muse have thought,
Than those who bravely for this COUNTRY fought?
(p. 134)

In keeping with the bardic traditions in Wales, Evans's conception of
the poet's role, even – or especially – when writing in English, is of
singing the glory of one's country and its past. Whereas English writers
struggled in various ways with the idea of patriotic poetry, for Welsh
writers such as Evans the connection was clear and unproblematic; of
the bards he writes: 'Their Country's love they sung, and in its cause /
To die was glorious, glorious its applause' (p. 134). This is a martial
Muse whose duty it is to inspire and record a country's courage in
battle, as did the bards of Ancient Greece:

Tyrtæus thus of old, a Bard renown'd,
Rouse'd the Greek's courage like a clarion's sound,
Such ardor did the poet's verse inspire,
From rank to rank they caught the sacred fire,
Steady as they mov'd, determined was their eye,
Bravely resolv'd to conquer or to die.
(p. 134)

As Evans notes, 'Nor did this Genius shine in Greece alone' (p. 135);
Wales can also boast a poetic heritage, consisting of 'the Bards that
grac'd the Celtic clime' with 'bold' and 'sublime' expression (p. 135).
It is in this role that Evans casts himself as he rehearses the history of
his native land in defiance of English caricature. In this instance, to
write in English is to show the English the very different role of the
poet in Wales.

A defining factor in Welsh history was the battle against the Saxons.
Most of the Welsh poems in this vein attack the Saxons who, even in
those English poems which centrally explore the era of the
British–Saxon conflict, simply do not figure or are mentioned as just
another of a series of invaders. In contrast, for Evans, editor of
Specimens, the bardic vocation was historically linked to the
celebration of victories over the Saxons:

Urien and Maelgwn, ancient heroes, shine
In thy fam'd odes, Taliesin the divine.
Old Llywarch and Aneurin still proclaim,
How Britons fought for glory and for fame,
Whole troops of Saxons in the field they mow'd,
And stain'd their lances red with hostile blood.
    LET annals tell how Cambria's princes fought,
The Saxon victories how dearly bought,
And how for liberty they bravely strove,
As if they had their sanction from above.

(p. 136)

The representation of the conflict between the Ancient Britons and
the Saxons constitutes another crucial difference between Welsh and
English versions of the Welsh past. In English poems, liberty may
have been a watchword for Whig opposition, but for Evans it means
the preservation of Welsh distinctiveness. As such, Welsh–English
historical relations are perceived as antagonistic, and this uneasy
relation was seen to be continued in contemporary historical writing
by Englishmen who, even if broadly sympathetic to Wales, inevitably
privileged England. This is not to say, however, that eighteenth-
century English poets uniformly glorified the Saxons at the expense of
the Britons. Indeed, as Rosemary Sweet has argued, 'the prevailing
attitude towards the Saxon period was deeply equivocal' and, at least
in the middle years of the eighteenth century, the Saxons were not
the focus of sustained literary or antiquarian interest.[54] Even for
the English, the Saxons were often seen as 'barbaric, rude, [and]
unedifying'.[55] The obvious exception was King Alfred, of whom
Evans writes: 'Let England in her Alfred's high renown / Boast of
a monarch worthy of her crown' (p. 136), while stressing that in
this instance it was Asser who taught Alfred all he knew.[56] In
general, though, for the Welsh, the Saxons unequivocally represented
the enemy.

    Not surprisingly, given his previous interest in the tradition, Evans
again uses the massacre of the bards to illustrate English tyranny and
Welsh heroism in resistance.

WHEN liberty was lost – and Cambria's pride,
The brave Llywelyn for his country dy'd,
When cruel Edward heavy burdens laid,
And like a vulture on his subjects prey'd,

Britons incens'd the tyrant's fetters broke,
And would no longer bear the slavish yoke.
> (p. 141)

Evans is responding specifically to the description of the bards and of
Edward I found in Joseph Cradock's *Letters from Snowdon* (1770). It is
clear why Evans was so incensed at the treatment of them, from the
following description of the bards at the time of Edward I:

> This vagabond poetical tribe, were formerly a great nuisance in this
> country, and we find divers acts of parliament and regulations made to
> suppress them. It is said that Edward I. cruelly destroyed them, it may be
> doubted whether it was not the greatest benefit he could do to the country.
> (Letter XIII, p. 83)

In the next letter (XIV), in the course of a discussion of the Welsh
language, the author acknowledges why Edward I may have been so
keen to exterminate the bards. Cradock comments that Welsh 'is the
language of a brave people' and 'Thus some account for the policy of
Edward I. who in order to enslave the people thought it a necessary
previous step to destroy the bards, who cultivated their language and
poetry' (p. 87). The connection between linguistic and cultural
preservation and patriotic independence is clearly perceived here: once
one is lost, the other follows. From Cradock's perspective, however, the
subduing of both national and political independence and cultural
buoyancy by submission to English rule is wholly positive. From his
perspective, to become 'civilised' Wales must lose its distinct national
identity and become one with England/Britain. For Evans, Edward I is
'cruel Edward' and his conquest is 'a slavish yoke' (p. 141); for
Cradock, the King is 'politic kind Edward' (Letter XXI, p. 142) and the
conquest a necessary civilising process. The representations of Edward
I thus epitomise the ways in which history could be interpreted in
completely contradictory ways in Wales and England.

   For Evans, the history of Wales also demonstrates the workings of
providence, as God cannot suffer 'tyrants' (p. 143) to be successful
indefinitely. The Glyndŵr rebellion and the Tudor accession both
prove this theory. Cradock's *Letters* present the Glyndŵr rebellion as
a minor internal conflict between Glyndŵr and Lord Rhythin
(pp. 143–4). For Evans, Glyndŵr's actions represent a torrent of
righteous fury against English dominance:[57]

The great Glyndŵr no longer could contain,
But, like a furious lion, burst the chain,
None could resist his force: like timorous deer
The coward English fled, aghast with fear.

(p. 142)

The Glyndŵr rebellion is, for Evans, a precursor of the accession of the Tudors who, in keeping with the practice of the other Welsh writers discussed in this book, are presented in glorious terms, as heaven-appointed deliverers of the Welsh from servitude who fulfil the prophetic promises of the bards:

THE day of liberty, by heaven design'd,
At last arose – benevolent and kind –
The Tudor race, from ancient heroes sprung,
Of whom prophetic Bards so long had sung,
Beyond our warmest hopes, the sceptre bore,
And brought us blessings never known before,
The English galling yoke they took away,
And govern'd Britons with the mildest sway.

(p. 143)

In what is by now familiar rhetoric, Evans describes the Tudor Union as a reuniting of Britain rather than an appropriation of Wales by England, despite the language clause of the Union. Evans also sings the praises of the Protestant succession, 'Good Edward's Days' and the 'golden reign' of Elizabeth I (p. 143). The Tudor era, attests Evans, also saw the beginnings of what was to become a flowering of scholarship on the Welsh language and Bible, shown in the work of Richard Davies (1501?–81), William Salesbury (c.1520–84?) and William Morgan (1545–1604):[58]

O MAY those days in future annals shine,
That made a Salesbury and a Morgan thine,
That made a Williams and a Davies toil,
Struck with the sacred Love of native soil,
To save our language, and with pious zeal
To tear away the Babylonian veil
That hid the truth, and bring the Gospel-light
To open view, and guide our footsteps right.

(p. 144)

Language, religion, literature and patriotic pride are all interlinked and politicised in terms of Protestant succession and Tudor union.

If the poem might seem to be moving towards a form of capitulation to unionist ideas of Britishness, then it is salutary to compare Evans's poem with the uses to which the Tudor union is put in the *Letters from Snowdon*:

> Thus were united under the same laws and same government, a people hitherto distracted with continual wars and enmity. And it is hoped, by every person that understands the real interest of the principality, and wishes to promote it, that every distinction between England and Wales, whether arising from a difference of manners and customs, the mode of administring justice, and executing the laws, or even in the language, may be intirely removed. (Letter XXI, p. 146)

Cradock sees the Union as a template for future treatment of Wales, which has to lose its language and culture in the interests of integration. As his remarks demonstrate, treatment of the Tudor Union is another bone of contention between Welsh and English writers. Welsh writers tend to use it as a way of asserting the return of the Welsh to a united Britain, in what was clearly a mythologising process. English writers, however, interpret the Union as a chance for the English finally to subdue the Welsh and bring them under English control. This is shown in the *Letters from Snowdon* and, equally blatantly, in Lyttelton's *Account of a Journey into Wales*. In the course of a description of the ruins of Welsh castles (specifically in Montgomery), Lyttelton adds that he is 'glad to think, that, by our incorporating union with the Welsh, this and many others, which have been erected to secure the neighbouring countries of England against their incursion, or to maintain our sovereignty over that fierce and warlike people, are now become useless'. [59]

As I have demonstrated in chapter 2, Jane Brereton and Nehemiah Griffith saw the Hanoverians as continuing the promise of the Tudor Union for Wales. Evans, too, was not above eulogising the Hanoverian monarchs. An earlier English poem, 'An Ode: On the Birthday of his Royal Highness George Prince of Wales', celebrated the birth of the eldest son of George III and Queen Charlotte on 12 August 1762 in the following terms:

> Great Cambria's Prince was born this day,
>   The honour of the nation;

> Britannia's future hope; the stay
>   And prop of Reformation.
> Come, let us then, with heart and voice,
> Proclaim from shore to shore our joys;
> Let no rebellious jarring noise
>   Disturb our acclamation.[60]

Despite these uncharacteristically pro-Hanoverian sentiments, by the early 1770s Evans's stance is nostalgia for a lost past: 'Mourn Cambria! Mourn, thy wretched state deplore – / Those golden days, alas! Are now no more' (p. 144). In rhetoric similar to that employed by Moses Williams in his St David's Day sermons (see chapter 1), and perhaps alluding to his own poem on Psalm 137 (see chapter 3), the Welsh are described as 'Israel's hapless sons' who complain of 'sore captivity' (p. 144). Importantly, Elizabeth's reign is praised for the way in which her pastors guarded the 'flocks' of Cambria, 'And taught the unwary stragglers to beware' (p. 143). By contrast, in the later eighteenth century, 'grievous wolves upon thy mountains prey' (p. 144), and 'strangers' come to preach in Wales in order to profit, not to guard.

This emphasis on the decline in the spiritual fortunes of Wales has a more immediate patriotic purpose: to lament the lack of Welsh-speaking pastors in Wales. The poem ends with an emphasis on the right to have the Gospel preached in Welsh:

> THE Gospel in your language you enjoy,
> I count it, Britons, as your chiefest joy –
> Sell not your birthright, 'tis a sacred trust,
> Be to yourselves, and to your County just –
> Thank Heaven, O Cambria! for the light divine,
> And may it ever in thy language shine,
> While sun and moon, and while the starry train,
> Adorn the sky and gild the heavenly plain;
> And may this feeble verse for ever prove
> How each brave Briton doth his COUNTRY LOVE.
> (p. 145)

Evans presents the right to worship in the vernacular as a 'birthright' and a 'sacred trust', enriched by the scholarship of Salesbury, Davies, Morgan and others. The 'light divine' must be kept shining through the Welsh language to prove the love of 'each brave Briton' for his country. However, as the *Letters from Snowdon* clearly illustrate, Evans and

other Welsh writers were fighting against a post-1707 unionist vision
which relied on a total absorption of any distinct Welsh national
identity. In *Considerations of the Illegality and Impropriety of Preferring
Clergymen Who are Unacquainted with the Welsh Language to Benefices
in Wales* (1768), John Jones has a more realistic view of the Tudor
Union. He appreciates 'the many reciprocal advantages resulting from
the Union', but argues that Henry VIII and Queen Elizabeth had the
same intention as Edward I with regard to Wales, 'to introduce the
English language and Customs there, both by planting colonies of
English, keeping garrisons, giving the Welsh encouragement to learn
their language, and to inlist in the English army' (p. 15). Yet, as Jones
notes of his countrymen, 'they could never prevail upon them to
submit to the most ignominious badge of slavery, the language of the
conquerors' (p. 16). Despite the widespread enthusiasm for the Tudors
among Welsh poets, there was also the realisation that to accept the
unionist vision on the terms of some English writers would be to lose
the Welsh language and, along with it, the entire Welsh past. Despite
his praise of the Tudors, Evans places a commitment to the Welsh
language and the preaching of the Bible in Welsh as the first
prerequisite of the patriot.

'An Ode to Cambria' (1782)
John Walters's 'An Ode to Cambria' in many ways exemplifies the
treatment of 'Cambria' in English-language poetry in the eighteenth
century, and is thus an appropriate text with which to conclude this
chapter.[61] It is also fitting that it was John Walters's father, also John
Walters, who had invented the Welsh word for patriotism – *gwladgarwch*
– in 1776.[62] The poem is printed in Walters's collection *Translated
Specimens of Welsh Poetry* (1782) and appears, at first glance, to be one
of the 'original pieces' noted in the full title.[63] Throughout the first half
of this short collection, Walters's debt to Evans's *Specimens* is clear, and
he is working in what is an identifiable eighteenth-century 'sub-genre' of
English-language imitations or versifications of Evans's prose
translations of bardic poetry.[64] Walters tries to do what Evans refuses to
attempt: metrical translation of ancient Welsh poetry. In doing so, it
could be argued that he 'Ossianises' the original poetry to fit eighteenth-
century tastes. Sometimes he does this in direct response to Evans, as
the poems on 'Nest, The Daughter of Howel' and 'The Ode of the
Months' make clear. These are very free imitative translations which are
indebted to Evans's English translations rather than the Welsh originals,

shown by the similar vocabulary used. These are not, therefore, translations as we would define them, but 'imitations', in the eighteenth-century understanding of the word. At other times the poems appear to have no direct original, but rely on the traditional themes, imagery and vocabulary of ancient Welsh verse, and in doing so veer perilously close to unintentional parody or pastiche. The two poems of this later type are 'Lewellin and his Bards. A Dialogue', which mingles the Edwardian invasion with the love story of Llewelyn and Elinor ('the lover with the king contends' (p. 7)), and 'An Ode to Cambria'.

If 'An Ode to Cambria' is a translation of anything it is closest to another of Evans's 'specimens': 'Arwyrain Owain Gwynedd' by Gwalchmai ap Meilyr (fl. 1130–80), otherwise known as 'Arddwyreaf hael o hil Rhodri' or 'The Battle of Tal Moelfre'. In his notes to the poem, Walters quotes from the English translation in Specimens about the battle, which is versified thus in the poem: 'A thousand banners waving high / Where bold Tan Moilvre meets the sky' (p. 10). Walters mingles these lines with references to the battle of 'Mailor' . . . fought with the English in the 12th century, by Owain Cyveiliog, prince of Powis, who composed the admired poem called Hirlas, or the Drinking horn on the victory he obtained' (note to line 26, p. 32). This poem is, of course, the opening text in Specimens. Overall, the poem is an address to Cambria in terms of a kind of amalgam of all the traditions apparent in Evans's choice of poems for Specimens. Walters ranges over the 'stately halls of kings' (p. 9), harp-playing, 'sparkling horns' and hospitality, 'warlike deeds' (p. 10) and 'chiefs invincible in fight' (p. 9). Into this recognisable mix of traditions he also adds 'maids for peerless beauty crown'd' (p. 9) who 'tam'd to love's refin'd delight / Those chiefs invincible in fight' (p. 9), Druids and more obviously eighteenth-century pastoral elements, such as shepherds tending 'their fleecy train' in pleasing Welsh vales of 'Innocence' which encourage 'indulging dreams' and the sport of 'rural lovers' (p. 11). Despite this last use of stereotypes worthy of the author of the Letters from Snowdon, it could be argued that what Walters is trying to do overall is to explore the poetic legacy of Wales from its earliest times through to the present as a form of 'bardic nationalism'. In this sense, as a 'free translation' of Evans's Specimens, the poem resonates with the poetry of Gray (and also the original verse of Evans himself) and provides further evidence of a discernible English-language poetic tradition developing in the eighteenth century which takes Welsh history and literature as its theme.

Throughout the poem Walters is concerned to mark out Cambria as a subject worthy of poetic record as well as to express the poetic voice's 'love of country'. He imagines calling up the 'ancient Genius' or poetic spirit of Wales, which, to reanimate 'the drooping land',

> Strikes the harp with glowing hand,
> Light spirits with aerial wings
> Dance upon the trembling strings.
> Oh, lead me thou in strains sublime
> Thy sacred hill of oaks to climb,
> To haunt thy old poetic streams,
> And sport in fiction's fairy dreams,
> There let the rover Fancy free,
> And breathe the soul of poesy!
> (p. 10)

It is as if Gray's last bard (or perhaps more fittingly his 'pale spectre') has returned to praise Wales. Like the other examples of English-language poetry on Wales, Walters insists on the appropriateness of Cambria as a poetic subject and as the inspiration for poetry. This inspiration is figured as coming directly from the bardic inheritance:

> Nor seldom, Cambria, I explore
> Thy treasures of poetic store,
> And mingle with thy tuneful throng,
> And range thy realms of ancient song,
> That, like thy mountains, huge and high,
> Lifts its broad forehead to the sky.
> (p. 11)

The landscape of Wales merges with the poetic tradition and becomes inseparable. As in the work of the bards, poetry is always tied to the politics of place and nation. In order to compound his vision of Cambria's rich poetic tradition, Walters provides a roll-call of the most famous Welsh bards, from Taliesin through Iolo Goch to Dafydd ap Gwilym, who are seen to revive the poetic fires of classical Greece:

> Whether, O prince of bards, I see
> The fire of Greece reviv'd in thee,
> That like a deluge bursts away;
> Or Taliesin tune the lay;

Or thou, wild Merlin, with thy song
Pour thy ungovern'd soul along;
   . . .
Whether, Iolo, myrtle-crown'd,
Thy harp such amorous verse resound
As love's and beauty's prize hath won;
Or led by Gwilim's plaintive son,
I hear him teach his melting tale
In whispers to the grove and gale.
(pp. 11–12)

So far, the poem has celebrated the more usual military triumph of Wales and cultural resilience of Cambria. By referencing the work of Dafydd ap Gwilym and Iolo Goch, Walters can highlight the presence of 'amorous verse' and 'melting tales' in Welsh poetry, factors more likely appeal to an eighteenth-century reader's more refined sensibilities. Despite this emphasis on a golden age of Welsh literature, the concluding sequence once again focuses on nostalgia and loss. As in the poems of Gray and Evans, the poet then turns away from the triumphs of the past to emphasise apathy, waste and ruin. Wales is no longer the repository of 'the sacred eulogies of song' (p. 12), but a place of cultural and literary desolation. The parallels with the decline of Greek and Roman culture are implicit here:

Thy spirit of renown expires,
The brave example of thy fires
Is lost; thy high heroic crest
Oblivion and inglorious rest
Have torn with rude rapacious hand;
And apathy usurps the land.
(p. 12)

Due to the 'waste of age' and war, the shores and mountains of Cambria no longer inspire poetry. This national decline, however, is also the result of the actions of 'Scolan', whose 'fiercer rage' (p. 12) completed the ravages already accomplished. In his notes to the poem, Walters explains that the legendary Scolan (or Ysgolan) was known for burning a library of Welsh books in the 'White Tower' after the Edwardian conquest of Wales in 1282:

The captive Welsh nobles, either hostages or prisoners of war, who were detained in the Tower of London, obtained permission that their libraries should be sent them from Wales, to amuse them in their solitude and confinement. This was a frequent practice, so that in process of time the Tower became the principal repository of Welsh literature. The present poverty of ancient Welsh manuscripts may be dated from the time when the History and Poetry of our country received a fatal blow in the loss of those collected at London. (note to line 18, p. 34)

He then quotes from 'a poem written in 1450' to illustrate his point:

The books of Cambria, and their villainous Destroyer,
Were concealed in the White Tower.
Cursed was the deed of Scolan,
Who committed them in a pile to the flames.
(p. 34)

Walters concludes by stating that at another time of national instability – the Owain Glyndŵr rebellion – more manuscripts were lost or 'so scattered and destroyed, "that there escaped not one (as William Salesbury relates) that was not incurably maimed, and irrecuperably torn and mangled"' (p. 35).

Walter's information about Ysgolan comes straight from Evan Evans's *Specimens*, where, in the notes to 'Ode of the Months' (also 'translated' by Walters), Evans had transcribed William Salesbury's account of the burning of the Welsh books and their further destruction at the time of Glyndŵr with the original quotation:

Llyfrau Cymru au llofrudd
Ir twr Gwyn aethant ar gudd
Ysceler oedd Yscolan
Fwrw'r twrr lyfrau ir tan
    Gutto'r Glyn. A.D. 1450

"The books of Cymru and their remains went to the White Tower, where they were hid. Cursed was Ysgolan's act in throwing them in heaps into the fire." (p. 44)

Evans conjectures that Gwilym Ddu was one of the few bards who escaped the martial law of Edward I and thus, as discussed in the previous chapter, this poem can be read as being used in the service of eighteenth-century bardic nationalism. It is clear where Walters gets his information from, but what is interesting is that he uses Ysgolan in particular as a way of framing a decline in Welsh poetic tradition, and thus adds (or re-emphasises) another layer of meaning to seemingly 'apolitical' or 'non-national' melancholic poems of loss. Significantly, the poem ends on a similar note to both 'On Seeing the Ruins of Ivor Hael's Palace' and 'A Paraphrase of the 137th Psalm' by Evan Evans, and also, therefore, to Gray's *Elegy*:

> Lo! silent as the lapse of time
> Sink to the earth thy towers sublime;
> Where whilom harp'd the minstrel throng,
> The night-owl pours her feral song:
> For ever sinks blest Cambria's fame,
> By ignorance, and sword, and flame
> Laid with the dust, amidst her woes
> The taunt of her ungenerous foes;
> For ever sleeps her warlike praise,
> Her wealth, dominion, language, lays.
>   (pp. 12–13)

Walters's poem foregrounds the staples of mid-eighteenth-century poems of melancholy: the passing of time revealing the futility of human grandeur, the symbolism of past greatness shown in the ruined towers, the lonely owl haunting the abandoned court/hall.[65] Like Evans again, and in this we can continue to trace a 'canon' of English-medium Welsh poetry in the mid to late eighteenth century, he then adds a specific Welsh context, which politicises the genre from a Welsh perspective. Ysgolan is the key to this vision. Cambria has lost her fame and cultural riches by her own 'ignorance', by war and by the flames into which Ysgolan is said to have thrown the Welsh manuscripts. As a result, she is at the mercy of her 'ungenerous foes'. There is a sense here that the Welsh are partially responsible for their own loss. As Philip Schwyzer suggests, Ysgolan is a 'figure for the wounds the Welsh inflict upon themselves' and thus joins a list of other 'great traitors' essential to nationalist narrative.[66] In this sense the bards themselves are in league with Ysgolan, as the absence of books means that their control over knowledge becomes complete and unassailable. However, the shadowy Ysgolan can also figure as the destroyer of 'cultural treasures by an enemy'.[67] This was the view of Richard Davies, who mentions Ysgolan in the preface to the Welsh New Testament of 1567, in the course of forwarding the theory that Wales had once 'possessed the whole Bible in the vernacular', since destroyed by the English (and Owain Glyndŵr).[68] Schwyzer's broader points about the nationalistic function of Ysgolan in the Tudor and Renaissance periods are also fruitful for thinking about eighteenth-century 'bardic nationalism'. He suggests that this mysterious figure in some way epitomises the Welsh national traditions: 'Ysgolan ensured that the Welsh past would remain irrecoverable, and thus that there would be no end to the nostalgic longing constitutive of nationalism.'[69] Again, this works in an eighteenth-century context and goes some way to explain the enduring popularity of the Edward I myth and Gray's *The Bard* with Welsh readers and writers. Schwzyer's further point that the lack of literate poetic culture could be made up for by 'oral tradition and collective memory' also holds good for the eighteenth century, as to emphasise the works of the bards is to emphasise primarily oral and communal literary utterances. Nevertheless, what Evan Evans was trying to do was to recover the manuscripts supposedly destroyed by Ysgolan and other national disasters. What is different about the eighteenth century is that Evans – and his interpreters/translators, like John Walters – are involved in creating new traditions and 'canons', which are built from the ashes of the past to emerge afresh through 'translation' in all its forms.[70] In yet another series of paradoxes, absence and destruction are the main subjects of a new English-language poetry of Wales, a body of patriotic poetry which reasserts bardic heritage, forges a new sense of national importance, and continues to evade appropriation by the English.

5

Narrating the Nation: Wales in Eighteenth-Century Fiction

Studies of the eighteenth-century novel have always been aware of its national dimension. As Britain's empire grew stronger as the century progressed, so too did a 'native' canon of novelistic writing which was seen to surpass other European literatures, most importantly that of France. However, as students of the novel also know, eighteenth-century fiction is predominantly seen, with the possible exception of the Scottish novelist Tobias Smollett, as an English phenomenon, dominated by the mid-century 'rivalry' between Henry Fielding and Samuel Richardson and then by the sentimental fiction so popular in the latter years of the century. However, in recent years, and partly as a result of the devolution debates in twentieth-century Britain, studies of eighteenth-century fiction have begun to explore the way in which novelists negotiated national identity from a more inclusively British perspective. Much of this important work has been written in response to issues of internal colonialism and post-colonial methodology. Literary scholars, such as Leith Davis, Murray Pittock, Janet Sorenson and Katie Trumpener, among others, have made important contributions to these debates in terms of English–Scottish literary dialogues (Davis), British national identities (Pittock), the role played by language in determining both internal nationalism and imperial identities (Sorenson), and bardic nationalism (Trumpener).[1] Further evidence of the increasing influence of such approaches for a study of the novel was the collection of essays on Scottish fiction printed together under the heading 'Internal Colonialism and the British Novel' in *Eighteenth-Century Fiction* (2002).[2] Janet Sorenson's introduction to these essays stresses that 'the political and cultural dynamics of internal colonialism has important implications for the ways in which we read eighteenth-century fiction' (p. 53). Attention to internal difference within Britain, Sorenson argues, opens up new ways for thinking about nation, empire and narration in eighteenth-century fiction and leads to complex reconfigurations of the particular roles played by the literary and cultural productions of 'Celtic peripheral spaces' (p. 58).

Despite the obvious importance of Wales to these debates, the studies mentioned above pay little or no attention to the Welsh context, either in terms of Wales's status as one of these 'Celtic peripheries' or in the light of recent bibliographical and literary-critical work on eighteenth- and nineteenth-century Welsh fiction.[3] As I have discussed in previous chapters, Katie Trumpener points to some suggestive Welsh paradigms as templates for her definition of 'bardic nationalism', but the bulk of her book deals with Scottish and Irish writing. Recent studies are starting to assess the impact of Welsh culture on Romanticism, but have, so far, mainly concentrated on poetic models and/or the influence of the Celtic world on the major Romantic poets: Blake, Coleridge, Southey, Wordsworth.[4] However, as the pioneering work of Jane Aaron, Andrew Davies and Moira Dearnley has demonstrated, not only is there a substantial body of fiction by writers of Welsh origin from at least the Romantic period, but also fiction with Welsh themes and locations was widespread throughout the eighteenth century. Given the slow but growing recognition of the significance of Wales to current debates concerning eighteenth-century British identities, it is clear that fiction by Welsh writers must be incorporated into such discussions if we are to have a fuller picture of the literary negotiation of Britain in the eighteenth century.

Are there valid reasons, however, for this critical neglect that go beyond national prejudices or blind spots? One reason is that the critical tradition of 'Welsh Writing in English' conventionally locates the beginnings of 'Anglo-Welsh' literary culture, and especially fiction, no earlier than 1915, the publication date of Caradoc Evans's *My People*.[5] In effect, the critical consensus has been that there was no novelistic tradition in Wales to speak of before the twentieth century. Another reason is the fact that there is no Welsh-language canon of novels in the eighteenth century alongside which an English-language tradition could develop and be compared. Nevertheless, in the last twenty years of the eighteenth century there was a rash of fiction which, although not necessarily written by Welsh-born authors, used Wales (and other Celtic countries) as setting and theme. This development was an outgrowth of the tourist interest in the newly fashionable appreciation of the once 'barbarous' Welsh landscape and lent itself to the growing popularity of the Gothic, pioneered by Horace Walpole's *The Castle of Otranto* (1764).[6] In keeping with this connection of tourist literature and fiction, perhaps the most important reason for critical neglect is the actual content and approach of the texts in question. In relation to women's writing, Jane Aaron argues that much of the fiction produced in the last years of the eighteenth century does not seem easily to fit the critical paradigms being developed to discuss the fiction of the 'Celtic peripheries'. She suggests that 'this neglect may have to do with the fact that, from the contemporary, twenty-first century point of view, these texts, paradoxically, are not Celtic enough' and do not write about Wales 'in ways which could be construed as supportive of its difference'.[7] Furthermore, the generic development of the 'Celtic Romantic novel' is implicated in a more widespread process of Anglicisation occurring towards the end of the eighteenth century, a process which affected both the content and the reception of these novels. Of Katie Trumpener's relative neglect of Welsh fiction in *Bardic Nationalism*, Aaron rightly points out that although there would be no shortage of texts for her to discuss which are 'located in Wales', it is a much more difficult task 'to find ones focusing on the type of aspiring nationhood that she ascribes to the Scottish and Irish fictions of the period'.[8]

Aaron's comments are based on nineteenth-century women writers, but her broader conclusions could equally apply to fiction written by both sexes in the eighteenth century (although gender issues remain important for analysing this fiction). Andrew Davies's extensive doctoral study of Welsh and Wales-related fiction, '"The reputed nation of inspiration": representations of Wales in fiction from the Romantic period, 1780–1829', endorses the perceived 'failure' of the Welsh novel in the eighteenth century, in particular in attempts to import antiquarian concerns into the novel.[9] Davies is successful in identifying some texts which attempt to use the novel form to explore antiquarian concerns. However, he concludes by viewing those fictional works which were directly inspired by Thomas Gray, for example, as representing 'a failed generic experiment'. After the advent of Walter Scott, Welsh antiquarian fiction petered out as a serious proposition: 'at no point after Evan Jones's *The Bard* (1809) does any writer attempt to fictionalise antiquarian narratives'.[10] Furthermore, as a whole, Davies reads the majority of pre-1800 Wales-related fictions, not as radical statements of separate Welsh identity, but as contributing to the further incorporation of Welsh identity in the service of a British nation-state and as dramatising 'the cultural and linguistic Anglicization of the Welsh aristocracy'.[11] Stephen Knight takes this even further in his delineation of eighteenth-century fiction from Wales as colonial 'first-contact texts', severely limited in their application for a Welsh audience:

> The early English-language fictions about Wales discussed by Dearnley, Aaron and Davies are basically imperial narratives with some first-contact features. It is clear that their major audience is in England and therefore they do not operate in any real way as texts that generate self-consciousness among English-speaking Welsh people.[12]

In this chapter I examine three authors who are starting to be seen, albeit in different ways, as having key positions in our understanding of Wales's place in eighteenth-century fiction: Tobias Smollett, Anna Maria Bennett and Edward 'Celtic' Davies. My broad aim here is to compare and contrast the way in which their novels address the concerns I have discussed in the book so far. How do these writers negotiate the place of Wales in post-1707 Britain, and what sort of roles is Wales seen to play in treatments of a British identity? Are there any connections between the antiquarian concerns and bardic nationalism found in the work of Evan Evans and his imitators? Are any of the key tropes of Welsh cultural nationalism at work in other literary genres also to be found in the fiction of the period, and do they work in the same way? Moreover, how do the generic demands of late eighteenth-century fiction reshape the ways in which Wales was imagined by writers, and how does gender inform these imaginings? Throughout this discussion, I revisit some of the critical claims made for these texts and re-examine the critical templates and reading strategies we might use to analyse such fictions. I begin with an examination of what has traditionally been seen as a key text for understanding British national identity, Tobias Smollett's *The Expedition of Humphry Clinker* (1771), through a focus on the nationality of the protagonist, the splenetic yet sentimental Welsh squire Matthew Bramble. I then move on to discuss Anna Maria Bennett's two Welsh novels, *Anna; or, Memoirs of a Welch Heiress* (1785) and *Ellen, Countess of Castle Howell* (1794), in the context of her Romantic treatment of Welsh and British identity. The chapter concludes with a discussion of what has been seen not only as the most successful attempt to incorporate Welsh antiquarian concerns into the novel, but also as a contender for the position of 'first Anglo-Welsh novel': Edward Davies's *Elisa Powell, or, Trials of Sensibility* (1795).[13]

Tobias Smollett, *The Expedition of Humphry Clinker* (1771)

As one of the major canonical novels of the eighteenth century, *Humphry Clinker* has received its fair share of critical attention. Traditionally seen as the epitome of Smollett's scatological and satirical genius, the novel has more recently been read as a text which is obsessed with the state of the nation, particularly with the rising tide of luxury and corruption stemming from developments in commerce, colonial expansion and concomitant class mobility. Unsurprisingly, given the book's structure as a domestic tour, Smollett's text has in recent years attracted comment in terms of its treatment of post-1707 Britishness and, in particular, in the light of the debates staged by the novel concerning the pros and cons for Scotland of the 1707 Union in the years since its inception. Understandably, given the author's natal identity and the book's main focus, it is Smollett's treatment of Scotland which forms the main subject of discussions of his negotiations of Britishness. Although most critics of Smollett mention in passing that the protagonist of the novel, Matt Bramble, and the whole travelling party are Welsh (Bramble is a Welsh squire of the estate Brambleton Hall, in Monmouthshire), this fact, and the novel's engagement with Wales overall, has rarely been an area for sustained commentary. Indeed, some critics seem to overlook the fact of Bramble's Welsh identity altogether, subsuming Wales under the name of England in a depressingly familiar manner.[14] Exceptions to this critical blind spot include the work of Moira Dearnley and Andrew Davies, and an article from 2002 by Sharon Alker which explores the way in which Smollett employs Wales as a mediator between England and Scotland.[15]

On first glance it is of course clear why the Welsh detail of *Humphry Clinker* has been underexplored, the simple reason being that, as the travellers themselves are Welsh, none of the action takes place in Wales. The point of the Bramble family tour is to explore places beyond Wales: they travel from Wales to Bristol Hotwells, Bath, then on to London, through Yorkshire and on into Scotland and the Highlands. However, this is in itself interesting, as the usual formula of the domestic tour would be the Londoner venturing beyond the capital to the Celtic peripheries. In these texts, such as the *Letters from Snowdon* discussed in the previous chapter, Wales is the object of cultural scrutiny as a foreign and alien culture. In *Humphry Clinker*, Wales is the traveller's norm or 'known', against which the other locations are compared and contrasted. In the first half of the book it is the urban centres of southern England – Bristol, Bath and London – which are the objects of bemused and shocked scrutiny. Matt Bramble declares: 'London is literally new to me'.[16] While attending a ball in Bath, Bramble faints, as a result, he tells his correspondent Dr Lewis, of 'the fouled air' (p. 65) resulting from the crowds of people, an atmosphere which is,

> A high exalted essence of mingled odours arising from putrid gums, imposthumated lungs, sour flatulencies, rank arm-pits, sweating feet, running sores and issues, plasters, ointments, and embrocations, hungary-water, spirit of lavender, assafœtida drops, musk, hartshorn, and sal volatile; besides a thousand frowzy streams, which I could not analyse. (p. 66)

In contrast to this suffocating mixture of odours from the mass of bodies crowded inside, the air of Wales is clean and pure. As Bramble declares: 'Such is the atmosphere I have exchanged for the pure, elastic, animating air of the Welsh mountains – *O Rus, quando te aspiciam!* [O my countryside, when shall I see you] – I wonder what the devil possessed me' (p. 66).[17]

As Bramble's use of Horace here suggests, the way in which he describes his Welsh home when first embarking on his journey is as an ideal, or, in Charlotte Sussman's terms, 'a compensatory fantasy' of 'self-sufficiency' and 'impenetrable national identity'.[18] The first letter of volume II, from Bramble to Dr Lewis, comprises a long harangue from the splenetic Bramble, based around a contrast between town and country. 'Shall I state the difference between my town grievances and my country comforts?' (p. 118), he begins, and proceeds to list the superior virtues of Brambleton Hall against the luxurious corruption of the town. Again, we are told the air in Wales is 'clear' and 'elastic' (p. 118), and there is room to move and quiet to enable peaceful sleep. As elsewhere in the novel, Bramble frames his praise of the countryside in terms of the self-sufficiency of his estate and what we would now term, in the days of 'food-miles', the traceability of his food supply:

> I drink the virgin lymph, pure and crystalline as it gushes from the rock, or the sparkling beveridge [*sic*], home-brewed from malt of my own making . . . my bread is sweet and nourishing, made from my own wheat, ground in my own mill, and baked in my own oven; my table is, in a great measure, furnished from my own ground. (pp. 118–19)

In contrast, in London there is barely 'room enough to swing a cat', the air is full of 'putrefaction', it is noisy, filthy, and the bread 'is a deleterious paste, mixed up with chalk, alum and bone-ashes; insipid to the taste, and destructive to the constitution' (pp. 119–20). Overall, London is seen by Bramble as a grotesque 'overgrown monster; which, like a dropsical head, will in time leave the body and extremities without nourishment and support' (p. 87). One pressing result of this for Bramble is the depopulation of the countryside and small farms, whose inhabitants and labourers swarm to the capital in vast numbers and end up being swallowed up by 'the grand source of luxury and corruption' (p. 87).

As Janet Sorenson and others have noted, Bramble's tirade against English urban corruption (the treatment of Scottish urban centres is in complete contrast) is typical of Tory-inflected inversions of centre and margin, which represented 'the centre, London, and the movement of goods and people towards it, not as the foundation of national identity in its ever-expansive accumulation of people and goods, but instead as the source of national corruption'.[19] As Sorensen adds, 'In this spatial model, the unbalanced circulatory movement by which a periphery merely gives to the core is devastating for the nation's periphery and, consequently, the entire nation.'[20] In *Humphry Clinker*, Smollett relocates the centre (or centres) of the nation in the 'stable and controllable space of the ancestral estate', symbolised by Brambleton Hall.[21] As Michael Rosenblum argues, the eventual 'Return to the Estate' movement of the 'Tour' reverses the drive to the centre and replaces 'sinister convergence' with a 'centripetal movement [which] flows outwards toward many centres – the country estates run by gentleman landowners'.[22] Urban commerce is replaced by what Rosenblum calls the 'myth of the paternal landowner', an ideal which is clearly articulated through Bramble's occasional remarks concerning his own benevolent approach to his estate.[23] Other examples include the failing estate of Baynard, which is then enthusiastically 'saved' by Bramble, and the perfect model of rural management and economy showcased in the Dennison estate. Sharon Alker suggests that by displacing the 'negotiation of British identity away from London', Smollett is also able to 'deconstruct the binary model of Anglo-Scottish relations that had emanated from the centre of the nation throughout the sixties'.[24] John Richetti goes slightly further and suggests that the ideal of the country estate represents a 'real' social alternative to London-centred Britishness: 'It is a romantic and pastoral alternative, to some extent, but Smollett expects his readers to see it as coherent and conceivable, not simply satire or comic fable but the moral and social renewal made possible by real travel though Great Britain.'[25]

Is it significant that this alternative national vision is Welsh? Is Wales being imagined by Smollett as the 'still sylvan heart' of the corrupt imperial nation that we saw dramatised in chapter 4 in Richard Rolt's *Cambria*? Does the symbolic purity of Wales purge the more corrupt aspects of the 'vortex' of the nation and, in doing so, add a more radical national spin to the otherwise Anglo-Tory emphasis on the centrality of the country gentleman and the country interest? Is it feasible that Wales functions as a symbol of 'hope for a potential British utopia where the peripheries and the centre can coexist in peace'?[26] Or is it that Wales is simply a neutral space which can avoid Anglo-Scottish confrontation and therefore act as a marker (more imaginatively powerful by its absence, perhaps) for how the nation should be? Andrew Davies's analysis of *Humphry Clinker* makes a convincing case for the deliberate significance of Smollett's choice of nationality for his country squire, making some intriguing connections between the figure of Bramble and Sir Watkin Williams Wynn (third baronet), most obviously through their mutual political independence. The specific construction of the archetypal Tory country gentleman as Welsh mainly derived from the prominent standing of Wynn as a political figure and made its way into a number of fictions as well as poems in the eighteenth century, including Sir Rowland Meredith in Samuel Richardson's *Sir Charles Grandison* and, as I will discuss, the novels of Anna Maria Bennett.[27] These parallels with Wynn are useful for thinking about what Smollett was trying to achieve in *Humphry Clinker*. By using Wales as a symbol of self-sufficiency, political independency and the regeneration of national virtue these states imply, it could be argued that, for Smollett, Wales functions as an ideal vision of Britain and thus plays an important, if mainly imaginary, role in one of the major fictional negotiations of Britishness in the eighteenth century. On the other hand, as Davies recognises, it could equally be argued that Welsh identity in the novel 'is subordinated to questions of Britain's internal unity and its European and colonial profile'.[28]

Such approaches offer fruitful points of entry for rethinking the significance of Wales in *Humphry Clinker*. What these readings leave out is the complicated role played by Matt Bramble and the fact that he is a satirical figure in a comic novel, not a straightforward mouthpiece for the author. Bramble is both a sharp (but often over-zealous) critic of contemporary urban life and a mediating figure between England and Scotland. What also needs to be taken into account is his development over the course of the novel, a development which John Richetti describes as moving from 'provincial outrage over metropolitan excess to productive participation in moral and social renewal, to private experiences that lead to an enlightened and moderate understanding of public life, and to a revived and balanced rural community'.[29] From this perspective, Bramble becomes an alternative figure for emergent Britishness, and his Welsh identity is clearly marginal to this broader process. Yet Bramble's implied experience of becoming British (as, in part, a reaction to the provincialisation which he himself represents at the beginning of the novel) is not as seamless as Richetti's assessment implies.[30] Renewed attention to Bramble's specifically Welsh identity reveals fissures in Smollett's attempt to reconcile his vision of ideal British unity. By dramatising Bramble's personal and physical regeneration through enlightened travel, Smollett also reveals some of the personal and private compromises that have to be made to accommodate a public unified nation.

Given the close connection between identity and naming, it is significant that Bramble's name is itself a source of confusion. The fact that he has two names points to a dual, and possibly divided, identity. Only when he is revealed as 'Matthew Loyd of Glamorganshire' can Humphry recognise him as his father: the 'secret' of Matt's previous Welsh name is connected to the secret of Humphry, who also, in turn, undergoes a metamorphosis into 'Matthew Loyd'.[31] Bramble had assumed his mother's name (Loyd) to inherit her estate in Glamorganshire, and then changed it back to his 'real name' when he sold his mother's property to 'clear [the] paternal estate' of Bramble Hall (p. 318). He has therefore lost his 'maternal' connection to Wales through his assumption of the more Anglicised paternal name of Bramble. The representation of Bramble's national identity also changes at different points and places in the novel. At an early stage in their journey, the travellers visit Squire Burdock in Harrogate, where they are positioned as naive provincials. The squire's wife (a first cousin of Matt's father) is an example of English prejudice against Welsh 'provinciality' and implies that, in Mrs Loyd, Bramble's father made a 'poor match in Wales' (p. 167). She then sneers at Liddy's enthusiastic description of a fellow guest as 'an angel': 'the lady of the house said in a contemptuous tone, she supposed Miss had been brought up at some country boarding school' (p. 168). Despite being on the receiving end of such attitudes, when the party reach Scotland, they initially seem to become more English-identified (or South – as opposed to North – British). The maid Win Jenkins, herself the possessor of a strong Welsh dialect, declares of the Scots that she cannot understand 'their lingo' (p. 220). Furthermore, Bramble's sister Tabitha, in a manner reminiscent of the anti-Welsh satires discussed in the previous chapter, thinks that they have to go across the sea to reach Scotland, showing her view of Scotland as unfamiliar and strange:

> She was so little acquainted with the geography of the island, that she imagined we could not go to Scotland but by sea; and after we had passed though the town of Berwick, when he [Lieutenant Lismahago] told her we were upon Scottish ground, she could hardly believe the assertion – If the truth must be told, the South Britons in general are woefully ignorant in this particular. What, between want of curiosity, and traditional sarcasms, the effect of ancient animosity, the people at the other end of the island know as little of Scotland as of Japan. (pp. 213–14)

However, the arrival in Scotland also leads to a reassertion of the party's Welshness. A few pages before her display of ignorance concerning the geography of Scotland, Tabby had asserted Matt's proud lineage from Llewelyn and as the namesake of his great-uncle 'Matthew ap Madoc ap Meredith' (p. 192). Similarly, in a letter from Jery Melford (Bramble's nephew) which asserts the difference between North and South Britons (thus conflating Wales with England), Jery also declares that he can understand Scotland better because of his knowledge of Wales. He thus draws a parallel between his homeland and the 'alien' Scots, and therefore makes a distinction between himself and the English which destabilises his 'South British' identity: 'If I had never been in Wales, I should have been more struck with the manifest difference in appearance betwixt the peasants and commonalty on different sides of the Tweed' (p. 214). Despite the travellers' status as 'tourists', the Welsh parallels make Scotland familiar. Jery Melford continually familiarises Scotland through a Welsh lens. The West Highlands are huge and imposing, but 'this prospect is not at all surprising to a native of Glamorgan' (p. 238). He declares: 'everything I see, and hear, and feel, seems Welch – The mountains, vales, and streams; the air and climate; the beef, mutton, and game, are all Welch'

(p. 240). Moreover, there are cultural and linguistic similarities. When asked by Jery where he can find game, a Highlander replies "*hu niel Sassenagh*," which signifies *no English*: the very same answer I should have received from a Welchman, and almost in the same words' (p. 240). Even more striking is the fact that, like Matt Bramble, their landlord, 'our Highland chief', has two names: one English (Douglas Campbell) and one Scottish, the latter 'distinguished (like the Welch) by patronimics': 'Dou'l Mac-amish mac - 'oul ich-ian' (pp. 240–1).

The possession of two names is an obvious mark of a double identity, which can be divided, conflicted and contradictory in other more complex ways. On the one hand, for example, Matt Bramble can assert that 'the Scots would do well, for their own sakes, to adopt the English idioms' if they are to do well in 'South-Britain' (p. 231). On the other, his admiration for Scotland is predicated on his Welshness. He declares that the Highland air 'cannot have a bad effect upon a patient born and bred among the mountains of Wales' (p. 235). Similarly, in his debate with Lismahago about the 1707 Union, Bramble becomes the mouthpiece for pro-Union Anglo-British sentiment, with no apparent sense that Wales's loss of independence could mirror the experience of the Scots, not only in terms of sharing a 'weeping climate'. In a manner similar to the laments for the loss of Welsh independence after the Edwardian conquest, Lismahago unequivocally declares that 'the Scots were losers by the union' because 'They lost the independency of their state, the greatest prop of national spirit' (p. 277). In response, Bramble takes the 'English' side, pointing out that Scotland has, after all, gained a place in the parliament of Great Britain. He argues that 'by the union the Scots were admitted to all the privileges and immunities of English subjects' (p. 277). Bramble also expresses an explicitly colonial view of Scotland when he asserts the benefits of establishing a fishery in Scotland, adding 'Our people have a strange itch to colonize America, when the uncultivated parts of our own island might be settled to greater advantage' (p. 256). Whereas Matt makes an 'anti-colonial' case here for national self-sufficiency, the Scottish Lismahago makes the 'internal' colonial connection explicit by asking in whose interests such developments will be made. Of Scotland's usefulness to England, he remarks: 'that country is more valuable to her in the way of commerce, than any colony in her possession' (p. 279). At the end of their conversation Matt is at a loss as to how to answer Lismahago and it is the Scotsman who gets the last word, as well as the hand of Matt's sister, Tabitha, in marriage.

As a result of his debates with Lismahago, Bramble is forced to admit the truth of his opponent's assertions, and confesses that, 'I cannot help now acquiescing in his remarks so far as to think, that the contempt for Scotland, which prevails too much on this side of the Tweed, is founded on prejudice and error' (p. 279). Significantly, in the light of the scrutiny of his own prejudices in Scotland, when he returns to the other side of the Tweed he encounters English prejudice against the Welsh, in the shape of Lord Oxmington, who functions in broader terms as an example of bad hospitality. Despite Bramble's previous identification with the English (or 'South Britons') and his call to eradicate regional accents and dialects, he is immediately classed as 'the Welshman' by the peer. Even though they superficially resolve their quarrel, the national animosity remains. Jery reports that Lord Oxmington 'went away in some disorder' and is of the opinion that 'he will never invite another Welshman to his table' (p. 285). Similarly, although the novel ends conventionally with a series of intermarriages between Welsh, English and Scots which are suggestive of harmonious union, the smoothness of the ending does not contain the more conflicted (and realistic) elements of Bramble's experience. Although the Welsh detail of *Humphry Clinker* has not attracted much modern critical attention, it is clear that Smollett's novel was an important influence on those writers who attempted to narrate the nation from a more distinctly Welsh perspective, as I shall now demonstrate.

Anna Maria Bennett, *Anna; or, Memoirs of a Welch Heiress* (1785) and *Ellen, Countess of Castle Howell* (1794)

In his study of the changing fortunes of the gentry in Glamorganshire (Matt Bramble's original home-county), Philip Jenkins describes 'a violent caesura' in the usual demographic profile of the county which, after about 1720, changed the 'composition and character of the Welsh gentry'.[32] The 'demographic crisis' was a result of the failure of gentry families to produce heirs, and thus their tendency to die out in the male line.[33] This lack of heirs inevitably led to a glut of heiresses who, Jenkins observes, were more likely to marry Englishmen and therefore give over their estates to English families.[34] The overall result of such development was 'the creation of a new elite oriented not to the county, but to England, to London, to the central government'.[35] Linda Colley endorses Jenkins's calculations, and adds that,

> In Monmouthshire, between 1700 and 1780, there were thirty-one failures in the male line affecting ten estates; and in Glamorgan, only ten of the

thirty-one great estates were occupied in 1750 by heirs in the male line of the head of the family of fifty years before.[36]

Colley interprets this development as representing increased political and economic opportunities for the Celtic elite, who 'did not in the main sell out in the sense of becoming Anglicised look-alikes', but 'became British in a new and intensely profitable fashion'.[37] By contrast, although he is sceptical of applying Michael Hechter's model of internal colonialism wholesale to Wales (in that the term 'colonial' implies 'Anglicization through state action – unthinkable by the eighteenth century'), Jenkins nevertheless suggests that something corresponding to 'internal colonialism' did happen in Glamorgan in the eighteenth century as a result of integration with England. Although he stresses that this was a result of the 'demographic crisis' discussed above, Jenkins describes the resulting transformation of Wales in ways that do indeed comply with Hechter's model: the weakening of traditional communities, the growth of absentee landlordism, and the decline of hospitality, literary patronage and bardic customs, caused by the indifference or hostility of the English incomers.

Anna Maria Bennett's two novels on Wales-related topics engage directly with these broad transformations but, as I shall demonstrate, the individual novels (written nine years apart) yield very different responses. *Anna* (1785) appears to present a romanticised ideal of Welsh–British integration, which would uphold Colley's thesis of profitable integration. In contrast, *Ellen* (1794) paints a much more pessimistic picture of the cost of becoming British and the fundamental inequalities between 'provincial' Wales and 'metropolitan' England. *Anna* is a story of inheritance, where the orphaned Anna of the title discovers her true identity as a Welsh heiress and returns triumphantly to her Welsh estate, secure of her place in Wales as well as in the British Establishment. *Ellen*, by contrast, is a tale of threatened disinheritance. Although the later novel also ends in typical romance fashion, with the happy marriage of the hero and heroine, throughout the text Wales and its fragile culture are presented as imperilled by the forces of Anglicisation rather than enriched by association with a newly inclusive British identity.

Despite their status as light entertainment, Bennett's romances, with their emphasis on the feminocentric seduction tale and the sentimental marriage plot, are actually a very appropriate form for exploring issues of national inheritance. Indeed, as a result of the decline in male heirs, female heiresses became more powerful players on the national marriage market. As its title implies, *Anna; or, Memoirs of a Welch Heiress* specifically engages with these contemporary questions of family lineage and ancestral inheritance in a number of ways. On the level of plot, Anna's life-story clearly lends itself to an exploration of these themes. Anna is an orphan who is brought up by the unscrupulous Methodist, Mr Dalton, then adopted by the proud and wealthy Mrs Melmouth, who admires her beauty. She is then sent to live with the Mansels (Mrs Mansel is her former governess) in Wales, where she meets the Herberts and Edwins of Llandore Castle. At the end of the novel, after undergoing attempted seduction, hardship, poverty and labour, Anna is revealed as Lady Ann Trevannion (Lady Cecilia Edwin is Anna's aunt) and returns to Wales as the wife of Charles Herbert of Llandore. This is a classic 'rags to riches' Cinderella plot, one which Moira Dearnley deems as 'powerful' in its depiction of female vulnerability, but 'patently absurd' overall.[38] Absurd and formulaic it may have been, but such plots were very common in the eighteenth century and *Anna* in particular was one of the most popular novels of its time. The trope of the 'orphan nation' seems to have been of especial pertinence to Wales-related fiction. As Andrew Davies notes, 'Of the twenty Wales-related sentimental novels and novels of sensibility identified between 1780 and 1830, the majority have female central focalisers and almost all of these are socially displaced orphans'.[39] If these demographic changes are taken into account, it could be argued that Anna, and other female characters like her, represents the dispossessed 'indigenous feudal class' of Wales who are in the process of being replaced 'by a new class of English landowners'.[40]

At the end of the first volume of *Anna*, the aristocratic Lady Edwin displays the traditional way of asserting lineage and family worth: a proud genealogy which is exclusively Welsh and in whose interests nationality outweighs class and financial interests. Lady Edwin is 'as family mad as her father was': 'she would almost expire at the thought of either of her children's marrying into one, whose pedigree did not reach as far as from hence to Llandore'.[41] Lady Edwin's father, the Earl of Trevannion (therefore Anna's grandfather), is described as,

A nobleman so strictly attached to his country, that he never but once in his life left it, to visit the court of London, and that was on the marriage of the then Prince of Wales – He was descended in a regular line from

Llewellin, Prince of South Wales, and every marriage and intermarriage in
his line of ancestry, were among the descendants of some or other of the
ancient Cambrian heroes. (I, p. 232)

His daughter inherits the 'family pride' and Welsh loyalties. She is
charitable to people from all countries, but in terms of family and
estate she is firmly Welsh:

> In other matters, her servants, her tradesmen, even her cattle must be Welch;
> nay, so attached was she to the Cambrian stream in her veins, she would, as
> she often declared, rather have chose to marry her children to the peasants
> of her own wild hills, than to nobles of any other country. (I, p. 234)

Economic and marital fidelity to Wales equals prosperity, which could
be read as a Welsh version of 'English self-sufficiency'. Therefore,
despite the clichéd employment of the Welsh obsession with genealogy,
Bennett is clearly signalling that the Edwins are ideal traditional
landowners. Sir William Edwin – yet another literary reincarnation of
Sir Watkin Williams Wynn (third baronet) – manages his estate in such
a way that his tenants prosper rather than suffer:

> He was, by inheritance from father to son, knight of the shire; and so well
> was he beloved, that his name carried the numbers for the town and
> country where Dennis Place stood – Though urged very much, he would
> not give up his seat for his own shire, many, very many, felt the
> philanthropy of his soul. Though no person living (the prime minister for
> the time being excepted,) ever found an enemy in Sir William Edwin, he
> was a constant railer at taxes; not because he paid them, but because his
> friends did; the country party was sure of *him*. (I, p. 236)

Sir William is firmly associated here with the Tory-inflected country
squire figure, reminiscent also of Smollett's Matt Bramble. As a result
of the loyalty of the Edwins, their estate is a vision of 'perfect order',
a microcosm of a flourishing and self-sufficient Wales which would
seem further to echo Smollett's connection between national
prosperity and the well-managed estate at the end of *Humphry Clinker*:

> While the tenants of every estate round him had their rents raised, his
> grew affluent at their old prices; hence gratitude induced those who had
> leases, and interested those who had not, to keep in perfect order and
> repair their several domains; their stock not being obliged to be parted
> with, at the requisition of a needy or cruel landlord, were numerous and

thriving, and the brow of contented, chearful industry, graced the door of every farm on their estate. (I, pp. 236–7)

Lady Edwin, who has control of most of the finances, is careful to pay all her bills promptly: 'no tradesman or artificer were suffered to leave the house without prompt payment of their bills' (I, p. 237). In this way, effective management of the estate translates into public status as well as private wealth. Due to their economical control of their finances the Edwins can be both rich and charitable:

> The riches of the Edwins were exaggerated by the world: the oeconomy of their well-regulated expences enabled them to do so many benevolent and even magnificent things, and their payments of all kinds were so punctual, that, ample as was their fortune, fame doubled it: the antient and honourable house of Trevannion was likewise universally known and acknowledged. (III, p. 56)

What is advocated here is the presence of a Welsh ruling class which puts the interests of Wales first. As a result of this national loyalty, Bennett suggests, aristocratic family pride is maintained alongside and in conjunction with the well-being of the tenant farmers and the community at large. This is an ideal vision which is a more obviously Welsh version of Smollett's 'compensatory fantasy' of domestic harmony. Llandore itself operates in a similar way. Although struck at first by what she perceives to be the barrenness of the landscape, Anna is then overwhelmed by its 'picturesque and romantic qualities' which makes the valley like 'fairy land' (I, p. 207). Anna's four years spent in domestic security at 'dear Llandore' are remembered throughout her hardships in London as a time of 'peaceful serenity' (IV, p. 219), which contrasts with the violence and corruption of the metropolis.[42] In the section of the novel set in Wales, then, Bennett presents a case against British incorporation. In her portrait of the Edwin family, she dramatises Welsh prosperity as reliant upon proud independence. Moreover, in the character of Anna, Bennett draws a firm connection between birth and worth which further endorses Lady Edwin's world-view. When Anna's uncle, Mr Mordant, returns from Jamaica and reveals her true identity as the daughter of a Trevannion, he makes a direct link between 'greatness of soul' and 'hereditary rights of blood': 'You are yet ignorant of the rank you are entitled to; munificence and greatness of soul are the hereditary rights of your blood; and Providence has amply supplied you with the means of being respectable as well as rich' (III, p. 269). In presenting Anna as a version of Lady Edwin (sharing faults as well as virtues), Bennett suggests that the Welsh heiress will continue Lady Edwin's mode of living and uphold her loyalty to the 'Cambrian stream' in their blood.

The novel ends when the newly married Anna and Charles return to Wales, where they are greeted joyfully by their 'tenants and vassals': 'The real heiress of Trevannion was met by the tenants and vassals of her estate, and followed through two counties by the acclamations and unfeigned joy of the honest, unconquered, tho' uncultivated, Cambrians' (IV, pp. 269–70). Lady Edwin's world-view is finally vindicated: 'The noble heiress soon became the idol of her country; and Lady Edwin exulted in the revival of her family dignity' (IV, p. 271). Sir William's estate is entailed on Charles, now Lord Trevannion, whose 'family was as ancient and respectable as that of Trevannion, of which indeed it was a branch' (IV, p. 267). Therefore, Charles is, in fact, not only Anna's choice but fortuitously also 'him most suitable to her situation' (IV, p. 268). They are born for each other in a romantic sense and a genealogical one. However, as Jane Aaron has noted, the new Lord Trevannion has a more general function: to 'cure' Sir Edwin of his 'insular' Welsh pride and promote a more inclusive British outlook, with loyalty to the political establishment and monarchy: 'Lord Trevannion, by degrees, divested Sir William Edwin of his prejudices, and changed his opposition to the minister, into a patriotic zeal for the good of his country, and the honour of his prince, which he at length convinced him were synonymous terms' (IV, p. 279). Although Lord Trevannion does show a particular interest in the fortunes of Wales, his broader concern is 'the nation at large':

> Himself, a watchful and independent guardian of the privileges and benefits of the nation at large, and his own country in particular, not urged by prejudice, nor restrained by interested considerations, he either supported, or opposed, men and measures, as they appeared to have in view the general good.
> (IV, p. 279)

Bennett presents an ideal here where Welsh specificity is still recognised, but without narrow 'prejudice'. The novel ends with a vision of domestic bliss and British national unity:

> Blest with the full gratification of their wishes in the possession of each other, and happy in a beauteous offspring, surrounding, like olive

branches, their hospitable board, they yet live, and may they long do so,
adored by each other,
Venerated by their Children,
Esteemed by their Friends,
Beloved and honoured by their Country. (IV, p. 280)

Jane Aaron interprets the shift in loyalties from Lady Edwin's firm commitment to all things Welsh to the Anglo-British sympathies of the new Lord and Lady Trevannion as evidence that the Trevannion gentry have 'switched sides'.[43] The new Lord Trevannion has 'succeeded in persuading his uncle that English rule is both rightful and beneficial for Wales'.[44] In Aaron's view, the inheritance of the Trevannion estate by Anna and her husband signals the wider processes of the Anglicisation of the gentry and the ideological hegemony of England over the rest of the Welsh nation. In contrast to Colley's insistence on the profits of being British, Aaron highlights the losses sustained by the decline of the Welsh gentry, losses which Bennett smoothes over through her focus on the happy union of Charles and Anna. However, it is precisely the text's status as romantic fantasy which goes some way to mitigate this view of Bennett's work as pro-establishment and Anglocentred. Despite Charles's pro-British sympathies, he and the virtuous Anna are both of Welsh descent and even a branch of the same family. Through the figure of her Cinderella-style heroine, Bennett presents an anachronistic fantasy of Wales as able to uphold its traditions, despite having to adapt to a new order. The strain involved in maintaining this fantasy of national reconciliation is suggested, however, by the various stories of seduction and failed marriages on the margins of the novel. These stories could be seen as representing the real fortunes of prominent Welsh families in the eighteenth century and offer, in anticipation of *Ellen*, a much more pessimistic picture of British unions.

Lady Edwin has so much faith in her rank that she thinks the blood of the Trevannions will secure virtue in her children, but this only works in the security of the 'family mansion, and its environs' (IV, p. 267). The temptations of the world mean that the Edwin children disappoint the expectations of their parents. Unlike the orphan Anna, who remains untainted by the metropolis, the privileged Cecilia Edwin is Anglicised and corrupted by London society. The spoiled and unpleasant Cecilia, betrothed to her cousin Charles Herbert, the future husband of Anna, elopes instead with the 'wild and dissipated' (IV, p. 271) second son of an Irish peer, Captain Dunbar. After the elopement, Lady Edwin mourns 'the depravity of her children' (IV,

p. 259), while Cecilia writes a letter to her mother explaining her actions and offers a positive view of the mixing of national bloodlines: 'the truth is, our blood has from generation to generation, by flowing in the same regular channel, at last wearied itself by its own sameness, and Mr. Dunbar assures me, *his* is no less respectable; so that a little change will be an advantage to both' (IV, p. 266). Such sentiments, which might be interpreted as British and pro-union in response to the views of Lady Edwin, are not supported by the overall message of the novel, however. Cecilia, the 'other' Welsh heiress, is clearly a negative character, whereas Anna (faithfully and chastely waiting for her Welsh husband) is the virtuous ideal.

The tension between idealism and reality which causes much of the textual inconsistency in *Anna* comes to the surface in Bennett's second novel on Welsh themes: *Ellen, Countess of Castle Howell*. If *Anna* ends with an ideal but precarious vision of Welsh–British coexistence, *Ellen* presents a more realistic picture of the fortunes of Wales in late eighteenth-century Britain. This novel is much more preoccupied with the loss of traditional Welsh culture than *Anna* and less romantic in its depiction of the marriage(s) of its Welsh heroine. Like all the fictions discussed in this chapter, the country estate plays a key symbolic role. *Ellen* opens with the description of the Merediths' estate, Code Gwyn, a 'large Gothic mansion' in the 'brown mountains of North Wales'.[45] The military background of the mansion is highlighted, as Bennett draws attention to its origins as a fort with 'turrets' and the 'nodding ruins' of four towers, separated from the mountain by 'an ancient stone bridge, the scene of many a bloody fray, when the gallant ancestors of the present family maintained their right against the inroads of the mountaineers' (I, p. 2).[46] The 'spacious hall' (I, p. 3), an important trope in the poetry of eighteenth-century Welsh writers, is the focus for the continuation of ancient tradition and faithful family retainers who congregate there:

> The hall appeared to be the bond of union between the heads of the family and the domestics – there the harper had his seat, and there the avocations and labours of the day constantly closed with a dance, in which all the younger part of the inmates mingled, without a frown on the brow of pride, or presumption in the bosom of poverty. (I, p. 3)

Despite this positive vision of traditional culture located in the ancestral hall, there is an overall sense of decay and decline, a sense that this culture can no longer sustain itself. As Francesca Rhydderch has argued, the figure of Sir Arthur Meredith, Ellen's grandfather, embodies and symbolises the decline of Welsh manhood and culture. He is in his seventies and 'apparently robust', but gout and 'chronic disease . . . made the use of a wheel-chair necessary' (I, p. 4).[47] In contrast to the physical and symbolic regeneration of Matt Bramble as a result of his travels by the end of *Humphry Clinker*, Sir Meredith is both static and moribund. Whereas Smollett could use an imagined Wales as an ideal fantasy of 'rural patriarchy' based on 'the mutual dependency of lord and retainer in the old feudal system', Bennett's representation of the Welsh estate is starkly realistic.[48] Lady Meredith is typical of the Welsh aristocracy in that she is the heiress of 'a noble Welch family, whose dignity far exceeded their wealth' (I, p. 4). The family have lived in the same way for generations, which means that they have never raised the rents. In stark contrast to the Edwins in *Anna*, however, this mode of living results in the potential obliteration of the family, rather than self-sufficient prosperity. Whereas the Edwins succeed in being faithful to all things Cambrian as well as fair to their tenants, the Merediths face extinction, due to what is presented as financial ineptitude: the tenants 'had grown into opulence, as their generous landlord, insensibly, became involved in difficulties' (I, p. 7). Bennett calls their approach 'supine negligence' (I, p. 159). As a result of the lack of proper financial management, the estate is in serious debt and the mortgages have been passed into the hands of a rich neighbour, John Morgan, whose sole aim in life is to reduce the family to ruin, as revenge for the suspected seduction of his late daughter by Sir Arthur's son, Edmund Meredith; a motive which is not revealed until the end of the novel. Whereas the pride of Lady Edwin in *Anna* strengthens the estate, Sir Arthur's pride fuels Morgan's anger further and therefore weakens Code Gwyn. Edmund is genuinely in love with Morgan's daughter, but 'Sir Arthur would not hear of a connection so degrading, notwithstanding the immense wealth of her father, and *his* views were much higher for his daughter' (I, p. 152). Edmund agrees, as he has 'inherited their pride of blood' (I, p. 152). Mr Morgan never forgives Sir Arthur and the Merediths. He also realises that their pride of blood no longer works in the new world of wealth: Mr Morgan 'knew enough of the world to be certain his daughter with 80,000l. would be received into families, whose blood might be traced up to the Conqueror, though the poor proud Code Gwyn family had the impertinence to remember his living in the hovel in which he was born' (I, p. 153). The choice the Merediths have to make is between being poor, proud and extinct, and marrying new wealth and surviving. This might be profit of a kind, but one inevitably steeped in loss. The ambivalence with which Bennett treats the class issues at stake in the decline of Code Gwyn typify what Katie Trumpener has identified as a common treatment of 'dispossession' in works of eighteenth-century cultural nationalism. Laments for the dispossession of the Meredith estate could, on the one hand, indicate a radical critique of property. However, from another perspective, and this is certainly true of *Ellen*, 'such laments often reflect not so much concern for tenant farmers as nostalgia for feudal privilege and a lost indigenous aristocratic culture'.[49]

The plot of *Ellen* revolves around the survival of Code Gwyn and its way of life. Ellen herself is another beautiful orphan, granddaughter of the Merediths, and it is her 'worth' as a marriage partner that is seen as the route to the survival of Code Gwyn. When Sir Meredith finally realises the extent and consequences of his debts to John Morgan, it is suggested that Ellen marry the neighbouring lord of Castle Howell, who, in return for this 'sacrifice' (I, p. 176), will pay off Code Gwyn's debts. At first Ellen refuses, but the family put pressure on her. Edmund writes a letter imagining the effect of her not marrying Lord Castle Howell: 'And the old Harper must have gone to the parish, and that, as he says, would be a sad thing for a man who had laced cloaths and played before my grandpapa's father, when he was knight of the shire' (I, p. 164).

Edmund plays on precisely the kind of longing for 'the hierarchal stability of a feudal past' which Trumpener describes as constitutive of bardic nationalism: the harper is, of course, a symbol of feudal loyalty, and the 'knight of the shire' echoes the Tory nostalgia of *Humphry Clinker*.[50] However, the survival of Code Gwyn is at the cost of Ellen's freedom and own inclination: she is in love with the apparently penniless pupil of her brother, Percy Evelyn (whom she marries at the end of the novel after he is revealed to be the rich son of John Morgan's daughter and one Lord Claverton, who throughout the novel has actually been in pursuit of Ellen himself).[51] By marrying Lord Castle Howell, Ellen will also save Castle Howell itself, as, due to the lack of an heir, it would automatically fall to the 'descendants from a second son', who is described as a libertine married privately to 'an artful and low-bred woman' (I, p. 118). It is not the passing of estates to English hands, but class anxiety which is represented as the major evil resulting from the lack of male heirs to inherit Welsh estates: 'the children of this low union were the presumptive heirs of Castle Howell' (I, p. 118).

However, although Bennett may seem to have hit on a perfect solution for national regeneration – the poor and ailing Code Gwyn being joined to the richer and stronger Castle Howell – the marriage of Ellen and Lord Castle Howell does not secure the harmonious union of two great Welsh houses. Instead, the marriage precipitates a sequence of events which not only threaten Ellen's reputation but almost lead to the disinheritance of her whole family line.

The disinheritance plot is driven by Ellen's transformation from a child of nature warbling Welsh airs in the mountains, playing the harp by ear and galloping bareback, to an educated and Anglicised young lady of fashion who is being shaped to fulfil her role as Countess of Castle Howell. Although admiring of Ellen's 'native graces' (I, p. 55), Lord Castle Howell also expresses concern as to 'her deficiencies in modern accomplishments' (I, p. 55), summarised as 'skills in music, drawing, reciting different languages and fine works' (I, p. 96). Accordingly, Ellen is sent away to boarding school in Bath and is shocked into a realisation of her own provincial 'inadequacies': she

> was confounded to see ladies, much younger than herself, perfect mistresses of accomplishments, for which she had but just begun to acquire a taste; comparing herself with her new associates, how ignorant, how contemptible did she appear. (I, p. 96)
>
> . . .
>
> The truth is, that though Ellen approached as near perfection as most heroines of her age, yet she certainly had a Welch accent, which, to the refined ears of Mrs Forrest [her teacher], and her ladies, sounded a little uncouth. (I, p. 97)

Jane Aaron has emphasised the national implications of Ellen's education and socialisation into fashionable English norms of femininity. She reads Ellen's relinquishing of her Welsh accent as a symbol of the painful process of Anglicisation.[52] For example, Ellen has to be separated from Winifred, her loyal Welsh maid, one of the faithful family retainers at Code Gwyn. This is because of Winifred's language, which, as a 'barbarous jargon of neither Welch nor English, but a bad mixture of both' (I, p. 97), threatens to stall Ellen's education and 'improvement'.[53] As Jane Aaron comments,

> It is in this kind of detailing, of processes one knows must have happened and of the complicated pain they involved, that makes up much of the interest of these texts for me. Ellen is made to feel ashamed of her

Welshness, while at the same time she does grieve over the estrangement from kinsmen which the espousal of English values entails. Saving Code Gwyn materially seems to mean, in that contemporary climate, betraying it culturally.[54]

On one level, the first volume of *Ellen* presents a nostalgic vision of the feudal Welsh past, centring on the figure of the harper as a symbol of traditional values and culture. The harper functions as a register for the fortunes of Code Gwyn as well as symbolising traditional culture. His demise was used as a threat to make Ellen marry Castle Howell, but there is an inevitable sense that he would have disappeared anyway. Despite the sentiment surrounding the harper, it is implied that Code Gwyn is too cut off from society and too backward-looking in its ways to flourish. Yet, like Smollett, Bennett also employs the idea of London as the seat of vice and Wales as symbolically virtuous: London and metropolitan standards are increasingly criticised as the novel progresses, just as Ellen gets physically weaker the more Anglicised she becomes. In the second volume a disgraced Ellen, who, due to her behaviour at the gaming table, is suspected of adultery by high society (she lets Lord Claverton pay her gambling debts), roams around England trying to find a safe place to have her child (Lord Castle Howell's heir). She is accompanied throughout by the faithful Welsh maid Winifred Griffiths, who puts all their sufferings down to the fact that they left Wales in the first place. She opines that 'the tivel's cloven foot covers all Englant I believe' (II, p. 48). Code Gwyn has also been further destroyed by Ellen's 'corruption' in the metropolis. Ellen's mother has since died of grief when hearing of Ellen's supposed disgrace, and as a result Code Gwyn's contented community of family and servants is shattered: 'even the loud and cheerful mirth, which used to echo in the servants hall was changed into gloomy whispers, and the harper's occupation was over' (II, p. 82). As a result, Ellen is exiled from her homeland. Lord Castle Howell realises his wife's innocence, but shortly after their reunion is killed by a fall from his horse, and it becomes apparent that he was in debt. A lawsuit is then brought against Ellen, for trying 'to pass a surreptitious heir on the world', by one of the low-bred Howells – Walter of Moor Bank (II, p. 152). Ellen and Winifred return to Wales as Ellen's innocence is proved, but the Castle Howell estate is deserted and everyone has been turned out of Code Gwyn by John Morgan.

Predictably, the novel ends with the restoration of Ellen's fortune and the happy marriage of Ellen and Percy Evelyn, who is revealed to be the son of Lord Claverton and John Morgan's daughter Elizabeth. As they approach the estate on their homecoming, Ellen and Winifred meet a crowd on the road which includes the harper of Code Gwyn, 'blind and lame, led by a grandson of the coachman's' (II, p. 172). The blindness and lameness of the harper symbolise the decline of the feudal past which must now give way to the modernising present. Due to their change of fortune, Ellen and her husband (whose real name is Horatio) are able to restore Code Gwyn. The mansion undergoes 'a complete repair, when Horatio and Ellen attended the house-warming, and the whole parish, rich as well as poor, commemorated the return of Sir Arthur, and his family to the place of their nativity' (II, p. 288). Although, like the harper, 'lame and almost blind', Mr and Mrs Griffiths return as butler and housekeeper. Despite this idealistic vision of repair and continuity, it is clear that the Countess and the 'Right Reverend Bishop Claverton', her husband, will not live at Code Gwyn. They return for the house-warming, but live in the 'polite world' of London, where Ellen's parties and her taste are 'the rage' amongst the fashionable world (II, p. 291). As a bishop, Horatio preaches before royalty, and Bennett manages a compliment to Queen Charlotte as the 'strangest character, ever heard of, A good wife, a tender mother, a sincere friend, a queen, and a Christian!' (II, p. 291). However, despite this overt praise of the British monarchy, the narrative voice at the end of this novel reveals a bitterness not present in the more romantic ending of *Anna*. Although Ellen and Horatio are one of the most admired couples 'in the most flourishing Kingdom, of the most enlightened World' (II, p. 292), it is suggested that other frailties are hidden under 'the impenetrable veil of IMMENSE RICHES' (II, p. 292). Indeed, the world in which the couple live at the end of the novel is precisely the fashionable urban world which has been criticised throughout the novel.

Although both are obviously romances, these two novels offer two quite different views of Wales's place in Britain in the late eighteenth century. Anna can initially be interpreted as a figure for Wales, orphaned by the loss of its gentry class and aristocracy. However, through the inheritance plot, whereby Anna is revealed as an heiress, Bennett dramatises a semi-reversal of the actual social forces described by Philip Jenkins, as the stories of cross-border marriages are pushed to the margins of the text. Anna receives an English education, but also learns Welsh when she lives in Llandore with Mrs Mansel. Although Anna only learns Welsh to be the interpreter of the poor, it is nevertheless the case that at the end of the novel the heroine who returns to Wales as the wife of a Welsh husband can also speak Welsh.[55] Significantly, in regard to Jane Aaron's arguments about international marriages as a form of national seduction of Wales by England, Anna resists all attempts at seduction until she can be united with her first love.[56] This is not to say that Bennett's vision is necessarily a radical one for Wales, in that she is arguing for a rejection of English values in favour of a separate Wales. Rather, this is a fantasy that one can be both Welsh and British with no losses involved, only profit and harmony for all concerned. *Ellen* punctures the British–Welsh unionist fantasy of *Anna*. In a reversal of Anna's fortunes, Ellen has to lose her Welsh accent to be accepted into English society. All the old retainers of Code Gwyn are lame and almost blind at the end of the novel, despite the material restoration of the mansion itself. The new union of Percy/Horatio and Ellen is London-based and a mix of new money with the blood of the English peerage. Whereas *Anna* is a novel about rightful inheritance being recognised, *Ellen* is concerned with the threat of disinheritance, not only of Ellen's son but of Wales's gentry class as a whole. In this context, although nostalgia is expressed for the feudal past of 'Ancient Britain', the continuation of this past is seen as untenable. *Anna* ends on a note of romantic optimism; *Ellen* closes with a note of pessimistic and bitter regret, but offers no solution. In many ways, then, the vision of Wales in *Anna* is no longer sustainable, even under the veil of romance. Bennett's more open-eyed account in *Ellen* presents a realistic account of what actually happened in eighteenth-century Wales as a result of 'happy unions', both marital and national.

Edward Davies, *Elisa Powell, or, Trials of Sensibility* (1795)

Given the author's natal identity and the antiquarian themes addressed in the text, *Elisa Powell* would seem to represent a bridge between the antiquarian concerns of eighteenth-century Welsh poetry and the novel. Throughout his life, Edward 'Celtic' Davies was passionately involved in antiquarian activity, shown by the publication of his *Celtic Researches* (1804) and *The Mythology and Rites of the British Druids* (1809). He was also a creative writer who, in addition to his one novel, produced two volumes of poems.[57] Like John Walters, he also attempted metrical English translations of both ancient Welsh poetry and the work of Dafydd ap Gwilym, samples of which he sent to the Gwyneddigion Society in 1791 and reprinted in *Elisa Powell*.[58] Davies was born in Wales (Llanfaredd in Radnorshire), but spent the majority of his life in Chipping Sodbury in Gloucestershire, as the master of the grammar school there. English was his first language, although he taught himself Welsh later in life. Therefore, as Moira Dearnley notes, his was in many ways the archetypal Anglo-Welsh experience, shaped by 'the loss of Welsh as his first language and his long exile in England'.[59] To some extent, Davies's personal circumstances are reflected in *Elisa Powell*: the antiquarian touches, the insertion of bardic poetry, and the device of the English 'outsider' as the main narrative voice. As such, it has been argued that the novel has a claim to be the 'first Anglo-Welsh novel'.[60] Yet, as Edward Davies discovered, the concerns of antiquarianism and Welsh bardic nationalism do not easily fit the generic frame of eighteenth-century fiction. Just as Anna Maria Bennett's use of a romance formula adds a set of generic limitations to her exploration of Welsh identity in a British context, Davies's text is as much a conventional novel of sensibility as it is a book which explores Welsh culture and the Anglo-Welsh predicament.

Elisa Powell is interesting precisely because of its exceptionality. Dearnley argues that this distinctiveness 'lies mainly in his [Davies's] handling of native culture – rare if not unique as subject matter in the eighteenth-century novel'.[61] *Elisa Powell* follows *Humphry Clinker* in its epistolary form but, in contrast to Smollett, Davies sets his fiction in Wales and changes the nationality of the main protagonist. Although the novel is advertised on the title-page as written in a series of letters 'collected by a Welsh curate', the bulk of the letters are written by an Englishman, Revd Henry Stanley, who has come to Wales to take up an estate in Builth Wells and who eventually falls in love with the titular Elisa Powell. Through his use of Stanley as the primary focal point, Davies presents the reader with an outsider's view of Wales, which owes much to tourist accounts of the period. Stanley is also, of course, an example of the appropriation of Welsh estates by the English. The novel begins with Stanley's first impressions of his new home, where his eye roves over the hills and 'waving woods' to the 'dusky, brown-peaked mountains, which at a solemn distance, mix with the mellow shades of the horizon'.[62] The reference point is self-confessedly the 'tours' of Henry Wyndham and William Gilpin: 'You may recollect that we have admired the landscapes of the principality, as exhibited to us in the tours of Wyndham, Gilpin and others' (I, p. 3). However, this is not wild Wales, but a 'chaste and delicate' landscape which will provide 'a delicious feast for the lover of nature!' (I, p. 4). Stanley's appreciation of the landscape here is primarily proprietary, as it serves as an introduction to his description of his estate, which 'embraces the banks of the Wye, and thence runs up a winding valley, well wooded, and watered by a pretty brook' (I, p. 4). Like Matt Bramble, Stanley focuses particularly on the pursuits of the country gentleman: 'rural sports' and 'a variety of game' (I, p. 5). The tourist's view of Wales is continued in Stanley's various excursions, where he delights in the 'highly picturesque scenery' (I, p. 25) and voyeuristically gawps at the 'fair CambroBritons' wearing 'deep beaver hats' in the pump-room, describing himself as 'a straggling Englishman' who fails to attract the notice of the Welsh. So far, it would seem that Davies is merely presenting Wales to the reader as a pleasant tourist attraction through voyeuristic English eyes.

Despite the tourist perspective and the recognisably Horatian construction of the Welsh country estate and rural life as self-sufficient and innocently pleasing (we see Smollett's influence again here), Davies introduces practical elements to Stanley's new venture as well as an ironic treatment of Stanley himself. Indeed, far from a complete identification with Stanley as an outsider figure, Davies often treats his protagonist with palpable ironic distance, which has relevance for his depiction of Wales and Welsh identity in the novel. From the outset, Stanley conveys the economic value of his estate, which comprises four farms and brings in '500*l.* per annum', which will place him 'in a respectable rank among the freeholders of Brecknockshire' (I, p. 4). In the second letter, Stanley describes his first meeting with the farmers whose leases were due to expire. Stanley debates the rent with them in his guise of 'landlord', where he is persuaded by the 'manly candour' of Mr Thomas, one of the farmers, to limit the rent increase to building a couple of rooms and stables on the land. As a result, Stanley and his farmers, who, apart from the persuasive Mr Thomas, speak only 'broken English' (I, p. 11), part on good terms. As ever, Stanley is quick to congratulate himself on his behaviour and the efficient running of his estate, which he plans to steward himself: 'What man, that has a competency, could purchase more real pleasure for fifty pounds a year, than shall I enjoy by seeing my estate in good condition, and securing the comfort of four industrious, worthy families?' (I, pp. 12–13). Despite his initial enthusiasm in aping the role of the paternal feudal landowner, Stanley's interest in business and agricultural management soon pales, as does his effusive appreciation of rural retirement. He begins by again congratulating himself that he has discovered 'the haunt of Happiness, that modest nymph who saunters in the rural shades and shuns the noise and bustle of the great world' (I, p. 20). His references to metropolitan centres like Bath are couched in terms of his virtuous rejection of corrupt luxury and fashionable affectation (Smollett again). Yet most of his afternoons are spent roaming the countryside rather aimlessly, as he soon discovers it can be a lonely place. He quickly admits that 'The delirium was of short duration' (I, p. 20) on having 'discovered that the place is no thoroughfare' and 'thinly inhabited by gentlemen' (I, p. 20). His discontentment is broken by meeting 'a brother sportsman' in the figure of the 'Brecknock attorney' Watkins (I, p. 27), but it is only on the arrival of the beautiful yet melancholy Elisa from Pembrokeshire that Stanley finally perks up and recasts himself as a doomed romantic lover. On one level, then, Wales might be said to function in this text in a manner similar to that found in *Humphry Clinker*: as a microcosm of the ideal nation, with the association of the Tory-inflected figure of the Anglicised country gentleman or squire with the well-run estate/nation.

The ironic treatment of Stanley as an overly idealistic yet ineffectual proponent of this image punctures its efficacy, however, and suggests that the reality is much more complex. It can be argued that in much of volume I of the novel, Davies concerns himself with the realities of eighteenth-century Wales and the negative processes of Anglicisation. Stanley is not treated entirely unsympathetically in this respect. In his role as participating observer the lessons he learns can be shared by the reader. One example is when he rides past 'a neat villa' and asks a passing 'countryman' if it is the residence of a gentleman. The man replies, '"A gentleman! No, sir, 'tis nothing but an Englishman"' (I, p. 21). Although Stanley initially laughs, he is forced to reconsider his reaction with the following reflection, which has echoes of Matt Bramble's debate over the Union with Lismahago in *Humphry Clinker*:

> Five centuries ago we Englishmen robbed the Welch of their national independence. In defence of it, they had valiantly fought, seven hundred campaigns: at last they were compelled to yield it up; but it was resigned with indignant, haughty submission. They have never forgiven us; and, at this present day, I sojourn among them – 'nothing but an Englishman'. (I, pp. 21–2)

Stanley's outsider status and naivety in some ways mean he can be (unintentionally) revealing. He realises, for instance, that although the

gentry are thoroughly (if reluctantly) Anglicised, the general populace
of Wales remains staunchly national:

> The gentlemen of the principality have, indeed, in a great measure,
> forgotten their nationality, and now enlist, with a tolerable grace, under
> the banner of their conquerors; but the populace still retain sufficient
> greatness of mind to contemn a refinement, which they consider as the
> badge of slavery, and to glory in their descent from the ancient Britons.
> (I, p. 22)

As a result of his encounter, Stanley is brought to consider the nature
of liberty. Like Matt Bramble again, he vacillates in his opinion of
conquest and union. On the one hand, he puts forward the economic
view that the Welsh are in fact 'much better secured' in material terms
than under 'their native princes' (I, p. 22). Thus, their resentment can
be seen as merely 'an imaginary yoke' (I, p. 23). Yet on the other hand,
he is forced to admit that 'Liberty must be something necessary to the
composition of human happiness . . . the loss of which for ever debases
the man in his own esteem' (I, p. 23). Stanley concludes with an implicit
understanding of the Welsh experience, that liberty is 'a gift from
heaven', only removed by 'the lust of conquest and dominion which, in
all ages, has filled the world with misery' (I, p. 23). In effect, through
his use of Stanley as a naive yet sympathetic observer, Davies forcefully
yet subtly makes the point about the pain and misery of the English
conquest of Wales. In this respect, the text differs sharply from
Smollett's use of Wales as an ideal neutral space in *Humphry Clinker*.

The novel addresses other matters of political import to Wales, most
markedly issues concerning absentee landlordism, the politics of
enclosure, the treatment of the poor, and related subjects familiar to
reader of *Humphry Clinker*: the ills of commerce, luxury and
colonialism. Halfway through volume I, Stanley relates a conversation
between Mr Powell and Dr Isaac Pemberton (an antiquarian friend of
Stanley's) concerning enclosure, which again recalls the debates
rehearsed between Matt Bramble and Lismahago. A local Welsh
freeholder, Mr Jones, is involved in a scheme to enclose the common
ground. Mr Powell views this action as robbing 'the poor of their
privilege of common' (I, p. 114). Dr Pemberton, however, is of the view
that waste land made the position of the common people worse.
Stanley remarks that a similar view was expressed to him by an English
farmer, who said this was particularly true of Wales. When asked by
the doctor why Wales was singled out, Stanley relates the man's

opinion: "'Here, in England," said he, "the very summits of the hills are cultivated and rendered fruitful; whereas, in Wales, they are suffered to remain wild and desolate, to the disgrace of the inhabitants, and the perpetuity of their proverbial poverty'" (I, p. 115).

The doctor responds with an extensive harangue on the subject of national agriculture, where each nation has deep-rooted 'prejudice in favour of long-established custom' (I, p. 116). He concludes that both England and Wales would benefit from enclosure, to provoke the idle poor to industry and remove the need for colonisation of other lands. Mr Powell is persuaded that enclosure may be a good thing, but 'doubts whether any plan of economy could relieve us from a burdensome poor, unless the government could, now and then, detach a superfluous half million of inhabitants, to colonise some unoccupied lands' (I, p. 127). Dr Pemberton realises the irony of this statement from a fellow Welshman, and declares that they are already losing from colonial expansion: 'we are now sufferers by the bad policy of our ancestors, in ablegating [*sic*] their poor to till the wilds of America; and maintaining them there at an enormous expense, while so much remained to be done at home' (p. 128). Although Mr Powell suggests that 'the colonisation of distant provinces generally included some commercial interest' for England, Dr Pemberton continues to argue that if agriculture is managed properly to support the nation, then 'commerce can claim but a secondary importance' (I, p. 130). Commerce, suggests Pemberton, mostly produces only luxurious excess, which allures people into 'a labyrinth of luxury' (I, p. 132), whereas 'ambitious agriculture . . . strengthens, domesticates, and unites the people' (I, p. 133). Only when agriculture is perfected, yet found still not to be sufficient, Pemberton concludes, can colonisation be justified.

It is significant that this critique of colonisation and imperial warfare comes from the mouth of the Welsh antiquarian Dr Pemberton who, throughout the text, is occupied in a search for the grave of Llewelyn, the last prince of Wales, whose downfall at the hands of Edward I ended Welsh national independence. Dr Pemberton had been taught both Welsh and the veneration of ancient culture and artefacts by his grandmother, and his youthful interest in coins has blossomed into antiquarian passion: he exits the text on a trip to Ireland to locate a copy of 'Aneurin's Gododin [*sic*], the most ancient British poem now extant' which he must have 'at any price' (II, p. 152). This quest is described by Stanley as his friend's 'golden dream'

(II, p. 154). However, although Dr Pemberton is a well-liked old friend, Stanley is frequently exasperated by him, and Pemberton often appears as a 'figure of fun' rather than veneration.[63] Watkins inadvertently bumps into him and thinks he is a giant: 'I had just time to observe an enormous pair of boots, a brown cloak that would have covered a haystack, and a huge umbrella mounted upon a pole as long and as large as one of Cromwell's pikestaves' (I, p. 38). Moira Dearnley suggests that Pemberton is Davies's attempt at 'personifying the recovery of Welsh history in the eighteenth century' (I, p. 164). She suggests that his giant size symbolises 'the absurd and unwieldy nature of his own [Davies's] grand obsession' (I, p. 166). As such, Pemberton serves as an uneasy 'alter ego' for Davies, one which is 'riven with self-doubt' (I, p. 165) and exposes antiquarianism to satirical scrutiny. Yet it is the Anglicised Welshman, Watkins, who has no idea of the significance of Llewelyn's grave, who describes Pemberton in this way, and it is only the easily bored Stanley who finds Pemberton tedious at times. Rather than trying to read the novel for forms of self-expression on Davies's part, it may be more fruitful to consider the representation of Dr Pemberton as mediated through Anglicised characters. Davies is perhaps suggesting that antiquarian concerns are increasingly seen as outdated and eccentric from an English perspective, but this does not necessarily reflect his own position or views. Indeed, on many other occasions in the text Pemberton's voice is one of authority, knowledge and wisdom. Nevertheless, it is clear that his presence in what becomes a novel of sensibility becomes untenable and, as Andrew Davies argues, he is 'airbrushed' out of the novel's conclusion.

Edward Davies's inclusion of a contemporary representation of a Welsh bard adds to the novel's originality, but a similar ambivalence is present in the portrait of Morgan ap Dewi, the 'celebrated harpist' (I, p. 167).[64] Tellingly, Davies narrates the journey to visit ap Dewi through the eyes of Stanley, who is characteristically full of stereotypical cultural expectations. Stanley describes the journey to ap Dewi's cottage as taking place through 'naked crags, gloomy woods and solitary glens' (I, p. 181). He is slightly taken aback when they see 'a neat white cottage', where the housekeeper informs them rather bathetically that 'this Cambrian Ossian' (Stanley's phrase) has gone to play his harp at a farmer's wedding (I, p. 181). The first view of the bard is similarly bathetic. Unlike the harper in Bennett's *Ellen*, who simply moulders away, ap Dewi has lost an eye and a leg in the American war of Independence, after leaving Wales for London as a result of being jilted by his mistress. Like many a countryman before him, ap Dewi is tricked into enlisting into the army (for three guineas), and ends up at the battle of Bunker Hill in Charleston, Massachusetts (17 June 1775), where the British suffered major casualties despite their overall victory. As a result of his injuries, ap Dewi is pensioned out of the army and makes his living by performing at various social occasions. Like Pemberton, ap Dewi is a figure of both sympathy and ridicule. As Dearnley notes, his epithalamium is mostly doggerel and his function is to entertain, not to express patriotic loyalty to Wales. However, Davies appears to be satirising English expectations of what the 'Cambrian Ossian' should be, rather than the bard himself. It is, after all, Stanley who again narrates the episode, and it is the gap between his expectations and the reality of the hardship of the bard's life which Davies exposes. Given the previous condemnation of overseas warfare and colonisation, it is also significant that ap Dewi is wounded in a war which has absolutely no gains for him personally and in which his valour is rewarded with physical mutilation. As such, *Elisa Powell* can be read in terms of the 'plot of cultural comparison' between Britain and her colonies which Katie Trumpener identifies as common to Romantic fiction. The mutilated body of ap Dewi thus functions as an implicit critique of empire, as he is a victim of the imperial violence which contrasts so dramatically with the 'protected . . . Welsh domesticity' that the novel dramatises elsewhere.[65]

Despite its potential as an Anglo-Welsh novel which deals with the state of the British nation from a Welsh perspective, *Elisa Powell* is read by both Dearnley and Davies as ultimately unsuccessful in its attempt to import bardic nationalism into the novel. Andrew Davies concludes that as the novel develops it drops its cultural and antiquarian interest and is principally concerned with the sentimental story of Elisa herself. Similarly, Moira Dearnley argues that Davies not only 'failed to produce an adequate fiction written at the interface of two cultures', but also failed to write well in the sentimental mode.[66] The second volume of *Elisa Powell* does indeed deal primarily with the sentimental decline of Elisa as a result of attempted rape and the deaths in her family. Stanley's role in relation to Elisa is as a 'man of feeling' who is drawn to her precisely because of, not despite, her sorrow and suffering. He soon gives up his pretensions to be a gentleman farmer and spends the rest of the novel swooning after Elisa. Given his status as a man of feeling, it is no surprise that Stanley engages in charitable acts: namely the relief of Sally Grifford, new mother of twins, whose Scottish husband has been press-ganged into land service as a soldier while in Bristol on business, mirroring the fate of Morgan ap Dewi. Despite the primary function of this story to exhibit Stanley's charitable nature to Elisa, this episode also reveals the brutal reality of eighteenth-century life. Sally's husband is pushed into the army to fight for Britain, yet as a Scotsman's widow she is not eligible for poor relief and is set for starvation and eviction until Stanley steps in. Similarly, although the story about the vivacious Maria Jones and her almost-rape by the son of a rich nabob is ultimately comic (she holds him up at gunpoint), it also reveals anxieties about the destruction of social stability as a result of imperial expansion and colonial gain. Therefore, although the national focus loses momentum, episodes like these continue to puncture and unsettle the sentimental plot.

Although perceived as a weakness, part of the uniqueness of *Elisa Powell* is precisely its status as a sentimental novel set in Wales with a sentimental Welsh heroine. Despite Stanley's expectations, in Wales he meets with civilised beauty and sensibility. Elisa herself is the product of a Welsh estate in Pembrokeshire and appeals to Stanley not only because of her attractively sorrowful mien, but also because of her cultivated taste. This taste is shown by her drawing-room:

> It was furnished with chairs, and hung with landscapes and figures of her own drawing, and needlework. It contained her own little library; a collection of moral essays, some volumes of popular sermons, about half a dozen of our best novels, a few chosen plays, and two or three of our most elegant poets, beside some music and French books. (I, p. 251)

Although she does play the Welsh harp, Elisa shows no other national characteristics. Her reading is conventional for a woman of her class, and we can be sure that the 'elegant poets' are not of Dr Pemberton's choosing. The problems facing Davies here are those of gender as well as genre. To write a novel which was attractive to sentimental tastes he had to create a heroine worthy of the genre and one who also complied with metropolitan and English expectations of feminine accomplishment. As I have shown, these expectations also inform the fiction of Anna Maria Bennett. Elisa has to be Anglicised in order to function as a sentimental heroine and attract the love of Stanley. As a result, Welsh cultural nationalism cannot be expressed in a genre which relies on feminine sensibility rather than heroic valour. This gendering of national characteristics also applies to Stanley, as his attempts to pursue a 'manly' (I, p. 109) career in farming give way to the stereotypical English sentimental lover, feminised and immobilised in 'listless apathy' (I, p. 93) by his excess of sensibility and idleness. As soon as he falls in love he is estranged from his idealistic pursuit of virtuous self-sufficiency. The national experiment of an Englishman becoming successfully naturalised in Wales (as opposed to colonising it) fails. Indeed, Stanley could not fulfil the generic and gendered expectations of the eighteenth-century novel of sensibility if he had succeeded in becoming a prosperous Welsh freeholder.

Such a reading of the novel ignores the role played by Maria Jones, however. In comparison to the rapidly fading Elisa, the real Welsh heroine of this novel is the feisty Maria, who sings the songs of Dafydd ap Gwilym (via Iolo Morganwg) and holds pistols to her abductor's head as well as constantly teasing the fastidious Stanley and her erstwhile suitor, Watkins. According to the generic rules of the sentimental novel, Maria cannot be the 'proper' heroine.[67] She is, nevertheless, an enticing alternative to the insipid Elisa. Maria is the 'daughter of a respectable freeholder' (the Mr Jones of the enclosure debate) from 'the other side of the county' (I, p. 30). When Stanley first sees her she is constructed as a potential love object, until superseded by Elisa. While on a fishing trip, Stanley sees her 'sitting alone, like the genius of the stream' and describes her as 'an object more engaging than all the trout in the Wye' (I, p. 29). She is frequently described as 'a charming girl', although she is 'highly accomplished in the art of teasing' (I, p. 31), which makes Stanley change the epithet to 'provoking' on occasions. Maria has the 'elegant accomplishments' expected of a young 'fine lady' (I, p. 35), but thankfully lacks that of fashionable affectation. In contrast to the 'pensive sensibility' (I, p. 95) and silence of Elisa, Maria has 'spirit' (I, p. 195) and is always singing her favourite songs, one of which is 'Address to the Summer', which she performs for Dr Pemberton, assuring him that her choice is 'a very old one, sir; it is a late translation, but the original is in Welsh, by David ap Gwillym, a bard who flourished, I do not know how many hundred years ago' (I, pp. 160–1). Although it is the amatory style of Dafydd ap Gwilym which draws Maria, not the martial ancient bards, her knowledge of the literature of her country marks again her difference from the Anglicised Elisa and her reading matter.

In effect, Maria provides a reverse image of Elisa. For example, the story of her abduction by the nabob provides a comic parallel, both to the story of the attempted rape of Elisa and to the more sinister seductive forces of the nabob figures in both *Anna* and *Ellen*. Although Maria's situation is arguably even more serious than Elisa's – she is forcibly taken away in a carriage – her taking control of the situation by turning his own pistols on her abductor allows the story to have a happy ending, compounded by the fortuitous appearance of Watkins on the scene to save her. The duel between Elisa's brother and her suitor, Weaver, is also paralleled in Maria's story. When her brother hears of the abduction he threatens to kill the nabob, but is happily assured that she has escaped unscathed and acts no further, unlike Charles Powell, who is imprisoned after fatally wounding Mr Weaver. Significantly for thinking about the national marriage plot as expressive of national allegiance, Maria and her father both reject the suit of the 'illustrious nabob' (II, p. 209) and his ill-gotten wealth, and it is implied that Maria and Watkins will eventually marry. In this respect, the attempted English–Welsh union of Stanley and Elisa is doomed to failure (Elisa dies), whereas the Welsh–Welsh union of Maria and Watkins survives into the future. They may not officially be the protagonists, but they do offer a more comic and optimistic alternative to the doomed Elisa and the wretched Stanley. Overall, Maria unsettles the sentimental mode of the novel just as much as she unsettles Stanley. Her ebullient presence suggests that Edward Davies himself realised the limitations of sensibility as a medium for his exploration of Welsh life and was forced to keep his real interests firmly in the margins of the text.

Despite their obvious limitations in the assertion of Welsh difference, then, the novels of Smollett, Bennett and Davies refute the view that Wales did not figure as a national trope in eighteenth-century fiction. In their obsession with the ancestral estate, the processes of Anglicisation, the politics of marriage and inheritance, colonial encounters, domestic spaces and, in the work of Bennett and Davies, the negotiation of what a Welsh heroine might, or might not, be in fiction, these three novels show us that Wales was indeed being considered in a national sense in the eighteenth-century novel and that certain key themes can be identified. The fact that these fictional negotiations of Wales are in many ways conflicted, deeply ambivalent and often highly idealistic does not necessarily point to generic failure or wholesale capitulation to English tastes. Indeed, it is precisely through paying attention to the ambivalence of these novels that we can more fully understand what was at stake in narrating the nation.

Notes

Introduction

1 Reprinted in Evan Evans, *Some Specimens of the Poetry of the Antient Welsh Bards, Translated into English* (Montgomery: Llanidloes, 1862), p. 163.

2 The majority of literary studies focus on Scotland. See, for example, Leith Davis, *Acts of Union: Scotland and the Literary Negotiation of the British Nation, 1707–1830* (Stanford: Stanford University Press, 1998); Robert Crawford, *Devolving English Literature* (Oxford: Clarendon Press, 1992). Murray Pittock's *Inventing and Resisting Britain: Cultural Identities in Britain and Ireland, 1685–1789* (Basingstoke: Macmillan, 1997) and Katie Trumpener's *Bardic Nationalism: The Romantic Novel and the British Empire* (Princeton: Princeton University Press, 1997) include some welcome discussion of the Welsh context, but the main focus is on Scotland and Ireland. Despite the inclusiveness of the titles, historical studies of Britain also mainly focus on Scotland and Ireland. See, for example, Jim Smyth, *The Making of the United Kingdom, 1660–1800* (Harlow: Pearson Education, 2001); Alexander Murdoch, *British History 1660–1832: National Identity and Local Culture* (Houndmills: Macmillan, 1998); Alexander Grant and Keith J. Stringer, *Uniting the Kingdom? The Making of British History* (London and New York: Routledge, 1995). Jane Aaron's ground-breaking work on Romantic and nineteenth-century Welsh women writers is a notable exception. See Aaron, *Pur Fel Y Dur: Y Gymraes yn Llên Menywod y Bedwaredd Ganrif ar Bymtheg* (Cardiff: University of Wales Press, 1998); also *Nineteenth-Century Women's Writing in Wales: Nation, Gender and Identity* (Cardiff: University of Wales Press, 2007). Wales has been extremely well served by its historians (see bibliography). I am referring here to those studies which specifically address British history and Britishness.

3 J. G. A. Pocock, 'British history: a plea for a new subject', *Journal of Modern History*, 47 (1975), 601–21. See also Pocock, 'The limits and divisions of British history: in search of the unknown subject', *American Historical Review*, 87 (1982), 311–16. For the most recent collection of essays which deal with 'archipelagic' history from a literary perspective, see Philip Schwyzer and Simon Mealor (eds), *Archipelagic Identities: Literature and Identity in the Atlantic Archipelago, 1550–1800* (Aldershot, Hants.:Ashgate, 2004).

⁴ Philip Schwyzer, *Literature, Nationalism and Memory in Early Modern England and Wales* (Cambridge: Cambridge University Press, 2004), p. 3. Another notable exception, which was published after this book went to press, is John Kerrigan's *Archipelagic English: Literature, History and Politics 1603–1707* (Oxford: Oxford University Press, 2008).

⁵ Linda Colley, *Britons: Forging the Nation 1707–1837* (repr. London: Pimlico, 1994), p. 11.

⁶ See, for example, Crawford, *Devolving English Literature*; Pittock, *Inventing and Resisting Britain*; Davis, *Acts of Union*.

⁷ Michael Hechter, *Internal Colonialism: The Celtic Fringe in British National Development 1536–1966* (London: Routledge and Kegan Paul, 1975). Another influential model of nationalism for literary scholars has been Benedict Anderson, *Imagined Communities: Reflections on the Origins and Spread of Nationalism* (rev. edn; London: Verso, 1991).

⁸ Colley, *Britons*, p. 6.

⁹ Ibid., p. 373.

¹⁰ Ibid., p. 6.

¹¹ Geraint H. Jenkins, 'Wales in the eighteenth century', in H. T. Dickinson (ed.), *A Companion to Eighteenth-Century Britain* (Oxford: Blackwell, 2002), pp. 392–402 (p. 398).

¹² Colley, *Britons*, p. 163.

¹³ Davies, *Acts of Union*, p. 6.

¹⁴ Ibid. Davies also reads Howard Weinbrot's assessment of British literature as being a *concordia discors*, in *Britannia's Issue: The Rise of British Literature from Dryden to Ossian* (Cambridge: Cambridge University Press, 1993), as another example of the 'Whig interpretation of British History' (p. 6).

¹⁵ Pittock, *Inventing and Resisting Britain*, p. 5.

¹⁶ Ibid., p. 6.

¹⁷ Ibid.

¹⁸ Colin Kidd, 'Integration: patriotism and nationalism', in Dickinson (ed.), *A Companion to Eighteenth-Century Britain*, pp. 369–80 (p. 370).

¹⁹ Ibid., p. 376.

²⁰ Ibid.

²¹ Rosemary Sweet, *Antiquaries: The Discovery of the Past in Eighteenth-Century Britain* (London and New York: Hambledon and London, 2004), p. 120.

²² See Jane Aaron, *Nineteenth-Century Women's Writing in Wales*, p. 10.

²³ Schwyzer, *Literature, Nationalism and Memory*, p. 95.

²⁴ Ibid., p. 6.

²⁵ Ibid.

²⁶ In 1718 Aaron Thompson published a new edition of Geoffrey of Monmouth's *History*. Sweet, *Antiquaries*, p. 122. Theophilus Evans's defence of the *History*, *Drych y Prif Oesoedd*, was published in 1716 with a second edition in 1740. An English translation by Revd George Roberts appeared in 1834 as *A View of the Primitive Ages* (Llanidloes: John Pryse).

²⁷ Sweet, *Antiquaries*, p. 121.

[28] Christine Gerrard, *The Patriot Opposition to Walpole: Politics, Poetry, and National Myth, 1725–1742* (Oxford: Clarendon Press, 1994).

[29] Philip Jenkins, 'Seventeenth-century Wales: definition and identity', in Brendan Bradshaw and Peter Roberts (eds), *British Consciousness and Identity: The Making of Britain, 1533–1707* (Cambridge: Cambridge University Press, 1998), pp. 213–35 (p. 219).

[30] Ibid., p. 220.

[31] For a further discussion of the different inflections of names/terms for Wales and the Welsh, see Philip Schwyzer's introduction to *Archipelagic Identities*, p. 2. See also Schwyzer, 'A map of Greater Cambria', in Andrew Gordon and Bernhard Klein (eds), *Literature, Mapping and the Politics of Space in Early Modern Britain* (Cambridge: Cambridge University Press, 2001), pp. 35–44.

[32] Belinda Humfrey, 'Prelude to the twentieth century', in M. Wynn Thomas (ed.), *Welsh Writing in English* (Cardiff: University of Wales Press, 2003), pp. 7–46.

[33] The first 'Anglo-Welsh' text is often said to be Ieuan ap Hywel Swrdwal's 'A hymn to the virgin' (*c.*1470). M. Wynn Thomas, 'Welsh writing in English', Microsoft® Encarta® Online Encyclopedia 2007, *http://uk.encarta.msn.com* © 1997–2007 Microsoft Corporation, All Rights Reserved. See also Roland Mathias, *An Introduction to Anglo-Welsh Literature* (Cardiff: University of Wales Press, 1970) and *Anglo-Welsh Literature: An Illustrated History* (Bridgend: Poetry Wales Press, 1986).

[34] Catherine Brennan, *Angers, Fantasies and Ghostly Fears: Nineteenth-Century Women from Wales and English-Language Poetry* (Cardiff: University of Wales Press, 2003); Moira Dearnley, *Distant Fields: Eighteenth-Century Fictions of Wales* (Cardiff: University of Wales Press, 2001); Andrew Davies, '"Redirecting the attention of history": antiquarian and historical fictions of Wales from the Romantic period', in Damian Walford Davies and Lynda Pratt (eds), *Wales and the Romantic Imagination* (Cardiff: University of Wales Press, 2007), pp. 104–21, and '"The reputed nation of inspiration": representations of Wales in fiction from the Romantic period, 1780–1829' (unpub. Ph.D. thesis, University of Cardiff, 2001).

[35] Jenkins, 'Wales in the eighteenth century', p. 398.

[36] See Geraint H. Jenkins, *The Foundations of Modern Wales, 1642–1780* (Oxford: Oxford University Press, 1993), esp. pp. 204–9. It is less easy to generalise about the medium of education in Wales in this period. On the one hand, the SPCK charity schools were intent on rearing 'a new generation of English speakers'. Ibid., p. 203. On the other hand, Welsh Methodism, especially through the indefatigable work of Griffith Jones, helped to preserve the Welsh language through using it as the medium of instruction. See ibid., pp. 380–1. However, on a higher social scale, it had also been the case that, from the reign of Henry VIII, the Grammar Schools in Wales produced mainly Anglicised alumni who attended university in Oxford and never returned to Wales. See Mathias, *Anglo-Welsh Literature*, p. 15.

[37] Lewis Morris is often termed a 'Welsh Augustan'. Goronwy Owen also consciously adopted an Augustan poetic mode alongside his reverence for the

traditional Welsh poetic forms and metres. See Jenkins, *Foundations of Modern Wales*, pp. 399–409.

[38] *www.bwrdd-yr-iaith.org.uk*

[39] Jenkins, 'Wales in the eighteenth century', p. 398.

[40] M. Wynn Thomas, 'Welsh writing in English', Microsoft® Encarta® Online Encyclopedia 2007, *http://uk.encarta.msn.com* © 1997–2007 Microsoft Corporation, All Rights Reserved.

[41] There is a volume on John Dyer in the 'Writers of Wales' series: Belinda Humfrey, *John Dyer* (Cardiff: University of Wales Press, 1980).

[42] See Walford Davies and Pratt (eds), *Wales and the Romantic Imagination*. The Iolo Morganwg project at the Centre for Advanced Welsh and Celtic Studies is producing excellent work on not only Iolo himself, but Welsh Romanticism more broadly. See, for example, Geraint H. Jenkins (ed.), *A Rattleskull Genius: The Many Faces of Iolo Morganwg* (Cardiff: University of Wales Press, 2005), and titles in the University of Wales Press series 'Iolo Morganwg and the Romantic Tradition in Wales'.

1 Anglo-Welsh Relations in Eighteenth-Century London

[1] Thomas Brereton, 'To my worthy Friend, the AUTHOR', commendatory poem prefixed to N. Griffith, *The Leek. A Poem on St. David's Day: Most humbly Inscribed to the Honourable Society of Ancient Britons* (2nd edn; London, 1718). All further references are to this edition and are cited parenthetically in the text.

[2] For a good introduction to the activities of the Cymmrodorion and the Gwyneddigion see Glenda Carr, 'William Owen Pughe and the London Societies', in Branwen Jarvis (ed.), *A Guide to Welsh Literature c.1700–1800* (Cardiff: University of Wales Press, 2000), pp. 168–86.

[3] *The Rise and Progress of the Most Honourable and Loyal Society of Antient Britons, established in Honour to her Royal Highness's Birthday, and the Principality of* Wales, *on St.* David'*s Day, the First of* March, *1714–15* (London, 1717). All further references are to this edition and are cited parenthetically in the text unless indicated otherwise. Sir Thomas Jones (d. 1731) was the first secretary and treasurer of the Society. He was knighted in 1715.

[4] *An Account of the Rise, Progress, and Present State of the Welsh Society, for Supporting a Charity School Erected in Gray's-Inn-Road, London* (London, 1793), 'The Master's Account', pp. 9 and 13.

[5] Thomas Jones, *The Rise and Progress*, pp. 18–19.

[6] Alexander Murdoch, *British History 1660–1832: National Identity and Local Culture* (Houndmills: Macmillan, 1998), p. 101.

[7] Prys Morgan, *The Eighteenth-Century Renaissance* (Llandybïe: Christopher Davies, 1981), pp. 7–8.

[8] See, for example, Benjamin Hoadley (Bishop of Bangor), *A Sermon Preach'd at St. James, Westminster, On St. David's Day, March I. 1716* (London, 1717).

⁹ All further references are cited parenthetically in the text. Wotton was a scholar in Edward Lhuyd's circle in the early eighteenth century. With the assistance of Moses Williams he published *Cyfreithjeu Hywel Dda* in 1730. See Morgan, *The Eighteenth-Century Renaissance*, p. 77.

¹⁰ *The Goodness and Severity of GOD, in his Dispensations, with respect unto the Ancient BRITAINS, Display'd: In a Sermon Preach'd to an Auditory of Protestant Dissenters, At Haberdasher's Hall in London, on March the 1ˢᵗ, 1716* (London, 1717). All further references are to this edition and are cited parenthetically in the text. Jeremy Owen (*fl.* 1704–44) was a Presbyterian minister. He resigned his pastorate of Henllan Amgoed in about 1715 because of 'Undefined but self-confessed laxity of conduct'. At the time he preached the above sermon he was resident in London. See *Welsh Biography Online* (National Library of Wales, 2007).

¹¹ John Evans, *The Christian Soldier; or, An early Instruction in the Christian Warfare, the surest Foundation of the Subject's Loyalty, and of the Servant's Fidelity* (London, 1750), p. 22. All further references are to this edition and are cited parenthetically in the text. At the time of the sermon Evans was one of the 'Chaplains of the Royal-Chapel at White-Hall' (title-page). Evans (1702–82) was an anti-Methodist cleric from Carmarthen, educated at Jesus College, Oxford. He had the Crown living of Eglwys Cymyn from 1730, but lived in London. His chaplaincy at Whitehall was a result of the patronage of Bishop Edmund Gibson. He was a founder member of the Honourable Society of Cymmrodorion. See *Welsh Biography Online* (National Library of Wales, 2007).

¹² The rhetoric of one body and one blood uniting the people of Britain echoes that used in some Jacobean unionist writing. See Philip Schwyzer, *Literature, Nationalism and Memory in Early Modern England and Wales* (Cambridge: Cambridge University Press, 2004), pp. 153–5. Interestingly, two examples of those writers who insisted on James I's British blood were Welshmen: George Owen Harry and William Harbert. Ibid., p. 155.

¹³ As Christine Gerrard notes, the image of intermarriage between Saxons and native Britons 'in a myth of peaceful integration' was central to Aaron Hill's plans for his opera *Hengist and Horsa; or, The Origins of England*. The opera was never written, but planned to present the love of Vortigern for Hengist's daughter, Matilda, as a route to such reconciliation. For the Welsh, such a plot-line would be unthinkable. See Christine Gerrard's excellent study, *The Patriot Opposition to Walpole: Politics, Poetry, and National Myth, 1725–1742* (Oxford: Clarendon Press, 1994), pp. 119–20.

¹⁴ Kathleen Wilson, *The Island Race: Englishness, Empire and Gender in the Eighteenth Century* (London and New York: Routledge, 2003), p. 7.

¹⁵ Ibid., p. 13.

¹⁶ See Colin Kidd, *British Identities before Nationalism: Ethnicity and Nationhood in the Atlantic World, 1600–1800* (Cambridge: Cambridge University Press, 1999) and *The Forging of Races: Race and Scripture in the Protestant Atlantic World, 1600–2000* (Cambridge: Cambridge University Press, 2006). Kidd, *British Identities before Nationalism*, pp. 187, 207.

[17] Ibid., pp. 194–5.

[18] Wilson, *The Island Race*, pp. 85–7. See also Roxann Wheeler, *The Complexion of Race: Categories of Difference in Eighteenth-Century British Culture* (Philadelphia: University of Pennsylvania Press, 2000).

[19] Kidd, *British Identities before Nationalism*, p. 207. The idea of Saxon liberty as a staple of English nationalism has its most familiar incarnation in the mythic theory of the 'Norman Yoke'. See Christopher Hill, *Puritanism and Revolution: Studies in Interpretation of the English Revolution of the 17th Century* (London: Secker and Warburg, 1958), pp. 50–122. As Hill notes, the Norman Yoke theory and the lauding of Saxon constitutionalism resurfaced in radical form at the end of the eighteenth century.

[20] Schwyzer shows that tropes of rebirth were common in Tudor nationalist rhetoric. *Literature, Nationalism and Memory*, p. 154. Gerrard also argues that 'Calls for a purged or reformed Church led by a Protestant king untrammelled by priestcraft recur repeatedly in Whig pamphlets of the Restoration', and adds that these were 'echoed in the messianic opposition Whig language of Patriot kingship during the 1730s'. *The Patriot Opposition to Walpole*, p. 25.

[21] The text tells us that George is descended from Elizabeth (daughter of James I) and her husband Frederick, King of Bohemia, 'who by a Providence favourable to this Nation, was a *Protestant*' (p. 63), and who produced Princess Sophia, 'a Protestant also' (p. 63). Sophia's marriage to Prince Augustus, Elector and Duke of Brunswick Lunenburgh ('a Protestant'), produced, of course, George I, 'who therefore is the next Protestant Prince in the whole World' (p. 63).

[22] Linda Colley, *Britons: Forging the Nation 1707–1837* (London: Pimlico, 1994), p. 46.

[23] Such stress on the need for loyalty might indicate a need to quash Jacobite feeling in Wales, especially with the presence of the hugely influential Sir Watkin Williams Wynn and his Jacobite society, the Cycle of the White Rose (founded 10 June 1710). However, traditionally the Welsh were seen as loyal subjects, and the text might also be emphasising this aspect of Welsh identity. For a discussion of both sides of the argument, see Geraint H. Jenkins, *The Foundations of Modern Wales, 1642–1780* (Oxford: Oxford University Press, 1993), esp. pp. 148–52.

[24] Examples of parallel texts include: William Wotton, *A Sermon Preached in Welsh before the British Society* (London, 1723), and P. Philipps, *Loyalty and Love, Recommended in a Sermon Preach'd at St. Paul's Covent Garden, in the British Language on St. David's Day* (London, 1716).

[25] There are exceptions, for example Moses Williams's sermons *Pregeth a Barablwyd yn Eglwys Grist yn Llundain, Ar Dyddgwyl Ddewi* (Llundain: 1718 and 1722) were printed only in Welsh.

[26] The so-called 'Language Clause' of the Act of Union (1536) declared that English should be the language of the courts and that 'no personne or personnes that use the Welsshe speech or langage shall have or enjoy any manner office or fees within the Realme of Englonde Wales or other the Kinges dominions'. See Janet Davies, *The Welsh Language* (Cardiff:

University of Wales Press, 1993), pp. 22–3. On the other hand, however, 1546 saw the printing of the first book in Welsh, by Sir John Prise of Brecon (1501/2–55): *Yny lhyvyr hwnn*. Furthermore, it has often been argued that the Protestant Reformation helped to preserve the Welsh language through translations of religious material into Welsh. For a summary of these arguments, see Davies, *The Welsh Language*, pp. 24–31.

[27] For example, Thomas Jones, *The British Language in its Lustre* (London, 1688). For further discussion of this issue, see Jenkins, *Foundations of Modern Wales*, especially chapter 6.

[28] For example, William Richards's *Wallography; or, the Briton describ'd* (London, 1682), repr. in 1753 as *Dean Swift's Ghost*, ed. J.T. See Jenkins, *Foundations of Modern Wales*, chapter 6. The same J.T. (John Torbuck) edited a collection in *c*.1740 titled *A Collection of Welsh Travels, and Memoirs of Wales*, which included reprints of Ned Ward's *A Trip to North-Wales* (London, 1701) and Edward Holdsworth's *Muscipula; or, The Welsh Mouse-Trap* (London, 1712). For a description of *Wallography* and a discussion of its publication history, see Michael Roberts, ' "A Witty Book, but mostly Feigned": William Richards's *Wallography* and perceptions of Wales in later seventeenth-century England', in Philip Schwyzer and Simon Mealor (eds), *Archipelagic Identities: Literature and Identity in the Atlantic Archipelago, 1550–1800* (Aldershot, Hampshire: Ashgate, 2004), pp. 153–65.

[29] The antiquity of the Welsh language had been suggested by the work of various lexicographers, philologists and antiquarians, for example John Davies, Mallwyd, *Antiquae linguæ Britannicæ* (1621), Paul-Yves Pezron, *L'Antiquité de la nation et de la langue des celtes* (1703), Edward Lhuyd, *Archæologia Britannica* (1707) and Theophilus Evans, *Drych y Prif Oesoedd* (1716). See Jenkins, *Foundations of Modern Wales*, pp. 223–5.

[30] Linda Colley, *Britons*.

[31] Owen's stance on the Welsh language prefigures that of William Gambold's preface to his Welsh grammar of 1727, which argues for a higher status for Welsh in the rapidly expanding print culture of the eighteenth century (although Gambold himself was heavily reliant on John Davies). Gambold laments the fact that Welsh is little known either abroad or in Britain, and adds: 'Yet herein the language as well as proprietors, did but share in the common fate of all conquered nations; for it is very obvious that the language of such must as well give way to the language of the conquerors, as the necks of the inhabitants must truckle under the yokes of their subduers.' *A Welsh Grammar, or, A Short and Easie Introduction to the Welsh Tongue* (Carmarthen, 1727), quoted in Morgan, *The Eighteenth-Century Renaissance*, p. 71.

[32] Brynley F. Roberts, 'Williams, Moses (1685–1742)', *Oxford Dictionary of National Biography* (Oxford University Press, 2004) (*http://www.oxforddnb.com/view/article/29532*, accessed 2 Sept. 2005).

[33] As many scholars have noted, Welsh history continued to rely on Galfridian traditions despite a strong tradition of scepticism in England. Evans's *Drych y Prif Oesoedd* was the most popular of the Welsh defences of Geoffrey of Monmouth's 'British History'. For a discussion of the text and other Welsh-

language histories of the early eighteenth century, see Jenkins, *Foundations of Modern Wales*, esp. pp. 246–8.

[34] Moses Williams, *Pregeth a Barablwyd yn Eglwys Grist yn Llundain, Ar Dyddgwyl Ddewi* (London, 1718), p. 12. All further references are to this edition and are cited parenthetically in the text. I am grateful to Aberystwyth University for granting me a Sir David Hughes Parry Award for translation services performed by Martin Davis at Afiaith. Prys Morgan discusses the Gomer myth as a replacement for the loss of Welsh historiography to the English. See 'Keeping the legends alive', in Tony Curtis (ed.), *Wales: The Imagined Nation: Studies in Cultural and National Identity* (Bridgend: Poetry Wales Press, 1986), pp. 19–41 (pp. 24–5).

[35] Williams also comments extensively on how agricultural methods can be improved in Wales. *Pregeth a Barablwyd yn Eglwys Grist yn Llundain* (1718), p. 15.

[36] Owen is clearly indebted to Gildas's *De Excidio Britanniae* ('Concerning the Ruin of Britain'), especially chapter 23. I am grateful to M. Wynn Thomas for alerting me to the parallels. Charles Edwards's *Y Ffydd Ddi-ffvant* ('The Unfeigned Faith', 1677 and further editions) is an example of a Welsh-language use of Gildas which makes the parallel between the Welsh and the Israelites. See Jenkins, *Foundations of Modern Wales*, p. 234.

[37] Owen actually appears to be alluding to Psalm 137: '1. By the rivers of Babylon, there we sat down, yea, we wept, when we remembered Zion. / 2. We hanged our harps upon the willows in the midst thereof'. As Katie Trumpener notes, Evan Evans was to use this psalm for more openly patriotic purposes or, in Trumpener's terms, to further a 'bardic nationalism' which works 'in resistance not only to the military conquest of Wales but also to the arrogant assumption of the English that other cultures are there to be absorbed into their own'. *Bardic Nationalism: The Romantic Novel and the British Empire* (Princeton: Princeton University Press, 1997), p. 2. Evan Evans, 'A Paraphrase of the 137th Psalm, Alluding to the Captivity and Treatment of the Welsh Bards by King Edward I', in *Some Specimens of the Poetry of the Antient Welsh Bards, Translated into English* (Llanidloes, 1862). See chapter 3 of the present study.

[38] Jenkins, *Foundations of Modern Wales*, p. 214.

[39] Philip Schwyzer has discussed the early seventeenth-century rehabilitation of Saxonism as the beginning of a specifically English national identity in this period. He sees this development, in part, as an explanation for the failure of the Jacobean unionist campaign, which relied on the increasingly discredited Tudor narratives of British nationalism. See Schwyzer, *Literature, Nationalism and Memory*, p. 172. For a detailed discussion of Saxonism in an eighteenth-century political context, see Gerrard, *The Patriot Opposition to Walpole*.

[40] Sir Richard Blackmore, *Alfred: an epick poem in twelve books. Dedicated to the Illustrious Prince Frederick of Hanover* (London, 1723). Although Blackmore makes the Saxon connection with Hanover, the majority of his dedication praises the House of Hanover in Whiggish terms almost identical to those employed by the Society of Ancient Britons, placing special

emphasis on reformed religion, the Protestant succession, anti-Catholic
sentiment and the 'ungrateful Rebellion' of the Pretender.

41 Rosemary Sweet, *Antiquaries: The Discovery of the Past in Eighteenth-Century
Britain* (London and New York: Hambledon and London, 2004), p. 189.

42 Ibid., p. 190. However, as Sweet acknowledges, the 'barbarity' of the Saxons
still posed problems for English scholars who, like some Welsh commentators
on the Ancient Britons, mixed equivocal admiration for Roman civilisation
with a desire to celebrate a 'national' past.

43 Morgan, *The Eighteenth-Century Renaissance*, p. 16.

44 E. G. Bowen, *Dewi Sant/Saint David* (Cardiff: University of Wales Press,
1983), p. 103.

45 Ibid.

46 Schwyzer notes Richard Davies's use of exactly the same quotation from
Taliesin for similarly anti-Rome purposes in his 'Epistol at y Cembru', which
prefaced his (and William Salesbury's) translation of the New Testament into
Welsh, *Testament Newydd* (1567). *Literature, Nationalism and Memory*, p. 93.
Like his eighteenth-century counterparts, Davies 'disposes of the charge that
Protestantism is an innovation, and brands Catholicism, by contrast, as a
Saxon imposition' (p. 91). See also Glanmor Williams, 'Some Protestant
views of early Church history', in *Welsh Reformation Essays* (Cardiff:
University of Wales Press, 1967), pp. 207–19. It is extremely likely that Davies
is Owen's source for this quotation, not the original text.

47 John Hughes, *An Ode for the Birth-Day of Her Royal Highness The Princess
of Wales* (London, 1716).

48 For an example of the connection of James I to Cadwaladr, see George Owen
Harry, *Genealogy of the High and Mighty Monarch, James, by the grace of
God. King of great Brittayne, &c. with his lineall descent from Noah, by divers
direct lynes to Brutus, first Inhabiter of this Ile of Brittayne; and from him to
Cadwalader, the last King of the Brittish bloud; and from thence, sundry wayes to
his Majesty* (London, 1604), and Schwyzer's discussion in *Literature,
Nationalism and Memory*, pp. 154–5. However, Owain Glyndŵr also claimed
descent from Cadwaladr as part of a distinctly anti-English rhetoric. In a letter
to the King of Scotland, he rehearsed the Brutus myth and declared: 'I, dear
cousin, am descended directly from Cadwaladr'. Quoted in R. R. Davies, *The
Revolt of Owain Glyn Dŵr* (Oxford: Oxford University Press, 1995), p. 158.

49 For example, *The Tears of Cambria. A Poem* (London, 1773), a later
anonymous poem inscribed to the Society, is actively critical of the
then Prince of Wales. The title alludes to Tobias Smollett's 'The Tears of
Scotland' (1746).

50 I have been unable to find biographical details about Nehemiah Griffith, but
he appears to have been part of a circle of London Welsh writers which
included the Welsh poet Jane Brereton and her literary husband Thomas. The
three poems are by Thomas Brereton, Thomas Griffith (presumably a
relation) and 'Melissa', Jane Brereton's pseudonym. Thomas Brereton's poem
is interesting biographically as he describes himself as a 'Cambro-Briton
born' (6), which adds weight to the supposition that he was from Flintshire,

not Cheshire (the *DNB* suggests both as possible birthplaces). Thomas wrote another poem inscribed to Griffith, *A Day's Journey from The Vale of Evesham to Oxford: In a familiar Epistle to N. Griffith Esq* (London, 1717?). Both Thomas and Jane Brereton were Whig supporters and anti-Catholic. The dedicatory poem to Griffith is included in Jane Brereton's *Poems on Several Occasions* (London, 1744) as '*To* Nehemiah Griffith, *Esq; Author of the Leek*'. See chapter 2 of the present study.

51 The miracle is related in chapter 52 of Rhigyfarch's *Life of St David* (*c*.1090). See the translation by A. W. Wade-Evans, *Life of St. David* (London: SPCK, 1923), pp. 26–7.

52 Bowen, *Dewi Sant/Saint David*, p. 13.

53 *Armes Prydein/The Prophecy of Britain. From the Book of Taliesin*, ed. Ifor Williams, English version by Rachel Bromwich (Dublin: Dublin Institute for Advanced Studies, 1982). All line references are to this edition and are cited parenthetically in the text. There is no way of knowing for sure if Griffith had read this poem, but given his antiquarian leanings and proximity to antiquarian circles, it is not unlikely.

54 Glanmor Williams, *Religion, Language, and Nationality in Wales* (Cardiff: University of Wales Press, 1979), p. 111.

55 Bowen, *Dewi Sant/Saint David*, p. 93.

56 See Williams, *Religion, Language, and Nationality in Wales*, p. 117.

57 In 'An ODE for Two Voices' by John Hughes, the voice of 'Cambria' focuses on Edward III's victory at Crécy as a marker of national pride. Cambria tells Fame 'When my great *Edward*'s Deeds thou shalt rehearse; / And tell of *Cressy*'s well-fought Plain'. Jones, *The Rise and Progress*, p. 47. Gerrard notes that Edward III at Crécy (along with Alfred and the Armada victories of Elizabeth) was part of the general 'patriotic romanticization of past political golden ages'. *The Patriot Opposition to Walpole*, p. 74. She goes on to trace the way in which Edward III and the Order of the Garter were later used to bolster the images of Frederick, Prince of Wales, and, in a more substantial way, his son George III (pp. 224–9). The motto of the Society of Ancient Britons, 'Ich Dien', also plays on the myth that this was first used by the Black Prince in his role as Prince of Wales.

58 Patricia Parker, 'Uncertain unions: Welsh leeks in *Henry V*', in David J. Baker and Willy Maley (eds), *British Identities and English Renaissance Literature* (Cambridge: Cambridge University Press, 2002), pp. 81–100 (p. 82). Overall, however, Parker argues that far from the leek serving as a symbol of straightforward loyalty to England, the play as a whole reveals 'much more subtle anxieties of incorporation and invasion linked with the ongoing instability of England's "borderers"' (p. 98). As Philip Schwyzer has noted, whereas *Henry V* has traditionally been read as a celebration of English national identity, the play is increasingly being viewed from an 'archipelagic' perspective which highlights fissures in the text's ostensible claims for 'a unified identity'. *Literature, Nationalism and Memory*, p. 128.

59 Williams (ed.), *Armes Prydein/The Prophecy of Britain*, pp. 14–15.

[60] Glanmor Williams, for example, makes the point that although writers such as Sir John Prise, Arthur Kelton, David Powel and John Dee enthusiastically defended the particular narratives of the Welsh – the myth of Trojan origins, the Ancient Britons, Arthur, and 'a revived and more glorious British monarchy' – English writers such as Spenser and Drayton also favoured the 'British' myths over an acknowledgement of 'the barbaric Saxons as their ancestors'. *Religion, Language, and Nationality in Wales*, p. 17. However, as Rosemary Sweet points out, in the eighteenth century 'English antiquaries experienced little difficulty in identifying their earliest ancestors as the ancient Britons, whilst simultaneously setting a disdainful distance between themselves and the modern heirs of the original Britons, the Welsh'. *Antiquaries*, p. 121. Thomas Gray's *The Bard* (1757) is obviously significant in this context, as I argue in chapter 3 of the present study.

[61] Schwyzer, *Literature, Nationalism and Memory*, p. 46.

[62] Morgan, 'Keeping the legends alive', p. 25.

[63] Schwyzer, *Literature, Nationalism and Memory*, p. 46, and Kirsti Bohata, *Postcolonialism Revisited*, 'Writing Wales in English' (Cardiff: University of Wales Press, 2004), p. 131. Bohata argues that English assimilation of Welsh traditions 'resulted in them being *lost* to Wales' (Bohata's italics) and that 'assimilation in this instance was a form of cultural robbery', comparable to the stealing of native stories in present-day post-colonial situations (p. 131).

[64] Schwyzer, *Literature, Nationalism and Memory*, p. 95. See the introduction to the present study.

[65] Examples of such writers would include Sir Richard Blackmore, Lord Bolingbroke, and Aaron Hill.

[66] As Christine Gerrard notes, the term 'Gothic' was extremely flexible for English writers in the early eighteenth century and could house Celts, Goths and Saxons all 'under the same Gothic roof'. *The Patriot Opposition to Walpole*, p. 112.

[67] Ibid., pp. 117–18.

[68] Ibid., p. 118 and n. 39, p. 118. See chapter 2 of the present study.

[69] Elements of the old British tradition did survive to serve different circumstances or political persuasions, such as Hanoverian Toryism. For a further discussion of these issues see chapter 4 of the present study.

2 The Poems of Jane Brereton

[1] *Poems on Several Occasions: by Mrs Jane Brereton. With Letters to her Friends, and an Account of Her Life* (London, 1744). All further references are cited parenthetically in the text.

[2] As I suggested in the previous chapter, Thomas Brereton may have been born in Flintshire. The family as a whole originated from Chester.

[3] Thomas Brereton died in February 1722, shortly after his wife's move to Wrexham.

[4] Jane Brereton appears very briefly in Meic Stephens (ed.), *The New Companion to the Literature of Wales* (Cardiff: University of Wales Press,

1998), p. 67, and in Raymond Garlick, *An Introduction to Anglo-Welsh Literature* (Cardiff: University of Wales Press, 1972), p. 57. More recently, two of Brereton's poems are included in Katie Gramich and Catherine Brennan (eds), *Welsh Women's Poetry 1460–2001* (Honno: Honno Classics, 2003). Brereton's poetry is also anthologised in Roger Lonsdale (ed.), *Eighteenth-Century Women Poets* (Oxford: Oxford University Press, 1989). Discussion of her work in an eighteenth-century context can be found in Christine Gerrard, *The Patriot Opposition to Walpole: Politics, Poetry, and National Myth, 1725–1742* (Oxford: Clarendon Press, 1994); Claudia N. Thomas, *Alexander Pope and his Eighteenth-Century Women Readers* (Carbondale and Edwardsville: Southern Illinois University Press, 1994); Sarah Prescott, *Women, Authorship and Literary Culture, 1690–1740* (Basingstoke: Palgrave, 2003) and 'The Cambrian Muse: Welsh identity and Hanoverian loyalty in the poems of Jane Brereton (1685–1740)', *Eighteenth-Century Studies*, 38, 4 (2005), 587–603.

5 Philip Jenkins, 'Seventeenth-century Wales: definition and identity', in Brendan Bradshaw and Peter Roberts (eds), *British Consciousness and Identity: The Making of Britain* (Cambridge: Cambridge University Press, 1998), pp. 213–35 (p. 216).

6 See Jenkins, 'Seventeenth-century Wales', and Geraint H. Jenkins, *The Foundations of Modern Wales, 1642–1780* (Oxford: Oxford University Press, 1993).

7 Peter Roberts, 'Tudor Wales, national identity and the British inheritance', in Bradshaw and Roberts (eds), *British Consciousness and Identity*, pp. 8–42 (p. 8).

8 Ibid., p. 8.

9 Ibid., p. 34.

10 Keith Thomas, *Religion and the Decline of Magic* (Harmondsworth: Penguin, 1978), p. 494.

11 Roberts refers specifically to 'John Davies of Hereford and John Owen the epigrammatist'. 'Tudor Wales', p. 37.

12 As Philip Jenkins notes of seventeenth-century Welsh writers, 'Love of one's native soil was at least a familiar literary device, and we frequently find Welsh correspondents in England or overseas pining for their native land, clamouring for one clod of good Welsh earth.' 'Seventeenth-century Wales', p. 217.

13 For further discussion of poetic comparisons between classical and native literary culture, see chapter 4 of the present study.

14 For a discussion of Henry Vaughan's poems '*Ad fluvium Iscam*' and 'To the River *Isca*' in this context, see M. Wynn Thomas's chapter, ' "*In Occidentem & tenebras*": putting Henry Vaughan on the map of Wales', in *Corresponding Cultures: The Two Literatures of Wales* (Cardiff: University of Wales Press, 1999), pp. 11–13.

15 Ibid., p. 12. Thomas also makes the point that Vaughan's identity is much more complex than that of a 'mimic man'. Like Brereton, his identity (particularly that of the 'Silurist') is 'highly complex': 'unionist though he

was, he was not English; nor was he simply, unambiguously and uncomplicatedly Welsh' (pp. 12–13). I am arguing a similar case for Jane Brereton in a different context.

16 See Prescott, *Women Authorship and Literary Culture*, and Bronwen Price, 'Verse, voice, and body: the retirement mode and women's poetry 1680–1723', *Early Modern Literary Studies*, 12, 3 (2007), 5, 1–44, *http://purl.oclc.org/emls/12-3/priceve2.htm*.

17 There are seven letters extant from Brereton to John Mellor of Erthig (dated 1729) and two poems by Brereton in the Clwyd Record Office, Hawarden, Call No. D/E/871. The letters mostly concern Mellor's help in assisting Brereton to sell bottles of her 'elixir' spirit. The poems are a 'Poem in Praise of John Mellor', in which Brereton speaks of terrible hardships she has endured, and 'To Mrs Whitmore, on the Death of her Son'. There is a further poem, 'On the Death of Mr Bethel Whitmore', signed C. B. (Charlotte Brereton?).

18 See D. Leslie Davies, 'Miss Myddelton of Croesnewydd and the Plas Power Papers: a preliminary appraisal', *TBHS*, 22 (1973), 121–65 (136–41). I am grateful to Mared Owen for pointing me to this article. Brereton's poetry would have struck a chord with the Myddeltons, a Tory family who, 'had rid themselves of the taint of Jacobitism by loyally defending the principles of the Glorious Revolution and proclaiming their enthusiastic support for the Hanoverian succession'. Jenkins, *Foundations of Modern Wales*, p. 151. In her poem *'Written in Mr Law's Treatise on Christian Pefection; being the Gift of Mrs Myddelton'* we see evidence of Brereton receiving books as gifts from Mary Myddelton.

19 See Mary Burdett-Jones, 'Dr Humphrey Foulkes: "the most intellectual of Edward Lhuyd's correspondents"', unpub. lecture delivered for the Aberystwyth Bibliographical Society. I am extremely grateful to Mary Burdett-Jones for inviting me to attend and allowing me to read her lecture, and for providing me with a copy of the dissertation to which Brereton responds in her ode, as well as other information about Foulkes. I am also very grateful to Geraint H. Jenkins for his help in tracking down the identity of the Foulkes to whom Brereton is referring.

20 William Speck, *Stability and Strife: England 1714–1760* (London: Edward Arnold, 1977), pp. 187–90.

21 Dustin Griffin, *Patriotism and Poetry in Eighteenth-Century Britain* (Cambridge: Cambridge University Press, 2002), pp. 34–5.

22 Linda Colley, *Britons: Forging the Nation 1707–1837* (London: Pimlico, 1994), p. 18.

23 Brereton's position here backs up Colin Kidd's assertion that there was no common 'Celtic' identity or interest between the Welsh, Irish and Scottish at least until the end of the eighteenth century: 'The Welsh . . . did not identify themselves with their fellow "Celts", but saw themselves as the descendants of the ancient Britons'. *British Identities Before Nationalism: Ethnicity and Nationhood in the Atlantic World, 1600–1800* (Cambridge: Cambridge University Press, 1999), pp. 186–7.

[24] Murray G. H. Pittock, *Inventing and Resisting Britain: Cultural Identities in Britain and Ireland, 1685–1789* (Basingstoke: Macmillan, 1997), p. 5. As Pittock notes, divisions within Protestantism, such as those between High Church Anglicans and Dissenters, were sometimes as fierce as anti-Catholic feeling.

[25] The image of the sea as symbolising the commercial strength of the British nation was widespread by the time Brereton was writing. See, for example, James Thomson's *Liberty* (1735), Part V. For a discussion of maritime imagery as constitutive in the formation of eighteenth-century British national identity, see Geoff Quilley, '"All ocean is her own": the image of the sea and the identity of the maritime nation in eighteenth-century British art', in Geoffrey Cubitt (ed.), *Imagining Nations* (Manchester: Manchester University Press, 1998), pp. 132–52.

[26] Carol Barash, *English Women's Poetry, 1649–1714: Politics, Community, and Linguistic Authority* (Oxford: Clarendon Press, 1996).

[27] Kathryn R. King, 'Political verse and satire: monarchy, party and female political agency', in Sarah Prescott and David E. Shuttleton (eds), *Women and Poetry, 1660–1750* (Basingstoke: Palgrave Macmillan, 2003), pp. 203–22 (p. 212). See also Abigail Williams, 'Whig literary culture: poetry, politics, and patronage, 1678–1714' (unpub. D.Phil. thesis, Oxford University, 2000).

[28] For a discussion of the debates raised by Whiggish women poets about the liberties of freeborn 'Englishwomen', see King, 'Political verse and satire', pp. 212–15. See also Carole Pateman, 'Conclusion: women's writing, women's standing: theory and politics in the early modern period', in Hilda L. Smith (ed.), *Women Writers and the Early Modern British Political Tradition* (Cambridge: Cambridge University Press, 1998), pp. 365–82 (p. 369).

[29] Judith Colton, 'Merlin's Cave and Queen Caroline: garden art as political propaganda', *Eighteenth-Century Studies*, 10, 1 (1976), 1–20 (2).

[30] Ibid., p. 2.

[31] Colton makes the point that Mother Shipton was 'a female Merlin' and, as such, Brereton's position as the prophetess 'Melissa' could be seen as comparable. Ibid., pp. 10–11. Mother Shipton was 'allegedly a Yorkshire contemporary of Cardinal Wolsey', but was first heard of in 1641 on the publication of *The Prophesie of Mother Shipton*. She remained popular until the nineteenth century and would have been well known at the time Brereton was writing. See Thomas, *Religion and the Decline of Magic*, pp. 465, 487. As Thomas points out, Mother Shipton's prophecies were published in the same year as Thomas Heywood's *Life of Merlin* (p. 487). For a contemporary assessment of Mother Shipton, see the *Gentleman's Magazine* (6 February 1736), 87–9.

[32] Gerrard, *The Patriot Opposition*, p. 169.

[33] Colley makes the point that, 'Written and spoken propaganda in support of the early Hanoverian kings has none of the poetry, and little of the rich, folkloric quality that characterizes some of the best Jacobite polemic.' *Britons*, pp. 48–9.

[34] Colton, 'Merlin's Cave', p. 13.

³⁵ Ibid., p. 13.

³⁶ For an in-depth discussion of the way in which both Court and Opposition writers responded to Merlin's Cave, see Gerrard, *The Patriot Opposition*, pp. 169–74.

³⁷ Ibid., p. 170. I am grateful to Andrew Hadfield for pointing me to *Orlando Furioso*.

³⁸ Brereton is thus placing herself in a long tradition of women who used the authority vested in them as prophets to speak on a range of religious and political issues. For a discussion of such traditions see Phyllis Mack, *Visionary Women: Ecstatic Prophecy in Seventeenth-Century England* (California: Berkeley, 1992).

³⁹ For a further discussion of Brereton in this context see Prescott, *Women, Authorship, and Literary Culture*, pp. 56–66.

⁴⁰ In this poem, Brereton also refers to Merlin as '*British Merlin*' (40), by which she appears to signify the Merlin of Welsh tradition. However, the overall point of the poem is to link this 'antient' Merlin to 'My honour'd modern *Cave*' (43). By calling her muse '*British*' at the start of the poem, Brereton is similarly implying both an ancient Welsh-British lineage and a 'modern' eighteenth-century British identity in her praise of Caroline. In doing so, she can suggest a connection between these two versions of 'Britishness' in terms of Welsh loyalty to the Hanoverian succession.

⁴¹ Brereton's Merlin is thus a composite figure comprising bardic, scientific and druidic elements. One visual influence may have been the engraving of 'The Chief Druid' from Henry Rowlands, *Mona Antiqua Restaurata* (Dublin, 1723). See Peter Lord, *The Visual Culture of Wales: Imaging the Nation* (CD-ROM; University of Wales Centre for Advanced Welsh and Celtic Studies: University of Wales Press, 2002).

⁴² Gerrard, *The Patriot Opposition*, p. 143.

⁴³ Colton, 'Merlin's Cave', p. 19.

⁴⁴ For example: John Dryden's 1691 revision of *King Arthur; or, The British Worthy* and Richard Blackmore's *Prince Arthur* (1695) and *King Arthur* (1697). Colton, 'Merlin's Cave', p. 14. After the appearance of Merlin's Cave, a flurry of literature appeared which discussed Merlin and his prophecies.

⁴⁵ Humphrey Foulkes (1673–1737), a graduate of Oxford, was a cleric (rector of St George near Abergele and later of Marchwiel, both parishes in Denbighshire) and antiquarian who wrote various unpublished dissertations on medieval history and literature as well as on philological topics. See *Welsh Biography Online* and Geraint H. Jenkins, *Literature, Religion and Society in Wales, 1660–1730* (Cardiff: University of Wales Press, 1978), p. 279. See also Caryl Davies and Mary Burdett-Jones, 'Cyfraniad Humphrey Foulkes at *Archæologia Britannica* Edward Lhuyd', in *Y Llyfr yng Nghymru / Welsh Book Studies* (forthcoming). Jane Brereton must have met Foulkes through Mary Myddelton.

⁴⁶ In general terms, the legal system in Wales before Edward was more enlightened than any in Europe regarding the position of women. See Dafydd Jenkins (ed.), *Hywel Dda: The Law* (Llandysul: Gomer, 1998). However, as a

widow herself, Brereton was particularly drawn to certain aspects of Edward's importation of English law to Wales. R. R. Davies comments, 'on two substantive issues of land law Edward introduced English customs which ran contrary to long-established Welsh practice: he allowed a woman to enjoy a third of her late husband's lands as dower (whereas dower in much of native Wales had hitherto been confined to moveable goods), and permitted females to succeed to land where the male line had failed'. *The Age of Conquest: Wales 1063–1415* (Oxford: Oxford University Press, 1987), p. 369. For a detailed comparison of Welsh and English law in relation to women, see R. R. Davies, 'The status of women and the practice of marriage in late medieval Wales', in D. Jenkins and M. E. Owen (eds), *The Welsh Law of Women* (Cardiff: University of Wales Press, 1980), pp. 43–114.

[47] Gramich and Brennan, *Welsh Women's Poetry*, p. xxvi.

[48] National Library of Wales, LIGC 10B. 'A dissertation on the Welsh Laws, &c.', pp. 175–217, formerly 1–41. I am grateful to Mary Burdett-Jones for this reference.

[49] Brereton's sentiments in her ode to George I are very similar to those in Thomas Brereton's poem *George: A Poem* (London, 1715)

[50] Brereton, '*To the Author of the foregoing* Verses'.

[51] Anne Williams was maid of honour to Queen Caroline from 1735–7. She was in office on 20 November 1737 on the death of the Queen. BL Add. MS 27543, fo. 3.

[52] 'homage, *n. a.*', *Oxford English Dictionary*, J. A. Simpson and E. S. C. Weiner (eds) (2nd edn; Oxford: Clarendon Press, 1989), *OED Online* (Oxford University Press, 1 September 2003), *http://dictionary.oed.com/cgi/entry/00181778*.

[53] 'reprisal, *n.* 1.', *Oxford English Dictionary*, J. A. Simpson and E. S. C. Weiner (eds) (2nd edn; Oxford: Clarendon Press, 1989), *OED Online* (Oxford University Press, 1 September 2003), *http://dictionary.oed.com/cgi/entry/00181778*.

[54] Jane Aaron's comments on the work of Felicia Hemans, a nineteenth-century Anglo-Welsh woman poet, are illuminating in this context. In her Welsh-oriented poetry Hemans's stance not only suggests a link with Brereton, but also helps to explain Brereton's particular dilemma as a Cambrian panegyrist of a united Britain: 'For Hemans . . . it is not a matter of the Welsh versus the English but of "Cambrians" or "Britons" versus "Saxons" only . . . In the interests of constructing the image of Britons as a united family . . . "the name of England" must not be defiled'. Jane Aaron, '"Saxon, Think not All Is Won": Felicia Hemans and the making of Britons', *Cardiff Corvey: Reading the Romantic Text*, 4 (May 2000); online: Internet (24 July 2003), *http://www.cf.ac.uk/corvey/articles/cc04_n01.html*, 1–8 (6). This article is a revised version of a paper originally presented at the 'Scenes of Writing, 1750–1850' conference, held 20–23 July 1998, in Gregynog Hall, Wales.

[55] The poems are drawn from two collections: *Epithlamia Oxoniensia* (1761) and *Gratulatio Solennis Universitatis Oxoniensis . . . Auspicatissime Natum* (1762). Roger Stephens Jones, 'Some Anglo-Welsh poems in honour of George III,

Queen Charlotte and the Prince of Wales', *Anglo-Welsh Review*, 27, 60 (Spring 1978), 87–97.

[56] Ibid., p. 97.

[57] Ibid., p. 91.

[58] The poem was originally published as a commendatory poem to the second edition of *The Leek* in 1718.

[59] Tony Conran, *Welsh Verse* (Bridgend: Seren, 1992), p. 72.

[60] Ibid., p. 72

[61] P. R. Roberts, 'The Union with England and identity of "Anglican" Wales', *Transactions of the Royal Historical Society*, 22 (1972), 49–70 (69).

[62] Ibid., p. 68.

[63] Ibid.

[64] The so-called 'Act of Union' of 1536, and the legislation of 1536–43 concerning Wales and England, continued to be popular with both Welsh and English commentators and were broadly seen as a positive gain for Wales. However, even those in favour of the Tudors agreed that the Act of Union adversely affected the language and literary culture of Wales, and by the early twentieth century the Act of Union was also seen as a complete disaster for Wales. For a clear summary of differing views of the Union over the centuries, see Glanmor Williams, *Wales and the Act of Union* (Bangor: Headstart History, 1992), pp. 38–49.

3 Evan Evans and the Rise of Welsh Bardic Nationalism

[1] M. Wynn Thomas, *Corresponding Cultures: The Two Literatures of Wales* (Cardiff: University of Wales Press, 1999), pp. 117–18.

[2] Jane Aaron has recently argued that Evans 'contributed to that cultural revival which in the second half of the eighteenth century helped to give birth to the modern concept of Welsh nationhood'. 'Bardic anti-colonialism', in Jane Aaron and Chris Williams (eds), *Postcolonial Wales* (Cardiff: University of Wales Press, 2005), pp. 137–58 (p. 141).

[3] Geraint H. Jenkins, 'Evans, Evan (1731–1788)', *Oxford Dictionary of National Biography* (Oxford: Oxford University Press, 2004), *http://oxforddnb.com/view/article/8955*, accessed 22 March 2005.

[4] M. Wynn Thomas and S. Rhian Reynolds, 'Introduction', in S. Rhian Reynolds (ed.), *A Bibliography of Welsh Literature in English Translation* (Cardiff: University of Wales Press, 2005), p. xiv.

[5] For definitions of these terms and a good general discussion of early Welsh poetry see J. E. Caerwyn Williams, *The Poets of the Welsh Princes* (Cardiff: University of Wales Press, 1978).

[6] Evan Evans, *Some Specimens of the Poetry of the Antient Welsh Bards* (London, 1764), Preface, p. iii. All page references are to this edition and are included in parenthesis in the text unless stated otherwise.

[7] Thomas and Reynolds, *A Bibliography of Welsh Literature in English Translation*, p. xiii.

[8] Charlotte Johnson, 'Evan Evans: Dissertatio de Bardis', *National Library of Wales Journal*, 22, 1 (1981), 64–91 (65). The translation of the *Dissertatio* runs from pages 76–90.

[9] Thomas, *Corresponding Cultures*, p. 118. See also Prys Morgan, *The Eighteenth-Century Renaissance* (Llandybïe: Christopher Davies, 1981).

[10] Thomas, *Corresponding Cultures*, p. 118. As Thomas notes, the phrase 'contributionism' is from Ned Thomas, 'Images of ourselves', in John Osmond (ed.), *The National Question Again: Welsh Political Identity in the 1980s* (Llandysul: Gomer, 1985), pp. 307–19.

[11] Thomas, *Corresponding Cultures*, p. 118.

[12] Thomas and Reynolds, *A Bibliography of Welsh Literature in English Translation*, p. xiv.

[13] Ibid., p. xv.

[14] Thomas, *Corresponding Cultures*, p. 118.

[15] Katie Trumpener, *Bardic Nationalism: The Romantic Novel and the British Empire* (Princeton: Princeton University Press, 1997), p. 4.

[16] Jane Aaron, 'Bardic anti-colonialism', p. 142.

[17] Johnson, 'Evan Evans', p. 75.

[18] I am grateful to Aberystwyth University for granting me a Sir David Hughes Parry Award for translation services performed by Martin Davis at Afiaith.

[19] For an excellent introduction to the field of 'Translation Studies' and the attendant critical issues, see Susan Bassnett, *Translation Studies* (London: Routledge, 1988).

[20] Johnson, 'Evan Evans', p. 71.

[21] In a different context, Michael Franklin has made a similar point about Evans's projected audience. See 'Sir William Jones, the Celtic revival and the Oriental renaissance', in Gerard Carruthers and Alan Rawes (eds), *English Romanticism and the Celtic World* (Cambridge: Cambridge University Press, 2003), pp. 20–37 (p. 27).

[22] For Macpherson and the Ossian controversy see, for example, Fiona Stafford, *The Sublime Savage: James Macpherson and the Poems of Ossian* (Edinburgh: Edinburgh University Press, 1988).

[23] Mary-Ann Constantine, 'Ossian in Wales and Brittany', in Howard Gaskill (ed.), *The Reception of Ossian in Europe* (London and New York: Thoemmes Continuum, 2004), pp. 67–90 (p. 72).

[24] Nick Groom argues that by 'printing the work as a large quarto', Evans made further use of the popularity of *Ossian* and also attempted 'to usurp *Ossian* with a new claimant for the British Homer: the ancient Welsh bard Taliesin'. *The Making of Percy's Reliques* (Oxford: Clarendon Press, 1999), pp. 96–7. I would argue that Evans is directly critical of Macpherson in more sophisticated ways. See, for example, Evans, *Specimens*, note h, 49–50.

[25] For a discussion of anti-Ossian feeling in Wales, see Mary-Ann Constantine, *The Truth against the World: Iolo Morganwg and Romantic Forgery* (Cardiff: University of Wales Press, 2007), pp. 85–7.

[26] M. Wynn Thomas offers a useful definition of the term 'Foundationalism' from a Welsh perspective on the BWLET.net web-page (Bibliography of

Welsh Literature in English Translation), in the section 'The ideology of Welsh–English literary translation'. In relation to the 'search for origins', he adds that, 'in the Welsh case, it began as an accompaniment to the discovery (counterpointed by the brilliant forgeries of Iolo Morganwg) of genuine, and genuinely old, poetical manuscripts that provided a culturally subordinated people with historical evidence of the previously "suspect" ancient authority of their "subaltern" culture'. *http://www.bwlet.net/index.htm.*

[27] For a discussion of the theoretical and linguistic issues surrounding 'Untranslatability', see Bassnett, *Translation Studies*, pp. 37–42.

[28] Constantine, 'Ossian in Wales and Brittany', p. 73.

[29] Groom, *The Making of Percy's Reliques*, p. 96.

[30] Four of the ten poems Evans includes are about Llewelyn ap Iowerth (c.1199–1240) or his grandson Llewelyn ap Gruffudd (1247–82), who both 'strove with remarkable determination . . . to convert the primacy of Gwynedd . . . into the leadership of a united native Wales'. R. R. Davies, 'Edward I and Wales', in Trevor Herbert and Gareth Elwyn Jones (eds), *Edward I and Wales* (Cardiff: University of Wales Press, 1988), pp. 1–10 (p. 4). See: Poem III 'Of David Benvras to Llewelyn the Great, Prince of Wales, A. D. 1240'; Poem IV 'To Llewelyn the Great, composed by Einion, the Son of Gwgan, about 1244'; Poem VII 'To Llywelyn ap Iorwerth, or Llewelyn the Great' by Llywarch Brydydd y Moch; Poem VIII 'To Llewelyn, the son of Gruffudd, last prince of Wales of the British line, composed by Llygad Gŵr, about the year 1270'.

[31] John Wynn, *The History of the Gwedir Family* (London, 1770). The spelling of Gwedir is Anglicised here. In his copy, now in the National Library of Wales, Evan Evans corrects it to Gwydir. Thomas Carte, *A General History of England*, 4 vols (London, 1747–55). All references are to this edition and are included in parenthesis in the text. Carte footnotes Wynn on p. 196, n. 5, when referring specifically to the massacre. See Roger Lonsdale's discussion of Gray's sources and influences in his introductory essay for *The Bard* in *The Poems of Thomas Gray, William Collins, Oliver Goldsmith* (London: Longmans, 1969), pp. 177–83. Edward D. Snyder usefully reprints the correspondence between Thomas Percy and Evans concerning Edward I and the sources for the tradition of the massacre of the bards. See 'Thomas Gray's interest in Celtic', *Modern Philology*, 11, 4 (1914), 559–79, correspondence on pp. 9–10. A. D. Carr suggests that the ambitious Sir John Wynn of Gwydir made up the story of the massacre of the bards to glorify his own family: his main objective in writing the *History*. Carr explains that, for Sir John, the story explained 'the lack of early poetry to his family, which did not emerge as patrons of the poets until the sixteenth century'. *Medieval Wales* (Basingstoke: Macmillan, 1995), p. 10.

[32] Geraint H. Jenkins, 'Historical writing in the eighteenth century', in Branwen Jarvis (ed.), *A Guide to Welsh Literature c.1700–1800* (Cardiff: University of Wales Press, 2000), pp. 23–44 (pp. 34–5).

[33] R. R. Davies, 'Edward I and Wales', pp. 7–8.

[34] Trumpener, *Bardic Nationalism*, p. 8.

[35] Note c, p. 48: 'The land of the Angles, i.e. England'.

[36] Jane Aaron makes a similar point in relation to the resilience of the alliterative *cynghanedd* poetic form (associated with the professional bards), which developed into even more elaborate configurations after the death of Llewelyn, 'as if in defiance of that formlessness into which their culture generally had been thrown'. 'Bardic anti-colonialism', p. 140.

[37] A translation by Charlotte Johnson of the *Dissertatio* is printed at the end of her article, 'Evan Evans'. All page references are to this translation and are included in the text.

[38] Edward Jones makes a similar point about Philip of Macedon and Edward I in *Musical Relicks of the Welsh Bards* (2nd edn; London, 1800), p. 20.

[39] For further discussion of the Tysilio myth, see Michael Franklin, 'The colony writes back: Brutus, Britanus and the advantages of an Oriental ancestry', in Damian Walford Davies and Lynda Pratt (eds), *Wales and the Romantic Imagination* (Cardiff: University of Wales Press, 2007), pp. 13–42. Franklin notes that 'the so-called *Brut Tysilio* is actually a fifteenth-century Welsh translation of Geoffrey's *Historia Regum Britanniae*' (p. 36).

[40] Jenkins, 'Historical writing in the eighteenth century', p. 30.

[41] See also Gerald Morgan, 'The Morris brothers', in Jarvis (ed.), *A Guide to Welsh Literature*, pp. 64–80 (pp. 72–3).

[42] Trumpener, *Bardic Nationalism*, p. 4.

[43] Ibid., p. 10.

[44] Ibid., p. 6.

[45] *The Bard*, in Lonsdale, *The Poems of Thomas Gray, William Collins, Oliver Goldsmith*. All further line references are to this edition and are included in parenthesis in the text.

[46] For a good summary of further literary treatments of the massacre, see Edward D. Snyder, 'Thomas Gray's interest in Celtic', and *The Celtic Revival in English Literature, 1760–1800* (Cambridge, MA: Harvard University Press, 1923).

[47] See Lonsdale's head-notes in *Poems* to 'The Triumphs of Owen' and 'The Death of Hoel'. Gray's other Welsh poems which used Evans's *Dissertatio* as the source are 'Caradoc' (also from the *Gododdin*) and 'Conan'.

[48] Ffion Llywelyn Jenkins, 'Celticism and pre-Romanticism: Evan Evans', in Jarvis (ed.), *A Guide to Welsh Literature*, pp. 104–25 (p. 104).

[49] M. Wynn Thomas has argued that 'there has been a strain of translation that seeks to dehistoricise and depoliticize the material by representing it as being primarily Celtic and only incidentally Welsh. There are many aspects to this practice, but it is obvious that in certain respects it represents the "othering" of Welsh language culture along the same exoticizing lines as those identified by Edward Said in his famous discussion of Orientalism'. *http://www.bwlet.net/index.htm*.

[50] See, for example, Howard D. Weinbrot, *Britannia's Issue: The Rise of British Literature from Dryden to Ossian* (Cambridge: Cambridge University Press, 1993).

51 R. R. Davies argues that in late thirteenth-century Wales, 'the prospect of creating a united native Welsh polity under a single prince was no longer an idealist dream, but a practical proposition. Indeed, during the decade 1267–77, it was briefly, if prematurely, realized'. 'Edward I and Wales', p. 3.

52 Trumpener, *Bardic Nationalism*, p. 6.

53 Weinbrot, *Britannia's Issue*, pp. 397–8.

54 Ibid., p. 398.

55 Dustin Griffin, *Patriotism and Poetry in Eighteenth-Century Britain* (Cambridge: Cambridge University Press, 2002), p. 166.

56 Ibid., p. 171.

57 Paul Odney, 'Thomas Gray's "Daring Spirit": forging the poetics of an alternative nationalism', *Clio*, 28, 3 (1999), 245–60 (257).

58 Ibid., p. 254.

59 Ibid., p. 257.

60 Alok Yadav makes the point about the 'anglocentric character' of eighteenth-century Britishness in 'Nationalism and eighteenth-century British literature', *Literature Compass* (electronic journal) (2004), *http://www.literature-compass.com/*. See also Yadav, *Before the Empire of English: Literature and Nationalism in Eighteenth-Century Britain* (Basingstoke: Palgrave, 2004).

61 Trumpener suggests that 'From a nationalist perspective, Gray's popularization of the legend of Edward as "bardicide" and his portrayal of the bard as a vengeful national hero seems more satisfactory than Macpherson's Ossian, a figure whom blindness and age have rendered at once venerable and feeble.' *Bardic Nationalism*, p. 8.

62 Dr David Powel's *The Historie of Cambria, now called Wales* (1584) was the major influence on later Welsh histories and historians. For a good summary of histories of Wales, see Carr, *Medieval Wales*, pp. 4–26. For Welsh prophecy see Margaret Enid Griffiths, *Early Vaticination in Welsh* (Cardiff: University of Wales Press, 1937), and R. Wallis Evans, 'Prophetic poetry', in A. O. H. Jarman and Gwilym Rees Hughes (eds), *A Guide to Welsh Literature, 1282–c.1550* (Cardiff: University of Wales Press, 1997), pp. 256–74.

63 Evan Evans, *The Love of Our Country, A Poem, With Historical Notes, Address'd to Sir WATKIN WILLIAMS WYNN of Wynnstay, Bt.* 'By a Curate from Snowden' (Carmarthen: J. Ross, 1772), in D. Silvan Evans (ed.), *Gwaith y Parchedig Evan Evans (Ieuan Brydydd Hir)* (Caernarfon/ Carmarthen: H. Humphreys, 1876), pp. 129–46 (p. 143). The poem was also sold by booksellers in London, Brecon, Swansea, Neath and Salop (Shropshire).

64 Yadav, 'Nationalism and eighteenth-century British literature', p. 5.

65 Philip Schwyzer, *Literature, Nationalism and Memory in Early Modern England and Wales* (Cambridge: Cambridge University Press, 2004), p. 84.

66 Jones, *Musical Relicks of the Welsh Bards*, pp. 20–1.

67 Like Gray, Drayton was an English poet deeply interested in Welsh culture. See I. Gourvitch, 'The Welsh element in the Polyolbion: Drayton's sources', *Review of English Studies*, 4, 13 (1928), 69–77, and Geoffrey G. Hiller, '"Sacred Bards" and "Wise Druides": Drayton and his archetype of the poet', *ELH*, 51,1 (1984), 1–15.

[68] In the introduction to the 1770 edition of *The History of the Gwedir Family*, the text is also framed by its relation to Gray's *The Bard*. The book has 'intrinsic value' because it 'hath given rise to an ode which will be admired by our latest posterity' (p. vi).

[69] Jenkins, 'Celticism and pre-Romanticism', p. 120. Snyder also draws attention to similar attitudes in travel writing of the period. In relation to Edward I's massacre, H. P. Wyndham in *A Tour through Monmouthshire and Wales* (2nd edn; London, 1781), for example, states that even though there may be regret for the poems lost in the massacre, comfort may be found 'in the reflection that it has given birth to one of the finest odes in the English tongue, the merit of which, alone, would probably surpass the ponderous volumes of all those that might have been written in the British language'. 'Thomas Gray's interest in Celtic', p. 578.

[70] Jenkins, 'Celticism and pre-Romanticism', p. 122.

[71] Ibid.

[72] Ibid., p. 124.

[73] Schwyzer, *Literature, Nationalism and Memory*, p. 95.

[74] There is some confusion over the dating and publication details of this poem. Katie Trumpener's reference in *Bardic Nationalism* locates it in the 1764 *Specimens* published by Dodsley. The poem does not appear in this edition. In addition, the version which Trumpener prints is incorrectly transcribed, with one section of the poem appearing out of sequence from all the other versions I have consulted. In 'Thomas Gray's interest in Celtic', Snyder dates the poem as having been composed between 1759 and 1764 (p. 571), based on the assertion that the poem is to be found 'in the appendix to the second edition of the *Specimens* (1762)' (n. 1, p. 569). No such volume exists: the *first* edition is from 1764. Snyder must be referring to the 1862 edition in which the poem made its first appearance. It has also been subsequently published in Evans, *Gwaith y Parchedig Evan Evans*, pp. 126–8.

[75] All line references are to the 1862 edition of *Specimens*, pp. 143–5, and are included in parenthesis in the text.

[76] Trumpener, *Bardic Nationalism*, p. 4.

[77] Ibid., p. 7.

[78] Many scholars have noted the link between nation-building, mapping and the representation of the nation's rivers in literature. See, for example, Richard Helgerson, *Forms of Nationhood: The Elizabethan Writing of England* (Chicago: University of Chicago Press, 1992). Two essays pertinent to my discussion here are Bernhard Klein, 'Imaginary journeys: Spenser, Drayton, and the poetics of national space', and Philip Schwyzer, 'A map of Greater Cambria', both in Andrew Gordon and Bernhard Klein (eds), *Literature, Mapping and the Politics of Space in Early Modern Britain* (Cambridge: Cambridge University Press, 2001), pp. 204–23 and pp. 35–44 respectively.

[79] The river Severn is highlighted throughout Geoffrey of Monmouth's *The History of the Kings of Britain* as marking the border between Wales and England, or the Saxons and the Ancient British. For those who were sceptical of Galfridian history, the status of the Severn was more unstable and

contested. Evans's use of 'Sabrina' may also allude to the nymph Sabrina in Milton's *Comus*. For excellent discussions of the symbolic significance of the Severn for Welsh–English politics, see Philip Schwyzer, 'A map of Greater Cambria' and 'Purity and danger on the west bank of the Severn: the cultural geography of *A Masque Presented at Ludlow Castle, 1634*', *Representations*, 60 (1997), 22–48.

[80] Trumpener, *Bardic Nationalism*, p. 8.

[81] Ibid.

[82] The editor of the poem in *Gwaith y Parchedig Evan Evans* also notes further allusions to English poetry. Line 3 alludes to Milton, line 4 to Goldsmith, and line 11 to Dryden (p. 126).

[83] Trumpener argues that, by ending the poem with the suicide of the last bard and not the witnessing of the murder of enemies' children (as in the original psalm), Evans 'blunts the full political force of the original'. *Bardic Nationalism*, p. 9. This 'displacement of political anger into cultural expression', she suggests, is typical of 'bardic nationalism' in general (p. 11). However, as I have shown, the poem does not end with the bard's suicide, despite the extensive use made of Gray's *The Bard*. In contrast to Trumpener, then, I am claiming a much less conciliatory stance for Evans.

[84] As part of the prefatory material to the poem Evans prints a copy (from John Brown's *Dissertation on the Union, and Power, Progressions, Separations, and Corruptions, of Poetry and Music* (London, 1763)) of a commission by Elizabeth I which led to the 'Congress of Bards' at Caerwys in 1567, a forerunner of the eisteddfod. The inclusion of this is partly to flatter Evans's dedicatee, Sir Roger Mostyn, whose family were patrons of the Congress, but Evans also mentions the 'Sylver Harp' (p. vi) as the prize given by the Mostyn family to the '*Chief* of *that Faculty*' of bards (p. vi). See Sally Harper, 'Instrumental music in medieval Wales', *North American Journal of Welsh Studies*, 4, 1 (2004), 20–42 (22).

[85] In *Gwaith y Parchedig Evan Evans*, lines 1–4, p. 52. The Welsh englynion version of the poem, 'Ar Lys Ifor Hael, O Faesaleg Yn Swydd Fynwy', is printed on pages 51–2.

[86] For further discussion of this model of patronage, see Constantine, *The Truth against the World*, p. 38, and Damian Walford Davies, *Presences that Disturb: Models of Romantic Identity in the Literature and Culture of the 1790s* (Cardiff: University of Wales Press, 2002), pp. 187–9.

[87] *Gwaith y Parchedig Evan Evans*, p. 51. Another famous example of Evans performing the bardic role is 'Hiraeth y Bardd am ei Wlad'.

4 Patriotic Poems of Eighteenth-Century Wales

[1] See, for example, Christine Gerrard, *The Patriot Opposition to Walpole: Politics, Poetry, and National Myth, 1725–1742* (Oxford: Clarendon Press, 1994), and Dustin Griffin, *Patriotism and Poetry in Eighteenth-Century Britain* (Cambridge: Cambridge University Press, 2002).

2 James Thomson, *Alfred. A Masque* (London, 1740). As Griffin notes, 'Rule Britannia' (1740) 'began life as the final ode in a masque about an English king', *Patriotism and Poetry*, p. 44.

3 Historians have served eighteenth-century Wales better in this respect than literary scholars. See, for example, works listed in the bibliography by Geraint H. Jenkins and Prys Morgan, among others.

4 There are exceptions, of course, such as the poet John Dyer, whose poetry has most recently been read in the context of 'imperial Georgic'. See Griffin, *Patriotism and Poetry*, chapter 7, and Rachel Crawford, *Poetry, Enclosure, and the Vernacular Landscape, 1700–1830* (Cambridge: Cambridge University Press, 2002). Other later examples of British-identified writers might include Edward 'Celtic' Davies and Felicia Hemans.

5 *Wallography* was reprinted in 1738 as *The Briton describ'd, or a journey thro' Wales*, as part of *A Collection of Welsh travels and memoirs of Wales*, and again in 1753 as *Dean Swift's Ghost*. All page references are to the 1753 edition and are cited parenthetically in the text.

6 Ned Ward, *A Trip to North-Wales: Being A Description of that Country and People* (London, 1701). All page references are to this edition and are cited parenthetically in the text. A further example of early-eighteenth-century anti-Welsh satire is Edward Holdsworth, *The Mouse-Trap: or, the Welsh engagement with the Mice* (London, 1709), first published in Latin as *Muscipula, sive kambromyomaxia* (Londini, 1709).

7 William Camden's *Britannia* (first published 2 May 1586) was a seminal antiquarian work which was constantly enlarged, edited and reprinted into the nineteenth century. It is described by the Oxford *DNB* as 'of the highest importance as a cultural icon affecting national self-image'. Camden was known for discrediting the myth of the Trojan origins of the Ancient Britons. Originally in Latin, *Britannia* was translated into English in 1610. Wyman H. Herendeen, 'Camden, William (1551–1623)', *Oxford Dictionary of National Biography* (Oxford: Oxford University Press, 2004), *http://oxforddnb.com/view/article/4431*, accessed 29 June 2007. John Speed was part of Camden's circle and provided the information about coins for the 1600 edition of *Britannia*. Sarah Bendall, 'Speed, John (1551/2–1629)', *Oxford Dictionary of National Biography* (Oxford University Press, 2004), *http://oxforddnb.com/view/article/26093*, accessed 29 June 2007.

8 The author is playing on the title of Speed's *The Theatre of the Empire of Great Britaine.*

9 Ezekiel Polsted, *Cambria Triumphans, or, A Panegyrick Upon Wales* (London, 1702). All page references are to this edition and are cited parenthetically in the text.

10 Jane Spencer, *Aphra Behn's Afterlife* (Oxford: Oxford University Press, 2000), p. 157.

11 See, for example, Abraham Cowley, 'On *Orinda*'s Poems: Ode' (1663); 'Philo-Philippa', 'To the Excellent *Orinda*' (1667); Delarivier Manley, 'To the Author of Agnes de Castro' (1696).

[12] For an opposite construction of Philips as a Welsh poet in a context favourable to Aphra Behn, see 'To Mrs. B on her Poems', by Daniel Ken[d]rick, in Aphra Behn, *Lycidas; or, The Lover in Fashion* (1688):

If we *Orinda* to your works compare,
They uncouth, like her countrys soyle, appear,
Mean as its Pesants, as its Mountains bare.

Quoted by Patrick Thomas (ed.), *The Collected Works of Katherine Philips*, vol. I, *The Poems* (Essex: Stump Cross Books, 1990), p. 27.

[13] John Owen (1564?–1628) was the author of eleven volumes of Latin epigrams which were published from 1606 to 1613. Meic Stephens (ed.), *The New Companion to the Literature of Wales* (Cardiff: University of Wales Press, 1998), p. 556.

[14] Griffin, *Patriotism and Poetry*, p. 18.

[15] See Richard Terry, *Poetry and the Making of the English Literary Past, 1660–1781* (Oxford: Oxford University Press, 2001), p. 54.

[16] Ibid., p. 55.

[17] Ibid., p. 54.

[18] John Husbands, 'Preface' to *Miscellany of Poems* (1731), quoted by Terry, *Poetry and the Making of the English Literary Past*, p. 139.

[19] All line and page references are cited parenthetically in the text.

[20] Griffin, *Patriotism and Poetry*, p. 73.

[21] Richard Rolt, *Eliza; a new musical entertainment; as performed at the New Theatre in the Hay-Market. Written by Mr. Rolt. The music composed by Mr. Arne* (London, 1754). *Eliza* was reprinted along with *Cambria* and other works in *Select Pieces, by the late R. Rolt* (London, 1772). In *Eliza*, Queen Elizabeth is figured as a Protestant champion driving out her Spanish enemies so that 'Britannia shall still be the queen of the main' (p. 53). Although similar to *Cambria* in its linkage of rural landscape with peace and liberty, in *Eliza* Britannia clearly means England, despite the lip-service paid to 'UNITED' Britons who 'BRAVE THE WORLD' (p. 71).

[22] Betty Rizzo, 'Rolt, Richard (*bap.* 1724, *d.* 1770)', *Oxford Dictionary of National Biography* (Oxford: Oxford University Press, 2004), *http://www.oxforddnb.com/view/article/24035*, accessed 10 July 2007.

[23] For a detailed discussion of this context, see Gerrard, *The Patriot Opposition to Walpole*.

[24] Ibid.

[25] Ibid., p. 9.

[26] Rosemary Sweet, *Antiquaries: The Discovery of the Past in Eighteenth-Century Britain* (London: Hambledon and London, 2004), p. 156.

[27] Sweet makes the interesting point that the Welsh antiquarians were not really interested in finding Roman remains in Wales, as they preferred to stress their resistance to Rome and the preservation of distinct native traditions. Ibid., p. 141.

[28] Ibid., p. 142.

[29] Rolt traces the lineage of Henry VIII from Cadwaladr and speaks favourably of the Union of Wales and England under his kingship: 'Wales was incorporated with England, its natives subjected to the same laws, made

capable of enjoying the same preferments, and endowed with like privileges and immunities as the English' (note to line 280, p. 22).

30 Griffin, *Patriotism and Poetry*, p. 36.
31 Ibid.
32 Richard Harding, 'Vernon, Edward (1684–1757)', *Oxford Dictionary of National Biography* (Oxford: Oxford University Press, 2004), p. 7, *http://www.oxforddnb.com/view/article/28237*, accessed 10 July 2007.
33 Ibid., p. 9.
34 Gerrard, *The Patriot Opposition to Walpole*, p. 9.
35 Sweet makes the point that 'English antiquaries experienced little difficulty in identifying their earliest ancestors as the ancient Britons, whilst simultaneously setting a disdainful distance between themselves and the modern heirs of the original Britons, the Welsh'. *Antiquaries*, p. 121.
36 Peter D. G. Thomas, 'Wynn, Sir Watkin Williams, third baronet (1693?–1749)', *Oxford Dictionary of National Biography* (Oxford: Oxford University Press, 2004), *http://www.oxforddnb.com/view/article/30155*, accessed 10 July 2007.
37 This regard is shown by the anecdote that when he went up to London 'it was customary for the Welsh gentry resident in London to meet him at Finchley and form a procession to escort him into town'. Ibid., p. 5.
38 Ibid.
39 Gerrard, *The Patriot Opposition to Walpole*, p. 212.
40 Thomas, 'Wynn, Sir Watkin Williams, third baronet', pp. 2–4.
41 Ibid., p. 3.
42 J. C. D. Clark, 'The politics of the excluded: Tories, Jacobites and Whig patriots, 1715–60', *Parliamentary History*, 2 (1983), 209–22.
43 Rizzo, 'Rolt, Richard (*bap.* 1724, *d.* 1770)', p. 1. On the difficulty of pinning down a Jacobite identity, see the introduction to Paul Monod, *Jacobitism and the English People, 1688–1788* (Cambridge: Cambridge University Press, 1989).
44 Gerrard, *The Patriot Opposition to Walpole*, p. 218.
45 Ibid., p. 142.
46 Ibid., p. 222.
47 Evan Evans, *The Love of Our Country, A Poem, With Historical Notes, Address'd to Sir WATKIN WILLIAMS WYNN of Wynnstay, Bt.* 'By a Curate from Snowden'(Carmarthen: J. Ross, 1772), in D. Silvan Evans (ed.), *Gwaith y Parchedig Evan Evans (Ieuan Brydydd Hir)* (Caernarfon/Carmarthen: H. Humphreys, 1876), pp. 129–46. All page references are to this edition and are cited parenthetically in the text. The dedication to Sir Watkin (fourth baronet, 1749–89) is in recognition of his patronage of Evans: between 1771 and 1778 he gave him a pension and use of the library at Wynnstay. This relationship was not to last, as Evans attacked Wynn in 1776 for his adoption of English as his language. See Geraint H. Jenkins, 'Evans, Evan (1731–1788)', *Oxford Dictionary of National Biography* (Oxford: Oxford University Press, 2004), p. 1, *http://www.oxforddnb.com/view/article/8955*, accessed 11 July 2007.

[48] The appointment of non-Welsh speaking clergy to Welsh benefices was an ongoing issue in the eighteenth century. For a full exposition of its contemporary significance see J. Jones, *Considerations of the Illegality and Impropriety of Preferring Clergymen Who are Unacquainted with the Welsh Language to Benefices in Wales* (Caernarvon: H. Jones, 1768).

[49] George Lord Lyttelton, *The History of the Life of Henry the Second, and of the age in which he lived, in five books* (London, 1767–71). In 1756 Lyttelton wrote a 'tour' of Wales, which was published in 1774 as an *Account of a Journey into Wales*. His account is described by the *DNB* as 'one of the earliest Romantic tourist accounts of Wales, containing a notable description of Mount Snowdon's sublimity'. Christine Gerrard 'Lyttelton, George, first Baron Lyttelton (1709–1773)', *Oxford Dictionary of National Biography* (Oxford: Oxford University Press, Sept. 2004; online edn, May 2006), *http://www.oxforddnb.com/view/article/17306*, accessed 14 June 2007.

[50] Joseph Cradock, *Letters from Snowdon: descriptive of a tour through the northern counties of Wales* (London, 1770). All page references are to this edition and are cited parenthetically in the text.

[51] In the section on Wales in volume II of *The History of the Life of King Henry the Second*, there are five uses of the word 'barbarous' to describe the Welsh, pp. 35–68. They are also characterised as vengeful, savage, anarchic and undisciplined, if valiant, prudent and cheerful.

[52] Aberystwyth NLW MS 1641 B, 2 vols, Miscellanies, vol. 1, pp. 308–9. The book belonged to Revd Walter Davies, 'Gwallter Mechain' (1761–1849).

[53] The library at Hengwrt in Llanelltyd 'contained the finest collection of Welsh manuscripts collected by one man', including *The Black Book of Carmarthen*, *The White Book of Rhydderch* and *The Book of Taliesin*. The collection stayed at Hengwrt until 1859. It is now catalogued in the National Library of Wales as Peniarth Manuscripts. See Stephens (ed.), *The New Companion to the Literature of Wales*, p. 756. Evans would have had connections to Hengwrt through the patronage of Sir Watkin Williams Wynn II (1771–8) of nearby Wynnstay. Aneirin Lewis, 'Evans, Evan (Ieuan Fardd or Ieuan Brydydd Hir) (1731–1788)', *Welsh Biography Online*.

[54] Sweet, *Antiquaries*, p. 190.

[55] Ibid.

[56] The Welsh monk Asser (from St David's) wrote the *Life of Alfred*, in which he is depicted teaching Alfred to read and translate. Patrick Wormald, 'Asser (d. 909)', *Oxford Dictionary of National Biography* (Oxford: Oxford University Press, 2004), *http://www.oxforddnb.com/view/article/810*, accessed 12 July 2007.

[57] For an extensive discussion of the ways in which Owain Glyndŵr has been used as a redeemer figure and nationalist symbol, see Elissa R. Henken, *National Redeemer: Owain Glyndŵr in Welsh Tradition* (Cardiff: University of Wales Press, 1996). Henken notes that Robert Vaughan of Hengwrt wrote a history of Glyndŵr in the 1660s (Aberystwyth, NLW Panton MS 53, pp. 49–60), p. 11. As she points out, the major treatment of Glyndŵr in the eighteenth century is by Thomas Pennant in his *Tours in Wales* (1778). *National Redeemer*, p. 11. My research suggests that Glyndŵr starts to crop up

more frequently as a symbol of national resistance in poetry from the mid century onwards. He also appears as a freedom fighter in Edward Jones, *Musical and Poetical Relicks of the Welsh Bards* (London, 1784), p. 88.

[58] The Renaissance humanist scholar William Salesbury is primarily known for his Welsh–English dictionary of 1547 (the first of its kind) and his contribution to the *Testament Newydd* of 1567. Richard Davies also contributed to the Welsh New Testament and wrote the famous preface 'Epistle to the Welsh', which included an essay on Welsh history and an '*apologia* for Welsh Protestantism, explaining how the pristine form of Christianity among the Welsh had been corrupted by Rome'. R. Brinley Jones, *William Salesbury* (Cardiff: University of Wales Press, 1994), p. 56. William Morgan completed the translation of the New Testament in 1588. I am yet to identify whom Evans is referring to as 'Williams'.

[59] *Account of a Journey into Wales*, in Henry Penruddocke Wyndham, *A Gentleman's Tour through Monmouthshire and Wales* (London, 1781), pp. 225–46 (p. 229).

[60] Evans (ed.), *Gwaith y Parchedig Evan Evans*, p. 72.

[61] John Walters (1760–89) was the eldest son of the more famous John Walters (bap. 1721, d. 1797), author of *An English–Welsh Dictionary* (1770–94) and *A Dissertation on the Welsh Language* (Cowbridge, 1771), which served as an appendix to the *Dictionary*. John Walters junior worked in the Bodleian Library, was headmaster of Ruthin School in 1784 and then rector of Efenechdid, Denbighshire. The two are treated under the same entry in the Oxford DNB: Richard Crowe, 'Walters, John (*bap.* 1721, *d.* 1797)', *Oxford Dictionary of National Biography* (Oxford: Oxford University Press, 2004), *http://www.oxforddnb.com/view/article/28644*, accessed 14 June 2007.

[62] John Walters senior invented the word for patriotism (*gwladgarwch*) in 1776 and the word for nationality (*cenedligrwydd*) in 1798. Geraint H. Jenkins, 'On the trail of a "Rattleskull Genius": introduction', in Geraint H. Jenkins (ed.), *A Rattleskull Genius: The Many Faces of Iolo Morganwg* (Cardiff: University of Wales Press, 2005), pp. 1–26 (p. 17).

[63] In S. Rhian Reynolds (ed.), *A Bibliography of Welsh Literature in English Translation* (Cardiff: University of Wales Press, 2005), the individual poems taken directly from Evans's *Specimens* are listed as translations ('Nest, the Daughter of Howel', and 'The Ode of the Months'). The other three poems which come under 'Translations' in *Translated Specimens* – 'The Praises of Lewellin the Great', 'Lewellin and his Bards' and 'An Ode to Cambria' – are not listed by Reynolds. Walters's (very) free translation of Llywarch Hen's elegy on the death of Cynddylan was printed as a 'specimen' in volume II of William Warrington's two-volume *The History of Wales* (1788), Book IX, pp. 310–12. The 'translation' is billed as an 'elegy', which suggests it is based on 'Marwnad Cynddylan'/'The Death Song of Cynddylan', although the actual poem is also similar to 'Stafell Gynddylan'/The Hall of Cynddylan'. Both poems are from the cycle of *englynion* known as *Canu Heledd/The Song of Heledd*. Walters's rendition is not listed by Reynolds. See Jenny Rowland, *Early Welsh Saga Poetry: A Study and Edition of the* Englynion (Cambridge:

D. S. Brewer, 1990), and Ifor Williams (ed.), *Canu Llywerch Hen* (Cardiff: University of Wales Press, 1935).

[64] For example, Anne Penny, 'Taliesin's Poem to Prince Elphin' and 'An Elegy on Neest' in her *Poems, with a Dramatic Entertainment* (1771), which also includes two fragments from 'Fingal'.

[65] The abandoned or ruined hall motif is also prominent in Walters's translation of Llywerch Hen in *The History of Wales*: 'No more the mansion of delight, / Cynddylan's hall is dark tonight' (p. 311).

[66] Philip Schwyzer, *Literature, Nationalism and Memory in Early Modern England and Wales* (Cambridge: Cambridge University Press, 2004), p. 83.

[67] Andrew Breeze, 'Sidney's *Apology for Poetry* and the Welsh bards', *Notes and Queries*, 46, 2 (June 1999), 198–9 (199). As Breeze notes, references to Ysgolan can also be found in the Black Book of Carmarthen and in Breton legend.

[68] Ibid., p. 198.

[69] Schwyzer, *Literature, Nationalism and Memory*, p. 84.

[70] Evidence of this 'canon' of original and 'translated' poetry being concretised by the nineteenth century can be found in, for example, John Pryse, *Breezes from the Welsh Mountains: A Scrap Book of Cambrian Prose and Poetry* (Llanidloes and London, 1858). Among Pryse's selection we find Evans's 'Captivity of the Welsh Bards', 'On seeing the Ruins of Ivor Hael's Palace', 'The Penitent Shepherd' and a selection from *Specimens*; Walters's 'Lewelyn and his Bards', 'The Praises of Llewelyn the Great', 'Nest, the daughter of Howel', 'The Ode of the Months', 'An Ode to Cambria' and a further selection of his poetry; as well as various 'translations' from the Welsh bards, 'Grongar Hill' by John Dyer and 'Farewell to Wales' by Mrs Hemans.

5 Wales in Eighteenth-Century Fiction

[1] Leith Davis, *Acts of Union: Scotland and the Literary Negotiation of the British Nation, 1707–1830* (Stanford: Stanford University Press, 1998); Murray G. H. Pittock, *Inventing and Resisting Britain: Cultural Identities in Britain and Ireland, 1685–1789* (Basingstoke: Macmillan, 1997) and *Celtic Identity and the British Image* (Manchester: Manchester University Press, 1999); Janet Sorenson, *The Grammar of Empire in Eighteenth-Century British Writing* (Cambridge: Cambridge University Press, 2000); Katie Trumpener, *Bardic Nationalism: The Romantic Novel and the British Empire* (Princeton: Princeton University Press, 1997).

[2] *Eighteenth-Century Fiction*, 15, 1 (2002), 53–8. All further references are cited parenthetically in the text.

[3] Most of the work on Welsh writers has been published since 2000. Exceptions include Jane Aaron, *Pur Fel Y Dur: Y Gymraes yn Llên Menywod y Bedwaredd Ganrif ar Bymtheg* (Caerdydd: Gwasg Prifysgol Cymru, 1998). The key study for the eighteenth-century novel is Moira Dearnley, *Distant Fields: Eighteenth-Century Fictions of Wales* (Cardiff: University of Wales Press, 2001).

[4] See Damian Walford Davies and Lynda Pratt (eds), *Wales and the Romantic*

Imagination (Cardiff: Cardiff University Press, 2007); Damian Walford Davies, *Presences that Disturb: Models of Romantic Identity in the Literature and Culture of the 1790s* (Cardiff: University of Wales Press, 2002); Gerard Carruthers and Alan Rawes (eds), *English Romanticism and the Celtic World* (Cambridge: Cambridge University Press, 2003).

5 Another pre-twentieth-century contender for being the first Anglo-Welsh novel is T. J. Ll. Prichard's *Twm Shon Catti* (1828). See Gerald Morgan, 'The first Anglo-Welsh novel', *Anglo-Welsh Review*, XVII, 39 (1968), 114–22; Sam Adams, *T. J. Llewelyn Prichard*, 'Writers of Wales' (Cardiff: University of Wales Press, 2000).

6 Jane Aaron, *Nineteenth-Century Women's Writing in Wales: Nation, Gender and Identity* (Cardiff: University of Wales Press, 2007), p. 9.

7 Ibid., p. 10.

8 Ibid., p. 11.

9 Andrew Davies, '"The reputed nation of inspiration": representations of Wales in fiction from the Romantic period, 1780–1829' (unpub. Ph.D. thesis, University of Cardiff, 2001).

10 Ibid., p. 149. As Davies notes, the obvious exception are the novels of Thomas Love Peacock. See also Davies's essay, '"Redirecting the attention of history": antiquarian and historical fictions of Wales from the Romantic period', in Walford Davies and Pratt (eds), *Wales and the Romantic Imagination*, pp. 104–21.

11 Davies, 'The reputed nation', p. 14.

12 Stephen Knight, *A Hundred Years of Fiction*, Writing Wales in English (Cardiff: University of Wales Press, 2004), p. 4.

13 Dearnley, *Distant Fields*, chapter 12.

14 In an otherwise excellent article, Charlotte Sussman consistently writes 'England' when the novel is actually referring to Wales. 'Lismahago's captivity: transculturation in *Humphry Clinker*', *ELH*, 61 (1994), 597–618.

15 Sharon Alker, 'The geography of negotiation: Wales, Anglo-Scottish sympathy, and Tobias Smollett', *Lumen*, XXI (2002), 87–103.

16 Tobias Smollett, *The Expedition of Humphry Clinker* (Oxford: Oxford University Press, 1998), p. 86. All further references are to this edition and are cited parenthetically in the text.

17 For an extensive discussion of Smollett's use of Horatian models, see Byron Gassman, '"Humphry Clinker" and the two kingdoms of George III', *Criticism*, 16 (1974), 95–108.

18 Sussman, 'Lismahago's captivity', p. 597. Sussman writes of 'English self-sufficiency'.

19 Sorenson, *The Grammar of Empire*, pp. 117–18.

20 Ibid., p. 118.

21 Michael Rosenblum, 'Smollett's *Humphry Clinker*', in John Richetti (ed.), *The Cambridge Companion to the Eighteenth-Century Novel* (Cambridge: Cambridge University Press, 1996), pp. 175–97 (p. 188).

22 Ibid., p. 185.

23 Ibid., p. 193.

24 Alker, 'The geography of negotiation', p. 99.

[25] John Richetti, *The English Novel in History 1700–1780* (London and New York: Routledge, 1999), p. 192.

[26] Alker, 'The geography of negotiation', p. 92.

[27] Davies, 'The reputed nation', p. 23.

[28] Ibid., p. 19.

[29] Richetti, *The English Novel in History*, p. 192.

[30] Davies, 'The reputed nation', pp. 28–9.

[31] Rosenblum, 'Smollett's *Humphry Clinker*', p. 188.

[32] Philip Jenkins, *The Making of a Ruling Class: The Glamorgan Gentry 1640–1790* (Cambridge: Cambridge University Press, 1983), p. xxi.

[33] Ibid., p. 39.

[34] Ibid., p. 41.

[35] Ibid., p. xxi.

[36] Linda Colley, *Britons: Forging the Nation 1707–1837* (London: Pimlico, 1994), p. 156.

[37] Ibid., p. 162.

[38] Dearnley, *Distant Fields*, p. 132.

[39] Davies, 'The reputed nation', p. 64.

[40] Trumpener, *Bardic Nationalism*, p. 20.

[41] Anna Maria Bennett, *Anna; or, Memoirs of a Welch heiress. Interspersed with anecdotes of a nabob, In four volumes* (London, 1785), vol. I, p. 230. All further references are to this edition and are cited parenthetically in the text.

[42] See Dearnley, *Distant Fields*, for an excellent discussion of the representation of Llandore in the novel which I do not wish to replicate (pp. 134–8).

[43] Jane Aaron, 'A national seduction: Wales in nineteenth-century women's writing', *New Welsh Review*, 27 (1994), 31–8 (33).

[44] Ibid. As Jane Aaron notes in another article, the generational difference between the two Lords mirrors the difference between the third baronet, Watkin Williams Wynn, and his son, Watkin Williams Wynn, the fourth baronet. 'Seduction and betrayal: Wales in women's fiction, 1785–1810', *Women's Writing*, 1, 1 (1994), 65–76 (73). See also Colley, *Britons*, p. 160.

[45] Anna Maria Bennett, *Ellen, Countess of Castle Howell. A novel in two volumes.* (Dublin, 1794), vol. I, pp. 2–3. All further references are to this edition and are cited parenthetically in the text. The first London edition (1795) was in four vols.

[46] For further discussion of the symbolism of the estate in Bennett's novels see Francesca Rhydderch, 'Dual nationality, divided identity: ambivalent narratives of Britishness in the Welsh novels of Anna Maria Bennett', *Welsh Writing in English: A Yearbook of Critical Essays*, 3 (1997), 1–17 (6–7), and Dearnley, *Distant Fields*, pp. 148–9.

[47] Rhydderch, 'Dual nationality, divided identity', pp. 8–9.

[48] Gassman, '"Humphry Clinker" and the two kingdoms of George III', p. 103.

[49] Trumpener, *Bardic Nationalism*, p. 30.

[50] Ibid., p. 14.

[51] Both *Anna* and *Ellen* feature nabob figures who try to seduce the heroine. Whereas Colonel Gorget in *Anna* comes to a bad end, the colonial adventurer

Lord Claverton is eventually accepted in his role as Percy's father. The different treatment of the nabob reflects the overall message of each novel. In the fantasy that *Anna* presents, Gorget is dispatched and his money is not incorporated back into the Welsh estate. The more realistic *Ellen* acknowledges the power (if not the propriety) of colonial gain and the desire for profit at home. For a discussion of the novels in this context, see Trumpener, *Bardic Nationalism*, pp. 168–74, and Rhydderch, 'Dual nationality, divided identity', pp. 12–15.

[52] Aaron, 'A national seduction', pp. 33–4, and Rhydderch, 'Dual nationality, divided identity', p. 7.

[53] The use of dialect may have been influenced by Win Jenkins in *Humphry Clinker*.

[54] Aaron, 'A national seduction', pp. 33–4.

[55] From the context in which Anna learns Welsh, it is clear that the Welsh language is associated by Bennett 'with a particularly disempowered economic and social position', whereas 'the ability to speak English' is presented in the novel as 'a marker of social superiority'. Rhydderch, 'Dual nationality, divided identity', p. 11. The loss of Welsh and the privileging of English was arguably the most pernicious effect of the Anglicisation of the Welsh gentry in the eighteenth century.

[56] Aaron, 'A national seduction'.

[57] These are *Aphtharte, the Genius of Britain* (Bath, 1784) and *Vacunalia* (London, 1788).

[58] Dearnley, *Distant Fields*, p. 163. As Dearnley notes, Davies was inspired by the (questionable) scholarship of William Owen Pughe, whose edition of Dafydd ap Gwilym (with Owen Jones), *Barddoniaeth Dafydd ab Gwilym*, was published in 1789. His translations, including that in *Elisa Powell*, were from this edition, but five of the nine were from the appendix, since recognised as the original work of Iolo Morganwg. See Moira Dearnley, '"Mad Ned" and the "Smatter-Dasher": Iolo Morganwg and Edward "Celtic" Davies', in Geraint H. Jenkins (ed.), *A Rattleskull Genius: The Many Faces of Iolo Morganwg* (Cardiff: University of Wales Press, 2005), pp. 425–42 (pp. 426–7).

[59] Dearnley, *Distant Fields*, p. 158.

[60] Ibid., p. 171.

[61] Ibid., p. 163.

[62] *Elisa Powell, or Trials of Sensibility* (London, 1795), p. 3. All future references are to this edition and are included parenthetically in the text.

[63] Dearnley, *Distant Fields*, p. 165.

[64] Andrew Davies highlights the realism in Edward Davies's portrait. 'The reputed nation', p. 117.

[65] Trumpener, *Bardic Nationalism*, p. 168.

[66] Dearnley, *Distant Fields*, p. 171.

[67] Rhydderch makes a similar point about the way in which the 'sympathetic portrayal' of Winifred Griffiths in Bennett's *Ellen* is superseded by 'English sentimental norms of beauty and social worth'. 'Dual nationality, divided identity', p. 11.

Bibliography

Manuscript Sources
BL Add. MS 27543, fo. 3.
Clwyd Record Office, Hawarden, Call No. D/E/871.
NLW MS 1641 B, 2 vols, Miscellanies, vol. 1, pp. 308–9.
NLW MS LIGC 10B, 'A dissertation on the Welsh Laws, &c.', pp. 175–217, formerly 1–41.

Primary Texts
Anon., *An Account of the Rise, Progress, and Present State of the Welsh Society, for Supporting a Charity School Erected in Gray's-Inn-Road, London* (London, 1793).
Anon., *The Tears of Cambria. A Poem* (London, 1773).
Bennett, Anna Maria, *Anna; or, Memoirs of a Welch Heiress. Interspersed with anecdotes of a nabob, In four volumes* (London, 1785).
Bennett, Anna Maria, *Ellen, Countess of Castle Howell. A novel in two volumes.* (Dublin, 1794; in 4 vols, London, 1795).
Blackmore, Richard, *Prince Arthur. An heroick poem, In ten books* (London, 1695).
Blackmore, Richard, *Alfred: An epick poem. In twelve books. Dedicated to the Illustrious Prince Frederick of Hanover* (London, 1723).
Brereton, Jane, *Poems on Several Occasions: by Mrs Jane Brereton. With Letters to her Friends, and an Account of Her Life* (London, 1744).
Brereton, Thomas, *George: A Poem* (London, 1715).
Brown, John, *Dissertation on the Union, and Power, Progressions, Separations, and Corruptions, of Poetry and Music* (London, 1763).
Carte, Thomas, *A General History of England*, 4 vols (London, 1747–55).
Cradock, Joseph, *Letters from Snowdon: descriptive of a tour through the northern counties of Wales* (London, 1770).
Davies, Edward, *Elisa Powell, or, Trials of Sensibility* (London, 1795).
Davies, Edward, *Vacunalia: consisting of essays in verse, on various subjects, with some translations* (London and Bristol, 1788).

Davies, Edward, *Aphtharte, the Genius of Britain* (London and Bath, 1784).

Dryden, John, *King Arthur; or, The British Worthy* (London, 1691).

Evans, D. Silvan, *Gwaith y Parchedig Evan Evans* (Caernarfon, 1876).

Evans, Evan, *Some Specimens of the Poetry of the Antient Welsh Bards, Translated into English* (London, 1764).

Evans, Evan, *Some Specimens of the Poetry of the Antient Welsh Bards, Translated into English* (Llanidloes, 1862).

Evans, Evan, *The Love of Our Country, A Poem, With Historical Notes, Address'd to Sir WATKIN WILLIAMS WYNN of Wynnstay, Bt.* 'By a Curate from Snowden' (Carmarthen, 1772).

Evans, Evan, *The Love of Our Country, A Poem, With Historical Notes* (2nd edn; Carmarthen, 1773).

Evans, John, *The Christian Soldier; or, An early Instruction in the Christian Warfare, the surest Foundation of the Subject's Loyalty, and of the Servant's Fidelity* (London, 1750).

Evans, Theophilus, *Drych y Prif Oesoedd yn ddwy ran* (Shrewsbury, 1716).

Evans, Theophilus, *A View of the Primitive Ages*, trans. Revd George Roberts (Llanidloes, 1834).

Ford, Patrick K. (ed.), *The Poetry of Llywerch Hen* (Berkeley: University of California Press, 1974).

Gambold, William, *A Welsh Grammar; or, A Short and Easie Introduction to the Welsh Tongue* (Carmarthen, 1727).

Geoffrey of Monmouth, *The History of the Kings of Britain*, ed. and trans. Lewis Thorpe (Harmondsworth: Penguin, 1978).

Griffith, Nehemiah, *The Leek. A Poem on St. David's Day: Most humbly Inscribed to the Honourable Society of Ancient Britons* (2nd edn; London, 1718).

Harry, George Owen, *Genealogy of the High and Mighty Monarch, James, by the grace of God. King of great Brittayne, &c. with his lineall descent from Noah, by divers direct lynes to Brutus, first Inhabiter of this Ile of Brittayne; and from him to Cadwalader, the last King of the Brittish bloud; and from thence, sundry wayes to his Majesty* (London, 1604).

Hoadley, Benjamin, *A Sermon Preach'd at St. James, Westminster, On St. David's Day, March I. 1716* (London, 1717).

Holdsworth, Edward, *Muscipula, sive kambromyomaxia* (Londini, 1709).

Holdsworth, Edward, *The Mouse-Trap: or, the Welsh engagement with the mice* (London, 1709).

Hughes, John, *An Ode for the Birth-Day of Her Royal Highness The Princess of Wales* (London, 1716).

Jones, Edward, *Musical and Poetical Relicks of the Welsh Bards* (London, 1784).

Jones, J. [John], *Considerations of the Illegality and Impropriety of Preferring Clergymen Who are Unacquainted with the Welsh Language to Benefices in Wales* (Caernarvon, 1768).

Jones, Thomas, *The British Language in its Lustre* (London, 1688).

Jones, Thomas, *The Rise and Progress of the Most Honourable and Loyal Society of Antient Britons, established in Honour to her Royal Highness's Birthday, and the Principality of* Wales, *on St.* David'*s Day, the First of* March, *1714–15* (London, 1717).

Lhuyd, Edward, *Archæologia Britannica, giving some account additional to what has been hitherto publish'd, of the languages, histories and customs of the original inhabitants of Great Britain* (Oxford, 1707).

Lonsdale, Roger (ed.), *Eighteenth-Century Women Poets* (Oxford: Oxford University Press, 1989).

Lonsdale, Roger (ed.), *The Poems of Thomas Gray, William Collins, Oliver Goldsmith* (London: Longmans, 1969).

Lyttelton, George Lord, *The History of the Life of Henry the Second, and of the age in which he lived, in five books* (London, 1767–71).

Owen, Jeremy, *The Goodness and Severity of GOD, in his Dispensations, with respect unto the Ancient BRITAINS, Display'd: In a Sermon Preach'd to an Auditory of Protestant Dissenters, At Haberdasher's Hall in London, on March the 1ˢᵗ, 1716* (London, 1717).

Owen, William, *The Heroic Elegies and other pieces of Llywarç Hen* (London, 1792).

Owen, William, *Barddoniaeth Dafydd ab Gwilym* (Llundain, 1789).

Penny, Anne, *Poems, with a Dramatic Entertainment* (London, 1771).

Philipps, P., *Loyalty and Love, Recommended in a Sermon Preach'd at St. Paul's Covent Garden, in the British Language on St. David's Day* (London, 1716).

Polsted, Ezekiel, *Cambria Triumphans, or, A Panegyrick Upon Wales* (London, 1702).

Poole, Edwin, *Old Welsh Chips,* January to December (printed 'For the Author', 1888).

Powel, David, *The Historie of Cambria, now called Wales* (London, 1584).

Pryse, John, *Breezes from the Welsh Mountains: A Scrap Book of Cambrian Prose and Poetry* (Llanidloes and London, 1858).

Richards, William, *Wallography; or, the Briton describ'd* (London, 1682), repr. in 1738 as *The Briton describ'd, or a journey thro' Wales* as part of *A Collection of Welsh travels and memoirs of Wales,* and again in 1753 as *Dean Swift's Ghost.*

Rolt, Richard, *Cambria. A Poem, in three books: illustrated with historical, critical and explanatory notes* (London, 1749).

Rolt, Richard, *Eliza; a new musical entertainment* (London, 1754).

Rolt, Richard, *Select Pieces, by the late R. Rolt* (London, 1772).

Rowlands, Henry, *Mona Antiqua Restaurata* (Dublin, 1723).

Smollett, Tobias, *The Expedition of Humphry Clinker* (Oxford: Oxford University Press, 1998).

Thomas, Patrick (ed.), *The Collected Works of Katherine Philips,* vol. I, *The Poems* (Essex: Stump Cross Books, 1990).

Thompson, Aaron, *The British History, translated into English from the Latin of Jeffrey of Monmouth* (London, 1718).

Thomson, James, *Alfred. A Masque* (London, 1740).

Torbuck, John [J.T.] (ed.), *A Collection of Welsh Travels, and Memoirs of Wales* (London, c.1740).

Walters, John, *An English–Welsh Dictionary* (London, 1770–94).

Walters, John, *A Dissertation on the Welsh Language* (Cowbridge, 1771).

Walters, John, *Translated Specimens of Welsh Poetry in English verse, With some original pieces and notes* (London, 1782).

Ward, Ned, *A Trip to North-Wales: Being a Description of that Country and People* (London, 1701).

Warrington, William, *The History of Wales*, 2 vols (London, 1788).

Williams, Ifor (ed.), *Armes Prydein/The Prophecy of Britain. From the Book of Taliesin*, English version by Rachel Bromwich (Dublin: Dublin Institute for Advanced Studies, 1982).

Williams, Ifor (ed.), *Canu Llywerch Hen* (Cardiff: University of Wales Press, 1935).

Williams, Moses, *Pregeth a Barablwyd yn Eglwys Grist yn Llundain, Ar Dyddgwyl Ddewi* (Llundain, 1718 and 1722).

Wotton, William, *A Sermon Preached in Welsh before the British Society* (London, 1723).

Wyndham, Henry Penruddocke, *A Gentleman's Tour through Monmouthshire and Wales* (London, 1781).

Wynn, John, *The History of the Gwedir Family* (London, 1770).

Secondary Sources

Aaron, Jane, *Nineteenth-Century Women's Writing in Wales: Nation, Gender and Identity* (Cardiff: University of Wales Press, 2007).

Aaron, Jane, 'Bardic anti-colonialism', in Jane Aaron and Chris Williams (eds), *Postcolonial Wales* (Cardiff: University of Wales Press, 2005).

Aaron, Jane, '"Saxon, Think not All Is Won": Felicia Hemans and the making of Britons', *Cardiff Corvey: Reading the Romantic Text*, 4 (May 2000); online: Internet (24 July 2003), *http://www.cf.ac.uk/corvey/articles/cc04_n01.html*, 1–8. This article is a revised version of a paper originally presented at the 'Scenes of Writing, 1750–1850' conference, held 20–23 July 1998 in Gregynog Hall, Wales.

Aaron, Jane, *Pur Fel Y Dur: Y Gymraes yn Llên Menywod y Bedwaredd Ganrif ar Bymtheg* (Caerdydd: Gwasg Prifysgol Cymru, 1998).

Aaron, Jane, 'A national seduction: Wales in nineteenth-century women's writing', *New Welsh Review*, 27 (1994), 31–8.

Aaron, Jane, 'Seduction and betrayal: Wales in women's fiction, 1785–1810', *Women's Writing*, 1, 1 (1994), 65–76.

Adams, Sam, *T. J. Llewelyn Prichard*, 'Writers of Wales' (Cardiff: University of Wales Press, 2000).

Alker, Sharon, 'The geography of negotiation: Wales, Anglo-Scottish sympathy, and Tobias Smollett', *Lumen*, XXI (2002), 87–103.

Anderson, Benedict, *Imagined Communities: Reflections on the Origins and Spread of Nationalism* (rev. edn; London: Verso, 1991).

Baker, David J. and Willy Maley (eds), *British Identities and English Renaissance Literature* (Cambridge: Cambridge University Press, 2002).

Barash, Carol, *English Women's Poetry, 1649–1714: Politics, Community, and Linguistic Authority* (Oxford: Clarendon Press, 1996).

Bassnett, Susan, *Translation Studies* (London: Routledge, 1988).

Bohata, Kirsti, *Postcolonialism Revisited*, Writing Wales in English (Cardiff: University of Wales Press, 2004).

Bowen, E. G., *Dewi Sant/Saint David* (Cardiff: University of Wales Press, 1983).

Bradshaw, Brendan and Peter Roberts (eds), *British Consciousness and Identity: The Making of Britain* (Cambridge: Cambridge University Press, 1998).

Breeze, Andrew, 'Sidney's *Apology for Poetry* and the Welsh bards', *Notes and Queries*, 46, 2 (1999),198–9.

Brennan, Catherine, *Angers, Fantasies and Ghostly Fears: Nineteenth-Century Women from Wales and English-Language Poetry* (Cardiff: University of Wales Press, 2003).

Carr, A. D., *Medieval Wales* (Basingstoke: Macmillan, 1995).

Carr, Glenda, 'William Owen Pughe and the London Societies', in Branwen Jarvis (ed.), *A Guide to Welsh Literature c.1700–1800* (Cardiff: University of Wales Press, 2000), pp. 168–86.

Carruthers, Gerard and Alan Rawes (eds), *English Romanticism and the Celtic World* (Cambridge: Cambridge University Press, 2003).

Clark, J. C. D., 'The politics of the excluded: Tories, Jacobites and Whig patriots, 1715–60', *Parliamentary History*, 2 (1983), 209–22.

Colley, Linda, *Britons: Forging the Nation, 1707–1837* (Yale: Yale University Press, 1992; repr. London: Pimlico, 1994).

Colton, Judith M., 'Merlin's Cave and Queen Caroline: garden art as political propaganda', *Eighteenth-Century Studies*, 10, 1 (1976), 1–20.

Conran, Tony, *Welsh Verse* (Bridgend: Seren, 1992).

Constantine, Mary-Ann, *The Truth against the World: Iolo Morganwg and Romantic Forgery* (Cardiff: University of Wales Press, 2007).

Constantine, Mary-Ann, 'Ossian in Wales and Brittany', in Howard Gaskill (ed.), *The Reception of Ossian in Europe* (London and New York: Thoemmes Continuum, 2004), pp. 67–90.

Corbett, Mary Jean, *Allegories of Union in Irish and English Writing, 1790–1870* (Cambridge: Cambridge University Press, 2000).

Crawford, Rachel, *Poetry, Enclosure, and the Vernacular Landscape, 1700–1830* (Cambridge: Cambridge University Press, 2002).

Crawford, Robert, *Devolving English Literature* (Oxford: Clarendon Press, 1992).

Cubitt, Geoffrey (ed.), *Imagining Nations* (Manchester: Manchester University Press, 1998).

Curtis, Tony (ed.), *Wales: The Imagined Nation: Studies in Cultural and National Identity* (Bridgend: Poetry Wales Press, 1986).

Davies, Andrew, '"Redirecting the attention of history": antiquarian and historical fictions of Wales from the Romantic period', in Damian Walford Davies and Lynda Pratt (eds), *Wales and the Romantic Imagination* (Cardiff: University of Wales Press, 2007), pp. 104–21.

Davies, Andrew, '"The reputed nation of inspiration": representations of Wales in fiction from the Romantic period, 1780–1829' (unpub. Ph.D. thesis, University of Cardiff, 2001).

Davies, Caryl and Mary Burdett-Jones, 'Cyfraniad Humphrey Foulkes at *Archæologia Britannica* Edward Lhuyd', in *Y Llyfr yng Nghymru / Welsh Book Studies* (forthcoming).

Davies, D. Leslie, 'Miss Myddelton of Croesnewydd and the Plas Power Papers: a preliminary appraisal', *TBHS*, 22 (1973), 121–65.

Davies, Damian Walford, *Presences that Disturb: Models of Romantic Identity in the Literature and Culture of the 1790s* (Cardiff: University of Wales Press, 2002).

Davies, Damian Walford and Lynda Pratt (eds), *Wales and the Romantic Imagination* (Cardiff: University of Wales Press, 2007).

Davies, Janet, *The Welsh Language* (Cardiff: University of Wales Press, 1993).

Davies, John, *A History of Wales* (London: Penguin, 1992; Harmondsworth: Penguin, 1994).

Davis, Leith, *Acts of Union: Scotland and the Literary Negotiation of the British Nation, 1707–1830* (Stanford: Stanford University Press, 1998).

Davies, R. R. and Geraint H. Jenkins (eds), *From Medieval to Modern Wales: Historical Essays in Honour of Kenneth O. Morgan and Ralph A. Griffiths* (Cardiff: University of Wales Press, 2004).

Davies, R. R., *The Revolt of Owain Glyn Dŵr* (Oxford: Oxford University Press, 1995).

Davies, R. R., 'Edward I and Wales', in Trevor Herbert and Gareth Elwyn Jones (eds), *Edward I and Wales* (Cardiff: University of Wales Press, 1988), pp. 1–10.

Davies, R. R., *The Age of Conquest: Wales 1063–1415* (Oxford: Oxford University Press, 1987).

Davies, R. R., 'The status of women and the practice of marriage in late medieval Wales', in D. Jenkins and M. E. Owen (eds), *The Welsh Law of Women* (Cardiff: University of Wales Press, 1980), pp. 43–114.

Dearnley, Moira, '"Mad Ned" and the "Smatter-Dasher": Iolo Morganwg and Edward "Celtic" Davies', in Geraint H. Jenkins (ed.), *A Rattleskull Genius: The Many Faces of Iolo Morganwg* (Cardiff: University of Wales Press, 2005), pp. 425–42.

Dearnley, Moira, *Distant Fields: Eighteenth-Century Fictions of Wales* (Cardiff: University of Wales Press, 2001).

Dickinson, H. T. (ed.), *A Companion to Eighteenth-Century Britain* (Oxford: Blackwell, 2002).

Dobin, Howard, *Merlin's Disciples: Prophecy, Poetry and Power in Renaissance England* (Stanford: California, 1990).

Evans, R. Wallis, 'Prophetic poetry', in A. O. H. Jarman and Gwilym Rees Hughes (eds), *A Guide to Welsh Literature, 1282–c.1550* (Cardiff: University of Wales Press, 1997), pp. 256–74.

Franklin, Michael, 'The colony writes back: Brutus, Britanus and the advantages of an Oriental ancestry', in Damian Walford Davies and Lynda Pratt (eds), *Wales and the Romantic Imagination* (Cardiff: University of Wales Press, 2007), pp. 13–42.

Franklin, Michael, 'Sir William Jones, the Celtic revival and the Oriental renaissance', in Gerard Carruthers and Alan Rawes (eds), *English*

Romanticism and the Celtic World (Cambridge: Cambridge University Press, 2003), pp. 20–37.

Garlick, Raymond, *An Introduction to Anglo-Welsh Literature* (Cardiff: University of Wales Press, 1972).

Gaskill, Howard (ed.), *The Reception of Ossian in Europe* (London and New York: Thoemmes Continuum, 2004).

Gassman, Byron, '"Humphry Clinker" and the two kingdoms of George III', *Criticism*, 16 (1974), 95–108.

Gerrard, Christine, *The Patriot Opposition to Walpole: Politics, Poetry, and National Myth, 1725–1742* (Oxford: Clarendon Press, 1994).

Gordon, Andrew and Bernhard Klein (eds), *Literature, Mapping and the Politics of Space in Early Modern Britain* (Cambridge: Cambridge University Press, 2001).

Gourvitch, I., 'The Welsh element in the Polyolbion: Drayton's sources', *Review of English Studies*, 4, 13 (1928), 69–77.

Gramich, Katie and Catherine Brennan (eds), *Welsh Women's Poetry 1460–2001*, (Honno: Honno Classics, 2003).

Grant, Alexander and Keith J. Stringer, *Uniting the Kingdom? The Making of British History* (London and New York: Routledge, 1995).

Griffin, Dustin, *Patriotism and Poetry in Eighteenth-Century Britain* (Cambridge: Cambridge University Press, 2002).

Griffiths, Margaret Enid, *Early Vaticination in Welsh* (Cardiff: University of Wales Press, 1937).

Groom, Nick, *The Making of Percy's Reliques* (Oxford: Clarendon Press, 1999).

Harper, Sally, 'Instrumental music in medieval Wales', *North American Journal of Welsh Studies*, 4, 1 (2004), 20–42.

Hechter, Michael, *Internal Colonialism: The Celtic Fringe in British National Development, 1536–1966* (London: Routledge and Kegan Paul, 1975).

Helgerson, Richard, *Forms of Nationhood: The Elizabethan Writing of England* (Chicago: University of Chicago Press, 1992).

Henken, Elissa R., *National Redeemer: Owain Glyndŵr in Welsh Tradition* (Cardiff: University of Wales Press, 1996).

Herbert, Trevor and Gareth Elwyn Jones (eds), *The Remaking of Wales in the Eighteenth Century* (Cardiff: University of Wales Press, 1988).

Herbert, Trevor and Gareth Elwyn Jones (eds), *Edward I and Wales* (Cardiff: University of Wales Press, 1988).

Hill, Christopher, *Puritanism and Revolution: Studies in Interpretation of the English Revolution of the 17th Century* (London: Secker and Warburg, 1958).

Hiller, Geoffrey G., '"Sacred Bards" and "Wise Druides": Drayton and his archetype of the poet', *ELH*, 51, 1 (1984), 1–15.

Hughes, W. J., *Wales and the Welsh in English Literature* (Wrexham: Hughes and Son, 1924).

Humfrey, Belinda, *John Dyer* (Cardiff: University of Wales Press, 1980).

Jarman, A. O. H. and Gwilym Rees Hughes (eds), *A Guide to Welsh Literature, 1282– c.1550* (Cardiff: University of Wales Press, 1997).

Jarvis, Branwen (ed.), *A Guide to Welsh Literature c.1700–1800* (Cardiff: University of Wales Press, 2000).

Jenkins, Dafydd (ed.), *Hywel Dda: The Law* (Llandysul: Gomer, 1998).

Jenkins D. and M. E. Owen (eds), *The Welsh Law of Women* (Cardiff: University of Wales Press, 1980).

Jenkins, Ffion Llywelyn, 'Celticism and pre-Romanticism: Evan Evans', in Branwen Jarvis (ed.), *A Guide to Welsh Literature c.1700–1800* (Cardiff: University of Wales Press, 2000), pp. 104–25.

Jenkins, Geraint H. (ed.), *A Rattleskull Genius: The Many Faces of Iolo Morganwg* (Cardiff: University of Wales Press, 2005).

Jenkins, Geraint H., 'Wales in the eighteenth century', in H. T. Dickinson (ed.), *A Companion to Eighteenth-Century Britain* (Oxford: Blackwell, 2002), pp. 392–402.

Jenkins, Geraint H., 'Historical writing in the eighteenth century', in Branwen Jarvis (ed.), *A Guide to Welsh Literature c.1700–1800* (Cardiff: University of Wales Press, 2000), pp. 23–44.

Jenkins, Geraint H., *The Foundations of Modern Wales, 1642–1780* (Oxford: Oxford University Press, 1993).

Jenkins, Geraint H., *Literature, Religion and Society in Wales, 1660–1730* (Cardiff: University of Wales Press, 1978).

Jenkins, Philip, 'Seventeenth-century Wales: definition and identity', in Brendan Bradshaw and Peter Roberts (eds), *British Consciousness and Identity: The Making of Britain* (Cambridge: Cambridge University Press, 1998), pp. 213–35.

Jenkins, Philip, *A History of Modern Wales 1536–1990* (London: Longman, 1992).

Jenkins, Philip, *The Making of a Ruling Class: The Glamorgan Gentry 1640–1790* (Cambridge: Cambridge University Press, 1983).

Johnson, Charlotte, 'Evan Evans: Dissertatio de Bardis', *National Library of Wales Journal*, 22, 1 (1981), 64–91.

Jones, R. Brinley, *William Salesbury* (Cardiff: University of Wales Press, 1994).

Jones, Roger Stephens, 'Some Anglo-Welsh poems in honour of George III, Queen Charlotte and the Prince of Wales', *Anglo-Welsh Review*, 27, 60 (Spring 1978), 87–97.

Kerrigan, John, *Archipelagic English: Literature, History, and Politics 1603–1707* (Oxford: Oxford University Press, 2008).

Kidd, Colin, 'Integration: patriotism and nationalism', in H. T. Dickinson (ed.), *A Companion to Eighteenth-Century Britain* (Oxford: Blackwell, 2002), pp. 369–80.

Kidd, Colin, *The Forging of Races: Race and Scripture in the Protestant Atlantic World, 1600–2000* (Cambridge: Cambridge University Press, 2006).

Kidd, Colin, *British Identities Before Nationalism: Ethnicity and Nationhood in the Atlantic World, 1600–1800* (Cambridge: Cambridge University Press, 1999).

Kidd, Colin, *Subverting Scotland's Past: Scottish Whig Historians and the Creation of an Anglo-British Identity, 1689–1830* (Cambridge: Cambridge University Press, 1993).

King, Kathryn R., 'Political verse and satire: monarchy, party and female political agency', in Sarah Prescott and David E. Shuttleton (eds), *Women and Poetry, 1660–1750* (Basingstoke: Palgrave Macmillan, 2003), pp. 203–22.

Klein, Bernhard, 'Imaginary journeys: Spenser, Drayton, and the poetics of national space', in Andrew Gordon and Bernhard Klein (eds), *Literature, Mapping and the Politics of Space in Early Modern Britain* (Cambridge: Cambridge University Press, 2001), pp. 204–23.

Knight, Stephen, *A Hundred Years of Fiction*, Writing Wales in English (Cardiff: University of Wales Press, 2004).

Mack, Phyllis, *Visionary Women: Ecstatic Prophecy in Seventeenth-Century England* (Berkeley, CA: University of California Press, 1992).

Mathias, Roland, *An Introduction to Anglo-Welsh Literature* (Cardiff: University of Wales Press, 1970).

Mathias, Roland, *Anglo-Welsh Literature: An Illustrated History* (Bridgend: Poetry Wales Press, 1986).

Merriman, James. *The Flower of Kings: A Study of the Arthurian Legend in England Between 1485 and 1835* (Lawrence: University Press of Kansas, 1973).

Monod, Paul, *Jacobitism and the English People, 1688–1788* (Cambridge: Cambridge University Press, 1989).

Morgan, Gerald, 'The Morris brothers', in Branwen Jarvis (ed.), *A Guide to Welsh Literature c.1700–1800* (Cardiff: University of Wales Press, 2000), pp. 64–80.

Morgan, Gerald, 'The first Anglo-Welsh novel', *Anglo-Welsh Review*, XVII, 39 (1968), 114-22.

Morgan, Prys, *The Eighteenth-Century Renaissance* (Llandybïe: Christopher Davies, 1981).

Morgan, Prys, 'Keeping the legends alive', in Tony Curtis (ed.), *Wales: The Imagined Nation: Studies in Cultural and National Identity* (Bridgend: Poetry Wales Press, 1986), pp. 19–41.

Murdoch, Alexander, *British History 1660–1832: National Identity and Local Culture* (Houndmills: Macmillan, 1998).

Newman, Gerald, *The Rise of English Nationalism: A Cultural History, 1740–1830* (New York: St Martin's Press, 1987).

Odney, Paul, 'Thomas Gray's "Daring Spirit": forging the poetics of an alternative nationalism', *Clio*, 28, 3 (1999), 245–60.

Parker, Patricia, 'Uncertain unions: Welsh leeks in *Henry V*', in David J. Baker and Willy Maley (eds), *British Identities and English Renaissance Literature* (Cambridge: Cambridge University Press, 2002), pp. 81–100.

Pateman, Carole, 'Conclusion: women's writing, women's standing: theory and politics in the early modern period', in Hilda L. Smith (ed.), *Women Writers and the Early Modern British Political Tradition* (Cambridge: Cambridge University Press, 1998), pp. 365–82.

Piggott, Stuart, *Ancient Britons and the Antiquarian Imagination: Ideas from the Renaissance to the Regency* (London: Thames and Hudson,1989).

Pittock, Murray G. H., *Celtic Identity and the British Image* (Manchester: Manchester University Press, 1999).

Pittock, Murray G. H., *Inventing and Resisting Britain: Cultural Identities in Britain and Ireland, 1685–1789* (Basingstoke: Macmillan, 1997).

Pocock, J. G. A., *Virtue, Commerce, and History: Essays on Political Thought and History, Chiefly in the Eighteenth Century* (Cambridge: Cambridge University Press, 1985).

Pocock, J. G. A., 'The limits and divisions of British history: in search of the unknown subject', *American Historical Review*, 87 (1982), 311–16.

Pocock, J. G. A., 'British history: a plea for a new subject', *Journal of Modern History*, 47 (1975), 601–21.

Prescott, Sarah, '"What Foes more dang'rous than too strong Allies?": Anglo-Welsh relations in eighteenth-century London', *Huntington Library Quarterly*, 69, 4 (2006), 535–54.

Prescott, Sarah, '"Gray's pale spectre": Evan Evans, Thomas Gray, and the rise of Welsh bardic nationalism', *Modern Philology*, 104, 1 (2006), 72–95.

Prescott, Sarah, 'The Cambrian Muse: Welsh identity and Hanoverian loyalty in the poems of Jane Brereton (1685–1740)', *Eighteenth-Century Studies*, 38, 4 (2005), 587–603.

Prescott, Sarah, *Women, Authorship and Literary Culture, 1690–1740* (Basingstoke: Palgrave, 2003).

Prescott, Sarah and David E. Shuttleton (eds), *Women and Poetry, 1660–1750* (Basingstoke: Palgrave Macmillan, 2003).

Price, Bronwen, 'Verse, voice, and body: the retirement mode and women's poetry 1680–1723', *Early Modern Literary Studies*, 12, 3 (2007), 5, 1–44, *http://purl.oclc.org/emls/12-3/priceve2.htm*.

Quilley, Geoff, '"All ocean is her own": the image of the sea and the identity of the maritime nation in eighteenth-century British art', in Geoffrey Cubitt (ed.), *Imagining Nations* (Manchester: Manchester University Press, 1998), pp. 132–52.

Reynolds, S. Rhian (ed.), *A Bibliography of Welsh Literature in English Translation* (Cardiff: University of Wales Press, 2005).

Rhydderch, Francesca, 'Dual nationality, divided identity: ambivalent narratives of Britishness in the Welsh novels of Anna Maria Bennett', *Welsh Writing in English: A Yearbook of Critical Essays*, 3 (1997), 1–17.

Richetti, John, *The English Novel in History 1700–1780* (London and New York: Routledge, 1999).

Richetti, John (ed.), *The Cambridge Companion to the Eighteenth-Century Novel* (Cambridge: Cambridge University Press, 1996).

Roberts, Michael, '"A Witty Book, but mostly Feigned": William Richards' *Wallography* and perceptions of Wales in later seventeenth-century England', in Philip Schwyzer and Simon Mealor (eds), *Archipelagic Identities: Literature and Identity in the Atlantic Archipelago, 1550–1800* (Aldershot, Hants.: Ashgate, 2004), pp. 153–65.

Roberts, Peter, 'Tudor Wales, national identity and the British inheritance', in Brendan Bradshaw and Peter Roberts (eds), *British Consciousness and Identity: The Making of Britain* (Cambridge: Cambridge University Press, 1998), pp. 8–42.

Roberts, P. R., 'The Union with England and identity of "Anglican" Wales,' *Transactions of the Royal Historical Society*, 22 (1972), 49–70.

Rosenblum, Michael, 'Smollett's *Humphry Clinker*', in John Richetti (ed.), *The Cambridge Companion to the Eighteenth-Century Novel* (Cambridge: Cambridge University Press, 1996), pp. 175–97.

Rowland, Jenny, *Early Welsh Saga Poetry: A Study and Edition of the Englynion* (Cambridge: D. S. Brewer, 1990).

Schwyzer, Philip, *Literature, Nationalism and Memory in Early Modern England and Wales* (Cambridge: Cambridge University Press, 2004).

Schwyzer, Philip and Simon Mealor (eds), *Archipelagic Identities: Literature and Identity in the Atlantic Archipelago, 1550–1800* (Aldershot, Hants.: Ashgate, 2004).

Schwyzer, Philip, 'A map of Greater Cambria', in Andrew Gordon and Bernhard Klein (eds), *Literature, Mapping and the Politics of Space in Early Modern Britain* (Cambridge: Cambridge University Press, 2001), pp. 35–44.

Schwyzer, Philip, 'Purity and danger on the west bank of the Severn: the cultural geography of *A Masque Presented at Ludlow Castle, 1634*', *Representations*, 60 (1997), 22–48.

Sitter, John (ed.), *The Cambridge Companion to Eighteenth-Century Poetry* (Cambridge: Cambridge University Press, 2001).

Smith, Hilda L. (ed.), *Women Writers and the Early Modern British Political Tradition* (Cambridge: Cambridge University Press, 1998).

Smyth, Jim, *The Making of the United Kingdom, 1660–1800* (Harlow: Pearson Education, 2001).

Snyder, Edward D., 'Thomas Gray's interest in Celtic', *Modern Philology*, 11, 4 (1914), 559–79.

Snyder, Edward D., *The Celtic Revival in English Literature, 1760–1800* (Cambridge, MA: Harvard University Press, 1923).

Sorenson, Janet, *The Grammar of Empire in Eighteenth-Century British Writing* (Cambridge: Cambridge University Press, 2000).

Sorenson, Janet, 'Internal colonialism', *Eighteenth-Century Fiction*, 15, 1 (2002), 53–8.

Speck, William, *Stability and Strife: England 1714–1760* (London: Edward Arnold, 1977).

Spencer, Jane, *Aphra Behn's Afterlife* (Oxford: Oxford University Press, 2000).

Stafford, Fiona, *The Sublime Savage: James Macpherson and the Poems of Ossian* (Edinburgh: Edinburgh University Press, 1988).

Stephens, Meic (ed.), *The New Companion to the Literature of Wales* (Cardiff: University of Wales Press, 1998).

Sussman, Charlotte, 'Lismahago's captivity: transculturation in *Humphry Clinker*', *ELH*, 61 (1994), 597–618.

Sweet, Rosemary, *Antiquaries: The Discovery of the Past in Eighteenth-Century Britain* (London and New York: Hambledon and London, 2004).

Terry, Richard, *Poetry and the Making of the English Literary Past, 1660–1781* (Oxford: Oxford University Press, 2001).

Thomas, Claudia N., *Alexander Pope and his Eighteenth-Century Women Readers* (Carbondale and Edwardsville: Southern Illinois University Press, 1994).

Thomas, Keith, *Religion and the Decline of Magic* (Harmondsworth: Penguin, 1978).

Thomas, M. Wynn, *Corresponding Cultures: The Two Literatures of Wales* (Cardiff: University of Wales Press, 1999).

Thomas, Ned, 'Images of ourselves', in John Osmond (ed.), *The National Question Again: Welsh Political Identity in the 1980s* (Llandysul: Gomer, 1985), pp. 307–19.

Thomas, Peter D. G., *Politics in Eighteenth-Century Wales* (Cardiff: University of Wales Press, 1988).

Trumpener, Katie, *Bardic Nationalism: The Romantic Novel and the British Empire* (Princeton: Princeton University Press, 1997).

Wade-Evans, A. W. (trans.), *Life of St. David* (London: SPCK, 1923) (by Rhigyfarch).

Weinbrot, Howard D., *Britannia's Issue: The Rise of British Literature from Dryden to Ossian* (Cambridge: Cambridge University Press, 1993).

Wheeler, Roxann, *The Complexion of Race: Categories of Difference in Eighteenth-Century British Culture* (Philadelphia: University of Pennsylvania Press, 2000).

Williams, Abigail, 'Whig literary culture: poetry, politics, and patronage, 1678–1714' (unpub. D.Phil. thesis, Oxford University, 2000).

Williams, Glanmor, *Wales and the Act of Union* (Bangor: Headstart History, 1992).

Williams, Glanmor, *Religion, Language, and Nationality in Wales* (Cardiff: University of Wales Press, 1979).

Williams, Glanmor, *Welsh Reformation Essays* (Cardiff: University of Wales Press, 1967).

Williams, J. E. Caerwyn, *The Poets of the Welsh Princes* (Cardiff: University of Wales Press, 1978).

Wilson, Kathleen, *The Island Race: Englishness, Empire and Gender in the Eighteenth Century* (London and New York: Routledge, 2003).

Yadav, Alok, *Before the Empire of English: Literature and Nationalism in Eighteenth-Century Britain* (Basingstoke: Palgrave, 2004).

Yadav, Alok, 'Nationalism and eighteenth-century British literature', *Literature Compass* (electronic journal) (2004), *http://www.literature-compass.com/*

Online and Electronic Resources

BWLET.net web-page (Bibliography of Welsh Literature in English Translation) *http://www.bwlet.net/index.htm*

Lord, Peter, *The Visual Culture of Wales: Imaging the Nation* (CD-ROM; University of Wales Centre for Advanced Welsh and Celtic Studies: University of Wales Press, 2002).

Oxford Dictionary of National Biography (Oxford University Press, 2004).

Oxford English Dictionary, ed. J. A. Simpson and E. S. C. Weiner (2nd edn; Oxford: Clarendon Press, 1989), *OED Online* (Oxford University Press) *http://dictionary.oed.com/cgi/entry/00181778*.

The Welsh Biography Online (National Library of Wales, 2004, 2007).

Index